Praise for
ALLIES AT WAR

"*In* Allies at War, *Phil Gordon and Jeremy Shapiro do a masterful job dissecting the recent rift between the U.S. and Europe over Iraq. More important, theirs is a timely demonstration that a new transatlantic compact is both possible and necessary for our common security.*"
> —Joseph R. Biden, Jr., Ranking Member, Senate Foreign Relations Committee.

"*An invaluable and lucid account of the present transatlantic crisis; and a compelling plea for putting that crisis behind us.*"
> —Robert Kagan, Author, *Of Paradise and Power: America and Europe in the New World Order*

"*A deservedly scathing indictment of an arrogantly unilateral policy and a sensible plea for an urgent strategic readjustment.*"
> —Zbigniew Brzezinski, former National Security Adviser

"Allies at War *is a superb but unsettling account of how the most successful alliance in history almost came apart over Iraq. The Americans and the Europeans have much to learn from this meticulously evenhanded account of a crisis both sides badly mishandled.*"
> —John Lewis Gaddis, Yale University

"*This is a great book, likely to become the definitive account of this period.*"
> —Charles Grant, Director, Center for European Reform

ALLIES AT WAR

AMERICA, EUROPE, AND THE CRISIS OVER IRAQ

PHILIP H. GORDON

AND

JEREMY SHAPIRO

A BROOKINGS INSTITUTION BOOK

McGraw-Hill

New York Chicago San Francisco Lisbon London
Madrid Mexico City Milan New Delhi San Juan
Seoul Singapore Sydney Toronto

The *McGraw·Hill* Companies

3 4 5 6 7 8 9 0 DOC/DOC 0 9 8 7 6 5 4

ISBN 0-07-144120-4

McGraw-Hill books are available at special discounts to use as premiums and sales promotions, or for use in corporate training programs. For more information, please write to the Director of Special Sales, Professional Publishing, McGraw-Hill, Two Penn Plaza, New York, NY 10121-2298. Or contact your local bookstore.

 This book is printed on recycled, acid-free paper containing a minimum of 50% recycled de-inked paper.

Library of Congress Cataloging-in-Publication Data

Gordon, Philip H.
  Allies at war : America, Europe and the crisis over Iraq / by Philip H. Gordon and Jeremy Shapiro.
    p. cm.
  ISBN 0-07-144120-4 (hardcover : alk. paper)
  1. European Union countries—Foreign relations—Iraq. 2. Iraq—Foreign relations—European Union countries. 3. European Union countries—Foreign relations—United States. 4. United States—Foreign relations—European Union countries. 5. United States—Foreign relations—Iraq. 6. Iraq—Foreign relations—United States.
I. Shapiro, Jeremy. II. Title.
  JZ1570.A57I724 2004
  956.7044'3—dc22

                                    2004000557

CONTENTS

ACKNOWLEDGMENTS

The authors would like to thank the many friends and colleagues who took the time to help us understand these events, relate their experiences and opinions, and offer constructive comments and criticisms. In addition to the many current officials on both sides of the Atlantic whom we interviewed for this project, we would like to thank Ron Asmus, Tony Blinken, Dan Byman, Ivo Daalder, John Lewis Gaddis, Charles Grant, Pierre Hassner, Robert Kagan, Michael O'Hanlon, Stephen Szabo, Strobe Talbott, and Justin Vaïsse for their generosity in reading various stages of the manuscript. We owe a special thanks to Jim Steinberg, who read several versions and gave liberally of his time, insights, and support. Ruxandra Popa, Jennifer Linker, and Marc Sorel provided invaluable and patient assistance in researching the book. Bob Faherty, Jeffrey Krames, and Stacy Rosenberg steered us skillfully through the publication process. We would also like to acknowledge the financial support of the German Marshall Fund of the United States and the Luso-American Foundation. Philip Gordon would like to thank Rachel, Noah, Benjamin, and Dinah Gordon for their indulgence of the time he spent at the computer instead of with them. Finally, we are most grateful to Amanda Cause, without whose unflappable calm, superb research skills, and constant encouragement we could not have completed this project.

INTRODUCTION

PRESENT AT THE DESTRUCTION

In the immediate aftermath of the September 11, 2001 terrorist attacks, Americans and Europeans surprised each other in positive ways. George W. Bush, who had faced vast protests during his first visit to Europe earlier that summer and was widely regarded there as an ill-informed cowboy, surprised the Europeans with his patient, careful, and proportionate action in Afghanistan. In turn, Europeans also broke with stereotypes, strongly supporting military action not only against the al Qaeda network but also against its Taliban hosts. European leaders pledged their "unlimited solidarity" with the United States, and within hours the North Atlantic Treaty Organization (NATO) allies invoked the Article V mutual defense clause. In a twist that few could have predicted before September 11, within a month America was conducting a major war halfway around the world, and the biggest problem for the European allies was that they wanted to send more troops than Washington was prepared to accept.

Less than a year and a half later, the U.S.-Europe clash over Iraq led to the most serious deterioration of transatlantic relations in recent memory. The dispute shook the alliance to its core and appeared to confirm the growing impression among scholars and policymakers alike that U.S. and European perspectives, interests, and even values had seriously diverged in the wake of the end of the Cold War. In March 2003 a significant majority of Americans—over 70 percent—supported President George W. Bush's decision to overthrow the Iraqi regime, while at least as large a share of Europeans opposed that decision. Some European governments—in Britain, Spain, Poland, and Italy, for example—overcame public opposition to support the American use of force, whereas others—primarily France, Germany, and Russia—strongly opposed it and denounced it as illegal, illegitimate, or misguided when it happened.

The dispute over Iraq ran so deep that it posed a challenge not only to transatlantic relations, but to the main institutions underpinning world order throughout the post-World War II period. The United Nations Security Council, the supposed arbiter of international peace and security, failed in March 2003 to reach a consensus on what to do about Iraq and was denounced as "irrelevant" by many Americans. NATO, the most successful and enduring military alliance in the history of the world, not only failed to unite over Iraq, but had great difficulty responding even to a request from one of its members, Turkey, to plan for its defense. The European Union, although in the midst of a constitutional convention to consolidate the continent's political unification, was profoundly divided. Indeed, the Iraq crisis exposed serious internal rifts among European governments over the future of European integration and the issue of how to deal with the United States.

By the time the war actually began in March 2003, the Iraq crisis was no longer just a result of transatlantic differences, but a significant *cause* of them. The crisis reinforced many of the worst transatlantic stereotypes—depicting the United States as unilateralist and militaristic in European eyes, and Europeans as unreliable and ungrateful allies in American eyes. Though clear majorities of Europeans still had a favorable opinion of the United States as late as summer 2002, by March 2003 such opinions were sharply down across the board—from 75 to 48 percent in Britain, 70 to 34 percent in Italy, 63 to 31 percent in France, 61 to 25 percent in Germany, 61 to 28 percent in Russia, and 30 to 12 percent in Turkey—and solid majorities in nearly all European countries expressed support for "more independent" foreign policies.

American opinions about the European countries that opposed the war were similarly affected. Between February 2002 and spring 2003, the number of Americans with favorable views of France fell from 79 to 29 percent, and those with favorable views of Germany fell from 83 to 44 percent. Throughout the spring of 2003, calls, instigated by commentators in the media and members of Congress, proliferated throughout the United States for a boycott of French and German goods, reciprocated to a degree in Germany and France of American goods. And even after the war's conclusion, Bush administration officials warned that there would be "consequences" for allies like France that failed to follow Washington's lead. By the summer of 2003, even mainstream columnists like Thomas L. Friedman of the *New York Times* were suggesting that French opposition to the war and to U.S. Iraq policy after the war meant that France was no longer just "our annoying ally" but actually becoming an enemy of the United States.

Bitter U.S.-European differences on matters of policy and global strategy are nothing new, of course. Episodes such as the 1956 Suez crisis, the French expulsion of American troops in 1966, the 1973 Arab-Israeli War, the debate over the "Euromissiles" or Central America in the early 1980s, are all reminders that the Atlantic alliance has always had to confront deeply divisive issues. What is striking today, however, is the growing sense among serious observers—clear even before the Iraq crisis broke out—that the very basis for a transatlantic alliance is eroding. Scholar Francis Fukuyama, who 13 years ago was declaring the triumph of common Euro-American values and institutions to be the "end of history," now speaks of the "deep differences" within the Euro-Atlantic community and asserts that the current U.S.-European rift is "not just a transitory problem." Historian Tony Judt believes that "we are witnessing the dissolution of an international system." Former Secretary of State Henry Kissinger worries that "if the existing trend in transatlantic relations continues, the international system will be fundamentally altered." Scholar Charles Kupchan believes that the United States and Europe may be headed "down the same road as Rome and Constantinople—toward geopolitical rivalry," and that the best they can do is pursue an "amicable divorce." Columnist Charles Krauthammer asserts that NATO—once the centerpiece of the transatlantic alliance—is "dead."

Not everyone agrees that the Atlantic alliance is finished. Former Clinton administration official Antony Blinken has written of a "false crisis over the Atlantic," analysts Ronald Asmus and Kenneth Pollack call for a "new transatlantic project," and the Brookings Institution's James Steinberg is cautiously optimistic about "salvaging transatlantic relations." In addition, key U.S. senators like Democrat Joseph Biden and Republican Richard Lugar have called for the partnership to be restored. But even the optimists recognize that there are real problems and challenges ahead. Longtime proponents of transatlantic cooperation, such as analyst Ivo Daalder, have begun to talk about the "end of Atlanticism" and warn that transatlantic relations are in "very serious trouble."

Probably the most powerful case that America and Europe are growing apart has been made by author Robert Kagan, whose summer 2002 *Policy Review* article "Power and Weakness" argued that it was "time to stop pretending that Europeans and Americans share a common view of the world." Kagan asserted: "On major strategic and international questions today, Americans are from Mars and Europeans are from Venus: They agree on little and understand one another less and less." The clash over Iraq certainly seemed to confirm his notion that when it comes to "setting national priorities, determining threats, defining challenges, and fashioning and implementing foreign and defense policies, the United States and Europe have parted ways."

There can be little doubt that the divisions revealed during the crisis in Iraq stem from real and growing structural differences between the United States and Europe—differences in capabilities, perspectives, and strategies. Yet we reject the conclusion that the breakup of the transatlantic alliance is therefore inevitable. We argue that it can and should be saved.

The alliance can be saved, we believe, because for all the transatlantic differences over Iraq and the war on terrorism, American and European interests and values—the ultimate drivers of long-term policy—remain highly similar. They were never identical—as demonstrated by the numerous and bitter disputes over global issues, and even over core approaches to dealing with the Soviet Union. But these very real differences never prevented the alliance from maintaining a successful overall strategy to confront the common challenge of the day or a sense that Americans and Europeans were fundamentally on the same side of history. Since the end of the Cold War, the allies' differing military capabilities and attitudes toward power have not prevented them from using force together—in Bosnia, Kosovo, and Afghanistan, for example—and continuing differences need not prevent such cooperation in the future. The image of a militaristic and unilateralist America and a pacifistic and inward-focused Europe certainly has a measure of truth to it, but it is also a caricature. The caricature, and the particular case of Iraq, obscures the fact that many Americans still place a high priority on international cooperation, legitimacy, and peaceful solutions to problems, just as many Europeans understand that force still plays a necessary role in international affairs. Iraq was in many ways the perfect storm; there is no reason to believe that the crisis it provoked will be anything like the norm in transatlantic relations.

We argue not only that the alliance can be saved, but that it should be saved. It is true that the new challenges are unlikely to unite the two sides of the Atlantic in the same way the Cold War did. And if "alliance" is defined to mean that members of the alliance share a precise view of the world and commit to pursuing all foreign policies together, then the transatlantic alliance is in fact dead. But in that case, as even a cursory review of NATO's history would show, it never existed in the first place.

Americans and Europeans may no longer be bound together by a common threat, but they continue to have an enormous continuing interest in maintaining the structures, expectations, habits, and commitment to cooperation inherent in the concept of a political alliance. For all its apparent power, the United States should not wish to take on the responsibility of maintaining international order and global security without the support of the most useful, prosperous, and like-minded allies it is likely to find anywhere—those in the widening European Union. The United States can and should pursue close cooperation with other major players such as Russia, India, Japan, Australia, and Israel. But the notion that these other relationships could adequately substitute for a permanent alliance with America's richest, most democratic, most longstanding, and—for all their pacifist tendencies—militarily most capable partners is absurd. All of the most critical twenty-first-century challenges—preventing terrorism and weapons of mass destruction proliferation, the transformation of the Middle East, the preservation of the environment, and the spread of democracy and free markets—require close cooperation between the world's two greatest repositories of democratic values and economic strength.

Critics of the alliance respond that they are not opposed to cooperation with Europe or anyone else, but that they believe such cooperation is better pursued on an ad hoc basis of mutual interest as appropriate: "The mission should determine the coalition," in Defense Secretary Donald Rumsfeld's famous formulation. Much U.S.-European cooperation could indeed proceed on such a basis even if transatlantic relations were to deteriorate further and attachment to the notion of alliance were to erode. But it would be misguided to assume—as many American theorists and administration officials apparently do—that cooperation would remain unaffected by deep mutual recriminations, antagonistic public perceptions, and the absence of any institutional structure. The leaders of Europe's democracies are still nearly all inclined to follow the lead of the United States when possible. But they will find it more and more difficult to do so if they cannot show that they are getting anything in return or if they feel they no longer have any voice in Washington.

The "end of the alliance" would not necessarily mean outright transatlantic hostility—anything like a new Cold War—but its eventual costs would nonetheless be high: an erosion of trust among leaders; domestic political pressures toward confrontation rather than cooperation; the end of NATO as an effective tool for common military actions; an escalation of trade conflicts; a diminishing willingness of either side to stand by the other in times of need; and, ultimately, political rivalry in the Middle East, Africa, and Asia. Europeans would face an America that no longer felt an interest in—and thus might actively seek to undermine—the united, prosperous Europe that Washington has supported for nearly 60 years. And Americans would find themselves dealing with monumental global challenges not only without the support and cooperation of their most capable potential partners, but perhaps even in the face of their opposition to American success. It is not the sort of environment in which leaders from either side should wish to operate.

Lessons from Iraq

That Americans and Europeans are not destined to go their separate ways is clear even when one considers the deep split over Iraq. While there were plenty of reasons for Americans and Europeans to disagree over Iraq in 2002–2003 (as they had for over a decade), a clash of this magnitude was in fact far from inevitable. It resulted not just from structural trends, but also from a strong degree of contingency, personality, misguided diplomacy, poor leadership, Iraqi unpredictability, and bad luck.

Clearly, the choices of both sides were shaped by the context. Americans, shocked by the tragedy of September 11 and exasperated after more than a decade of trying to enforce UN Security Council Resolutions on Iraq, concluded by 2002 that the only way to deal with the Iraq problem was to change the regime by force. Their new sense of vulnerability led them to accept the argument that regime change in Iraq was necessary, and the unprecedented power of the United States, together with the historical optimism of Americans, encouraged people to believe that regime change—and Iraqi democracy—were possible.

Europeans did not deny that Iraq was a problem, but they disagreed about the solution. Accustomed to both vulnerability and terrorism, lacking the military power even to contemplate large-scale invasions, and convinced from their own historical and colonial experiences that stabilizing a postwar Iraq would be nearly impossible, Europeans feared that the risks of an invasion outweighed the benefits.

Yet despite these differences, as late as December 2002 there was still a chance that a clash within the alliance would be avoided, and the United States and its traditional allies would end up supporting a unified policy. As we show in the story of the Iraq crisis in Chapters 4 and 5, if Iraq had blatantly violated the November 2002 UN Security Council Resolution giving it a "final opportunity" to disarm—for

8

example, by blocking the access of UN weapons inspectors, refusing to destroy any prohibited weapons found, or being found in possession of large stocks of prohibited weapons—even France would have gone along with military action. Similarly, more and better cooperation from Iraq—by explaining what happened to its past weapons of mass destruction programs and fully cooperating with inspectors—would have made it very difficult for the United States to launch a war, at least in the near term. Instead, the Iraqis cooperated somewhat, but not fully, and the result was a series of decisions and miscalculations that turned a legitimate dispute about a difficult problem into a crisis that threatened the very existence of the Atlantic alliance.

In early 2003 the Bush administration, certain that justice was on its side, launched a war of choice in Iraq. The decision to bring an end to Saddam Hussein's regime within the year, and by force if necessary, was made as much as a year beforehand, and with little input from allies. In January 2003, at the latest, Bush made a second decision: that both Saddam and the allies had exhausted all of the chances they deserved to avoid war, and that the United States would now use force to remove Saddam, almost regardless of what happened after that. A large number of Americans supported those decisions, but there was nothing inevitable about them. The administration certainly could have chosen a different course at either point.

Instead, Bush deployed massive military forces to the Gulf region, knowing that the deployment could not be sustained indefinitely; exaggerated Iraqi links with terrorist groups and weapons of mass destruction capabilities; and berated longstanding allies that were not prepared to support the war. He meanwhile failed to sufficiently engage key players, and in fact actually managed to alienate Russia, Turkey, and Germany, whose enduring opposition to the war bolstered the defiance of France. Bush's underestimation of European and world opposition to the war, and his belief that respect for American power would lead others to follow him despite their expressed differences, also led to the mistaken decision in early 2003 to pursue a second UN resolution specifically authorizing war. That decision was made despite the fact that France and Germany were telling the administration that pursuing an explicit authorization for war would only lead to a major diplomatic clash—as it did. Bush's deeply conservative political and philosophical orientation, so distant from that of many Europeans, also greatly exacerbated the problem. His decision to define the conflict as part of a struggle between good and evil and as an example of a new American doctrine of "preemption" changed the debate from one about how to deal with Iraq to a debate about international order and America's management of it.

Misguided decisions and unnecessary provocations in France and Germany also contributed to the Iraq clash. Facing difficult legislative elections in September 2002, German Chancellor Gerhard Schröder reversed the Atlanticism he had pursued during his first three years in office, which included providing an unprecedented level of German military support for American-led military actions in Kosovo and Afghanistan. Instead, Schröder chose to campaign shamelessly and relentlessly against the United States and a possible war in Iraq. Bush's unwillingness to forgive Schröder for doing so then drove the German chancellor increasingly into the arms of the French, which helped Jacques Chirac maintain his own antiwar position.

France signed on to UNSC resolution 1441 in November 2002, knowing it was running a real risk that Iraqi intransigence might oblige Paris to go along with—and maybe even participate in—another Iraq war. But over time, several factors changed France's calculation: Weapons searches failed to turn up any sign of weapons of mass destruction (WMDs), Iraqi cooperation with inspectors proved greater than France had expected, European public opinion became increasingly antiwar, and, perhaps most important, Germany, Russia, Turkey, and several members of the Security Council maintained their opposition. Under those circumstances, Chirac decided in January 2003 to stand up to the United States, even though he knew by then that stopping the war was highly unlikely.

Contrary to what many Americans thought, France's decision to threaten to veto American-led military action against Iraq was not the inevitable result of reflexive French resistance to American hegemony. Only a year before, Paris had strongly supported U.S. military action in Afghanistan, just as it had backed the NATO wars in Kosovo and Bosnia before that. Nor was France's opposition the result of French commercial interests, as was widely alleged, which in fact would have been better served if France had joined the coalition and demanded some of the spoils. Rather, the fierce French opposition to the war resulted from a combination of factors that all pushed France in the same direction: a genuine belief that the war was a strategic mistake, an unwillingness to give the United States a blank check for the management of world affairs, and a desire to reestablish Franco-German leadership of the EU by taking a stand that was highly popular with public opinion throughout Europe. France's ambitious Gaullist president thus not only chose to oppose the war, but he launched a high-profile campaign to try to stop it. The style with which Chirac went about opposing the United States, reinforced by his flamboyant foreign minister, Dominique de Villepin, also made the clash far worse than it needed to be—or than it arguably would have been had a different French government won the elections that had taken place less than a year before.

There were thus clearly powerful structural, cultural, and historical factors that led America to launch a war on Iraq while most of Europe opposed it. But it was the philosophies, personalities, decisions, and mistakes of the leaders who happened to be in office in 2001–2003 that led to the depth of the transatlantic clash over Iraq.

The outcome of the Iraq experience, while itself deeply damaging to the sense of solidarity and trust that must underpin any alliance, carries important lessons for both sides in the transatlantic alliance. The Americans who thought that U.S. decisiveness alone would suffice to bring about followers learned that this was not the case, and they paid for that lesson when it turned out that the European allies could deny them legitimacy and support during and after the war. The aftermath of the crisis—with the United States facing violent resistance, and bearing the overwhelming share of the financial and human burdens of coping with that resistance—should be enough to convince Americans that even superpowers sometimes need allies, and therefore need to take allies' legitimate concerns into account. An American approach that assumed that decisions about global peace and security were for Washington alone to make ended up needlessly alienating potential allies and fueling resistance to U.S. leadership. The next time there is such a crisis, American leaders might think more carefully before equating dissent with disloyalty, denouncing allies' motives, and attempting to "punish" them for lack of devotion to the cause.

There were also lessons for Europeans. Those who hoped to use opposition to U.S. policies as a rallying cry to forge greater European unity found that rather than a powerful and united EU, their approach produced only European divisions and weakness. Although it's not often apparent from the anti-Americanism of the daily European press, most European statesmen retain a basic understanding that behind the arrogance of any particular U.S. administration, American power and U.S.-European cooperation continue to underpin the unprecedented freedom and prosperity that Europeans enjoy and expect. In the face of this reservoir of goodwill and support for American leadership, any attempt to build EU unity against the United States—at least in current circumstances—is likely to fail.

It may be that leaders on both sides of the Atlantic will continue to act as if the alliance were not worth preserving. Perhaps without the stark simplicity of the Cold War to remind them of their common interests, European and American leaders will fail to see why an alliance needs to be maintained. But that would be a colossal failure of leadership, not a predetermined outcome. To conclude that the Iraq crisis was the inevitable result of irreconcilable interests or worldviews would make the permanent breakup of the alliance into a self-fulfilling prophecy.

Alliance and World Order

The enduring value of the transatlantic alliance must also be considered in a wider context. The U.S.-European relationship has served us so long and so well that we often forget the critical role it plays in providing overall global peace and stability. That alliance, in fact, functions as the bedrock of an international order born out of the tragedies of war and the Great Depression that marked the first half of the twentieth century. After World War II the United States took the lead in establishing a community of democratic nations that began as the Western Alliance and, especially after the fall of Soviet Empire, became in effect the foundation of world order. That order permitted a subset of countries, particularly the United States and the Western European nations, to achieve a level of prosperity and security unparalleled in world history. It was, in short, a spectacular and unprecedented achievement, principally of the United States, but one that would not have been possible without the active support of like-minded allies, particularly within Europe. Americans that have grown up with the Atlantic alliance have become so accustomed to it that they cannot even imagine a world in which our European partners were actively hostile to America's aims in the world.

From a historical standpoint, however, the most remarkable aspect of the current international system is the level of amity that exists between the world's leading military and economic powers, principally the United States, the larger nations of Europe, and Japan. If the need to maintain the alliance is not taken seriously in Washington, however, there is a real possibility that the historical tendency of nations to balance against the most powerful country in the system—a tendency that has not applied when it comes to the United States—might reassert itself. Particularly after the Iraq crisis, many Americans view France as a country determined to create a Europe—perhaps aligned with Russia and other powers—that would be a hostile counterweight to the United States. The perception is exaggerated, but it is encouraged by French rhetoric about multipolarity and the dangers of U.S. exceptionalism. The recent evolution of U.S. policy, however, risks not only encouraging the French to believe their own rhetoric, but, more seriously, could lead all of Europe to behave in the future like France already does.

The United States has faced this dilemma before. Arguably, at the end of World War II when the institutional foundations of the current world order were laid, the United States was even more powerful, relative to other nations, than it is today. As the title of former Secretary of State Dean Acheson's memoirs, *Present at the Creation*, implies, the statesmen of the day understood that they were, almost in a biblical sense, recreating the world. But Acheson and the other architects of that new world order were wise enough to see that in a global, generational struggle—then against communism, today against fundamentalist Islamic terrorism—the wisest course would be to set up a system to which others would rally. To win their hearts and minds was more important than to compel their obedience—an understanding that retrospectively explains more than any other single factor the essential solidity of NATO and the essential fragility of the Warsaw Pact.

At the start of the Cold War, maintaining this world order required the United States to forego the temptation to rule alone on the back of its immense power, but the constraints it accepted were limited and easily worth the price. The postwar institutions—including the United Nations, the International Monetary Fund (IMF), the General Agreement on Tariffs and Trade (GATT) and later the World Trade Organization (WTO), and NATO—from the start recognized the inescapable role of power in international politics, a recognition that was reflected in their structures and rules. Nevertheless, this hard-

14

headed notion of power was also nuanced by the recognition that excessively powerful states have tended to undermine their own legitimacy and overreach. It thus provided the incentive of a mechanism—indeed, several mechanisms—that could provide long-term legitimacy and consent for the most powerful states, in return for some limited constraints on their short-term freedom of action. The constraints of the system thus exist for the benefit of the powerful as well as the weak.

The enormous power of the United States today, particularly in military terms, and the new sense of vulnerability after September 11, have made these constraints chafe on American policymakers more than ever before. But it would be a mistake to base U.S. policy on the assumption that current American power makes the transatlantic alliance an unnecessary impediment to U.S. freedom of action. Acting on the premise that Washington does not need allies—or that it will find more compliant or more important ones elsewhere—could ultimately erode the reservoir of international legitimacy and consent to U.S. preeminence that has always served as a critical component of American power. In so doing, it might cost the United States the support and cooperation of those most likely to be useful to it in an increasingly dangerous world. No conceivable degree of U.S. military technology or defense spending could make good that loss.

Renewing the Alliance

The Western Alliance vitally needs a new vision of American leadership and transatlantic purpose. At the most basic level, leaders on both sides will have to rediscover the value of diplomacy and move beyond the gratuitous mutual insults and self-righteousness that was the hallmark of all too much of the Iraq debate. But they must do more than that. They need a new agenda for joint action toward common goals. That new agenda, detailed in Chapter 7, must at a minimum include a common effort to reconstruct Iraq, commitment to a long-term project to promote change in the Middle East, consolidation of the antiterror coalition forged after 9/11, and a revitalization of NATO based on more significant and more efficient European contributions. These challenges are vast, but they are no more unachievable—and no less important—than was the coordination of Western strategy during the Cold War.

As they pursue these common goals, leaders on both sides will have to recognize—better than they did during the Iraq debate—the costs of failing to maintain the basic norms and standards of alliance. Europeans must recognize that their security now depends more than ever on developments beyond their borders (and therefore on cooperation with America), and they must take more seriously American concerns about new challenges like weapons of mass destruction and terrorism. Failure to do so will not only allow such problems to grow, but will also fuel the very American unilateralism that Europeans resent, and which undermines the institutions they value—like the European Union and the UN. Americans, in turn, will have to resist the temptation to take advantage of their country's massive power by refusing to accept any constraints on U.S. freedom of action. If they do not, they will increasingly find themselves—as in Iraq after the war—bearing far too great a share of the burdens of international security alone.

Europeans and Americans are not destined to go their separate ways. But they could end up doing so if policymakers on both sides of the Atlantic act on the assumption that fundamentally different worldviews now make useful cooperation impossible or unnecessary. The reality is that despite their differences, in an age of globalization and catastrophic terrorism, no two regions of the world have more in common—or more to lose—if they fail to stand together in an effort to promote common values and interests around the globe. Now is certainly not the time to start pretending that either the United States or Europe can manage on its own.

PART I

THE ALLIANCE BEFORE IRAQ

Chapter
___
1

FROM COLD WAR
TO CLINTON

That the United States and Europe are clashing today over the management of world politics should not come as a surprise. The divisions across the Atlantic hardly started with, or were unique to, the crisis over Iraq. Indeed, the history of the Atlantic alliance is largely the history of its internecine struggles. A list of book titles published since the 1950s on crises or conflicts in the alliance, as historian Geir Lundestad has discovered, fills more than nine full pages.

Since the very inception of the alliance, its members have done all they can to maintain a common strategy within Europe, but they have often disagreed on approaches to the rest of the world. Whether in Indochina, Suez, Vietnam, the Middle East, or Central America, the NATO consensus was often stretched to the breaking point. Despite these almost continuous disputes, the Atlantic alliance persevered and prospered. By the 1990s it had become the most successful and endur-ing alliance in world history.

As a result of this success, those of us who have grown up in the post–World War II period have come to take the close alliance with Western Europe for granted. In the late twentieth century, transatlantic crises took on an almost ritualistic aspect in which a deep faith in the alliance allowed both sides to engage in brinkmanship in intra-alliance disputes with little fear that permanent damage would done be. Each successive crisis, battle-hardened diplomats would casually say, was "the worst transatlantic crisis since the last one." The assumption of continuity held because whatever else divided America and Europe, there was a mutual understanding that the Soviet threat was the central geopolitical challenge of the time, Europe was the primary terrain on which that threat had to be confronted, and West Europeans were the primary allies of the United States.

The Atlantic alliance that emerged and developed during this half century was not solely based on the need for defense against an outside threat. By the late 1960s, particularly, with the prospect of a Soviet invasion of Western Europe highly unlikely, the notion of an Atlantic alliance was clearly sustained by something more than a European need for American military power. The very success of alliance had cre-ated a belief in the idea that NATO might serve as the military foun-dation of a security community of democratic nations, one that could eventually spread its gifts of security, stability, and democracy throughout the world. After some soul searching in the early 1990s, that belief—as well as NATO's ultimate persistence, expansion, and first operational deployments in the Balkans after 1995—encouraged the notion that the Atlantic alliance had over time outgrown any need for the Cold War glue.

That notion is now open to question again. The Iraq crisis that tore the alliance apart during 2002–2003 has brutally reopened old ques-tions about the role of the Cold War in the formation and maintenance of the alliance. The sense of ritualized brinkmanship of transatlantic disputes remains, but with Europe no longer directly dependent for its security on the United States, and with the key issues for American foreign policy now outside of Europe, the ability of the alliance to weather such disputes is no longer guaranteed.

Can the United States and Europe maintain an alliance when their mutual strategic interests are not as obvious as when Soviet divisions lined the Elbe? A review of the origins and functioning of the alliance during the Cold War shows why doing so will not be easy. But it also shows how the democratic alliance built in the postwar period offered both sides advantages that transcend its original purpose. The threat to Western interests today may be a different one, but the ways in which transatlantic leaders managed to forge common strategies despite disparate strategic perspectives and roles, maintain public support and legitimacy, and ultimately defeat their common enemy carries important lessons for the present day.

An Alliance of Unequals

Americans like to look back on World War II as the event that finally shook them out of their historical isolationism and got them permanently involved in European affairs. According to this founding myth, Americans in 1945 realized the error of the isolationist path they had taken after World War I, committed themselves to permanent involvement in Europe, and then went on to establish a stable and democratic Western Europe firmly under a U.S.-led NATO umbrella. In fact, far from demonstrating America's natural involvement in European affairs, the immediate aftermath of World War II shows the depth of resistance to such involvement.

By the end of World War II the United States was not only present in Europe, but found itself practically running half of it. Even at this point, however, it was not obvious to Americans that they should remain a European power. A powerful American school of thought, one held by Franklin D. Roosevelt himself (and which has strong echoes in the United States today), saw Europe not as America's potential strategic partner, but as a continent whose time on the international stage had passed. "Roosevelt's outlook," historian John L. Harper has noted, "combined an old American confidence in his country's moral superiority and destiny, an animosity toward the European state system, and a finely honed instinct to divide and rule. . . . His vision of Europe was of a continent reduced to a state of weakness and irrelevancy, in effect retired from its long and checkered career at the center of world politics." For Roosevelt and many others, the United States would share the duties of running the world with Britain, the Soviet Union, and China, not with a continental Europe that had caused nothing but trouble throughout their lives.

Roosevelt-style disdain for Europe combined with traditional isolationism to create a powerful constituency for political and military withdrawal from Europe. Far from wanting to take on a leadership role of a "Western alliance" that did not yet exist, most Americans, exhausted by four years of total war, wanted only, as Averell Harriman put it, "to settle all our difficulties with Russia and then go to the movies and drink Coke."

By the end of 1946, of the over 1.6 million U.S. troops that had been in Germany when the war ended on May 8, 1945, only 170,000 remained. There was little appetite for taking on a permanent political role on the continent, let alone engaging in a close political, military alliance. Even involvement in Europe's second fratricidal war in 20 years was not enough to shake the United States out of the notion that entangling alliances were to be avoided at all costs.

This attitude changed only with the rise of the communist threat. Real or potential Soviet or communist advances from 1946, when instability threatened Greece and Turkey, until 1948—when communists forcibly ousted the Czechoslovak government, threatened to win elections in France and Italy, and launched a blockade of Berlin—gradually obliged the Americans to respond. Indeed, until the beginning of the Korean War in June 1950, American leaders continued to worry about gaining support for a permanent involvement in Europe. That involvement could only be sold to the public by persuading Americans that, in Truman's words, their very "way of life" was at stake. The administration's need to oversell its case was famously admitted by Secretary of State Dean Acheson, who later described the administration's need to make its points "clearer than the truth."

The response, formulated jointly by like-minded leaders on both sides of the Atlantic, came in the form of policies—the launch of the Marshall Plan, U.S. support for European integration, and the foundation of the Atlantic alliance itself—that were intended to commit the United States irrevocably to Europe. They represented a conscious decision to reconstruct an economically competitive but interdependent Europe that could aid the United States in the struggle against the Soviet Union, demonstrating a willingness to subordinate parochial economic interests to shared geopolitical goals, specifically the integration of Germany and the containment of the Soviet Union. The institutions themselves aimed to create a constituency for U.S. involvement in Europe on both sides of the Atlantic, thus raising the costs for both sides of dissolving the partnership.

The institutions of the Atlantic alliance, including NATO, reflected the democratic nature of their constituent parts. The founders of the alliance elaborated formal rules that asserted the sovereign equality of each of the members, including the powerful United States. According to historian John Lewis Gaddis, "familiarity with federalism discouraged the view that strength could override the need for negotiation and compromise. Without stopping to consider that it might have been otherwise, Truman and Eisenhower handled NATO as much as they did the Congress of the United States: by cutting deals instead of imposing wills."

Despite the recognized need for compromise, however, the Atlantic alliance was a never a relationship of equals—a point often overlooked today. In practice, it rested firmly on U.S. power and accorded a special role to the United States. That role did not entitle Washington to dictate to its partners in the manner of the Warsaw Pact. Rather, it meant that the alliance operated along certain norms of behavior that represented a compromise between the democratic principles embodied in its formal mechanisms and the realities of the power imbalance between the United States and Europe.

According to these norms, the United States would consult and listen to its allies, seeking some measure of international or at least multilateral legitimacy before taking any action. At least where core European interests were directly engaged—on issues like military strategy, nuclear weapons, or relations with the Soviet Union—the norms would in a sense allow U.S. allies into the American domestic political forum and the internal debates of the U.S. government. America's postwar leaders set out not to rule an empire or even to run an alliance based solely on realpolitik, but to build a voluntary Atlantic community in which all members felt they had a stake.

In the open political maelstrom of U.S. politics, the process of building such a community translated into some real—if difficult to quantify—European influence on important U.S. decisions. Thus, for example, when the United States decided after the beginning of the Korean War in 1950 that German rearmament was a strategic necessity, vigorous French objections and counterproposals were taken into account. Although initially highly skeptical, the United States ended up supporting the French alternative, the European Defense Community (EDC), only proceeding with German rearmament and admission to NATO when the French themselves rejected the EDC in 1954.

Similarly, when the Soviets deployed SS-20 intermediate range nuclear missiles in Europe in the 1970s, a move that had few direct strategic implications for the United States, Europeans were able to persuade the Americans to respond on their behalf. European influence brought about the so-called dual-track decision in 1979 to deploy American Pershing and cruise missiles in Europe and to embark simultaneously on arms control negotiations with the Soviets on Intermediate Nuclear Forces.

Even after the dialogue and lobbying Europeans might still have serious objections to American policy, and European public opinion might still oppose U.S. policy. But if the U.S. government asserted that a given action was critical for American and Western security, European leaders effectively agreed to manage their public opinion or, at worst, to stand aside or to criticize U.S. actions. But they did not actively oppose or impede them. This pattern can be seen in a host of issues that divided the alliance during the Cold War and throughout the Clinton administration—from the Vietnam War in the 1960s, to the debate over whether to deploy cruise missiles in Europe during the 1980s, to Clinton's policy toward Iraq in the 1990s. According to John Lewis Gaddis, "The logic linking all of these decisions was that of politics: the *balancing* of competing interests within a system all had an interest in sustaining."

The most serious Cold War crisis in the alliance, the 1956 Suez Crisis, revealed the danger of a lack of norms for resolving serious strategic disputes within the alliance. The genesis of this crisis was a plot hatched by the UK, France, and Israel, each for their own reasons, to undo Egyptian President Gamal Abdel Nasser's nationalization of the Suez Canal. The plot involved an Israeli attack on Egypt that would provide a pretext for Britain and France to intervene to separate the parties if and when Egypt refused a UN peacekeeping force. All went essentially as planned—the Israelis attacked, and British and French troops stood poised to occupy the canal. But Washington had not been consulted and, as Secretary of State John Foster Dulles put it, did not want to be linked to Europe in "any areas encroaching in some form or manner on the problem of so-called colonialism." (This American attitude was not so different from that of the Europeans today who do not want to be part of what they see as an American empire.)

The U.S. government vociferously objected to the Suez invasion and introduced a Security Council resolution calling on all members to refrain from helping Israel in its action against Egypt or from any intervention in the region—a measure clearly aimed at France and Great Britain. The U.K. and France vetoed the resolution, voting against the United States in the Security Council for the first time. When an agreement to withdraw was not forthcoming, the United States began dumping the British currency, undermining the value of the pound and effectively blackmailing the British into agreeing to a withdrawal from the canal.

Suez was a dramatic crisis for the alliance, and it was the Cold War crisis that most resembles the Iraq crisis of 2002–2003, both in the depths of the bitterness it created and in its potential implications for future policy. In the case of Suez, in fact, not only did a NATO ally *seek* to constrain military action by it partners, as France and Germany did to the United States in 2003, it actually *succeeded* in doing so, forcing the British and French into a humiliating withdrawal. British Prime Minister Anthony Eden had expected the United States to approach the issue "in the spirit of an ally" and to back the British. But the American action showed that such backing had a limit when U.S. and British interests diverged. In this sense, the Suez crisis demonstrated the limits of alliance even in the presence of the Soviet threat.

The depth of that crisis and its potentially dire implications for all sides led to several distinct lessons and results. The British determined that the best way to influence and further their interests was to depend on the "special relationship"; that is, working within the U.S. political process to ensure that satisfying both U.S. and British interests would never again require an open clash. The French drew the opposite conclusion. They determined that U.S. and French interests outside of Europe could not be reconciled and that, according to Pierre Melandri, "the Americans would not hesitate to leave them in the lurch." Thus, the French resolved to pursue an autonomous foreign policy and to obtain the means to carry out such policy—including independence from NATO and the development of their own nuclear force.

In the end, however, as Douglas Stuart and William Tow have pointed out, France and Britain "had no choice but to remain in the U.S. sponsored Western security system," and the United States "had no choice but to forgive (if not forget) the misbehavior of France and Britain." By demonstrating the dangers of intra-alliance disputes, the Suez crisis set the standard concerning what should be avoided, and led leaders to develop ways to deal with disputes that could allow for their resolution in a manner short of outright coercion.

Intra-alliance disputes in the 1960s, particularly between the United States and France, perversely help demonstrate the fundamental solidity of the alliance and its leaders' commitment to manage their differences. France was not willing to systematically accept American leadership of NATO, suggesting instead that a Directorate of the United States, Britain, and France should jointly manage global security affairs. When the United States refused to accommodate France's aspirations, de Gaulle in March 1966 took what seemed the ultimate step—withdrawal of France from NATO's military structure and the expulsion of NATO headquarters and all 26,000 U.S. troops from French soil.

As an alternative, France committed itself to a strategy designed to use an independent nuclear force, German power, and European integration to amplify French influence and balance American power. Ironically, one of de Gaulle's main arguments in pushing for a more independent France was that nations that do not play a real role in their own defense eventually develop a strategic culture of dependence. This was the fate American neoconservative writer Robert Kagan suggested Europe had suffered in his 2002 analysis of European "weakness."

Despite the seriousness of de Gaulle's challenge, the French withdrawal was less threatening to the overall purpose of the alliance than

Suez had been because both sides recognized and refused to cross certain limits in the dispute. The French challenge to U.S. control of NATO was possible because France accepted that, whatever the position of France within the NATO military structure, the United States was committed to defending Western Europe—and therefore France—in the event of Soviet aggression. Whenever de Gaulle had serious worries about the unity of the alliance—for example, during the Berlin crises and the Cuban Missile Crisis—he firmly supported the Americans. In striking contrast to the French position on Iraq in 2002–2003, de Gaulle publicly declared his backing for the U.S. position during the 1962 missile crisis and even told the American envoy sent to brief him—former Secretary of State Dean Acheson—that he did not need to see the U.S. intelligence on Soviet missiles in Cuba. "I trust you," de Gaulle told Acheson.

American restraint toward France was also relevant. Many of President Johnson's hard-line advisers called for retaliation against France for its withdrawal from NATO's military structure. On receiving the official demand to withdraw American troops, Secretary of State Dean Rusk asked sardonically if that included the dead ones in the cemeteries. Public opinion ran strongly against the French and people began boycotting French products and pouring French wine into the streets, again just as in 2003. But Johnson kept his cool, declaring, "When a man asks you to leave . . . you take your hat and go." In contrast to the Soviet Union when Hungary tried to distance itself from the Warsaw Pact in 1956, the United States accepted the sovereign French decision to withdraw.

This mutual restraint in the face of the partial defection of one of its strongest members demonstrated just how ingrained the notion of an alliance—larger in concept than just NATO's integrated military structure—had already become by the mid-1960s. Even after formal withdrawal, France continued to cooperate militarily with NATO and with the United States. Beginning with the Ailleret-Lemnitzer agreement in 1967, which gave France an important reserve role in allied defense, a series of agreements over the next 20 years brought France ever closer to NATO. These agreements ensured that in the long run, France's withdrawal from NATO's military structure had little practical meaning for the struggle against the Soviet Union. Similarly, French and European criticism of American interventions in Vietnam and elsewhere in the developing world was frequent and vituperative, but the Europeans did nothing to actually impede U.S. actions.

By the 1970s, with the Soviet threat to Western Europe largely gone and the more salient issues now falling outside of NATO's area of responsibility in Europe, alliance unity became harder to maintain. Divergences, particularly on the Middle East, occurred more frequently, and the principles of consultation and compromise established after Suez were not only challenged, but were often violated outright. Whereas in the 1950s and 1960s it was the French and British arguing that principles of solidarity should lead allies to support each other when one nation had vital interests at stake, now, after Vietnam, it was the Americans who were demanding solidarity.

Henry Kissinger, who was Secretary of State at the time, complained in his memoirs about Europe's unwillingness to follow the American lead: "[Europe's] legalistic argument was to the effect that obligations of the North Atlantic Treaty did not extend to the Middle East. But . . . our case for allied cohesion was based not on a legal claim, but on the imperatives of common interest. When close allies act toward one another like clever lawyers [and] if they exclude an area as crucial as the Middle East from their common concern, their association becomes vulnerable to fluctuating passion." But Kissinger's pleas for alliance unity on global issues had no more success than the French and British calls for American support decades before.

Thus, during the October 1973 War in the Middle East, nearly all the European allies distanced themselves from the U.S. policy of support for Israel. The UK and France even agreed on a joint declaration criticizing it. French Foreign Minister Michel Jobert complained that the European allies were neither consulted nor informed, particularly about an American decision to issue a global military alert, and criticized that Europe had been treated as a "nobody." The Europeans, except Portugal and the Netherlands, denied base access rights to U.S. transport aircraft on their way to resupply the Israelis, forcing them to fly an extra 1000 to 2000 miles. In response, Kissinger called the Europeans "craven" and "contemptible."

Still, even during this serious crisis, transatlantic consultations and efforts to find common ground were extensive, if unsuccessful, and European opposition to the U.S. actions had clear limits. The Europeans did nothing to prevent the resupply operation, the Germans looked the other way as the U.S. military used bases in Germany for refueling, and the French government went so far as to hold aerial defense exercises to camouflage the American planes passing overhead from a critical public.

During the first Reagan administration, 1981–1985, European-American relations in many ways foreshadowed the clashes that would emerge in 2002–2003. To much of European public opinion, the hawkish new U.S. President seemed to represent an irresponsible cowboy culture whose control over a vast nuclear arsenal put their very existence at risk. Reagan soon fulfilled their worst expectations by denouncing the Soviet Union as an "Evil Empire," calling for the deployment of a missile shield that threatened to destabilize the nuclear balance, and standing up to significant public resistance to the deployment of intermediate-range nuclear missiles on German soil. Polls showed that a majority of West Germans opposed the NATO deployments, and public protests mounted, culminating in an estimated one million West Germans demonstrating against American policy in the largest street protests in the Federal Republic's history. Once again, however, the logic of alliance and the dictates of the Cold War prevailed, and the German government allowed deployment of the missiles.

These various and nearly continual crises highlight the fractiousness of a democratic alliance. But at the same time they show its essential solidity and, in most cases, the willingness on both sides to adhere to certain norms. These norms included recognition of and respect for specific allies' vital interests, a commitment to consultation to ensure that allies did not surprise each other, and, especially on out-of-area issues, at least a grudging recognition of and deferral to America's special responsibilities and privileges. All of these norms fit within the notion of a democratic alliance modified to deal with a membership of sovereign states of different capabilities and the real and evident threat they all faced.

The fall of the Berlin Wall and the demise of the Soviet Union in 1989–1991 removed that threat. But the end of the Cold War also raised real questions about the future of the alliance that was created to fight it. Henry Kissinger has rightly observed that the architects of the Atlantic alliance "took it for granted that the prize for victory in the Cold War [would be] a lasting Atlantic partnership" and that they "would have been incredulous had they been told that victory in the Cold War would raise doubts about the future of their creation." But that is precisely what happened, and it would be left to a new set of leaders to prove that the old partnership could be preserved.

Learning to Live Without the Cold War

As the 1990s began, the constraints on intra-alliance disagreement loosened significantly. Europe was no longer directly dependent for its security on the United States, and the key issues for American foreign policy now lay outside of Europe, where transatlantic security cooperation had always been most difficult. It thus should not have been surprising that the immediate aftermath of the Cold War was a rocky period for the alliance.

In 1992, American voters turned their backs on a president whose career had been dominated by international affairs and elected a president with no foreign policy experience and an expressed determination to "focus like a laser" on the economy. In strong contrast to what would become U.S. foreign policy only 10 years later, early in Bill Clinton's presidency the administration placed higher priority on the domestic economy and fiscal solvency than on its international ambitions. As Undersecretary of State for Policy Peter Tarnoff famously explained in May 1993, "It is necessary to point out that our economic interests are paramount. . . . With limited resources, the United States must define the extent of its commitment commensurate with those realities." Tarnoff was officially reprimanded for putting the point so starkly, but in many ways he was simply stating the obvious: that with the Cold War over, a deeply indebted United States was going to give higher priority to its economic interests than to its foreign policy agenda.

The Clinton administration was initially inclined to emphasize domestic priorities because the disappearance of the Soviet Union made geopolitical considerations seem remote. With Europe no longer the central strategic region for the United States, the new administration consciously attempted to redirect U.S. attention and resources toward an economically rising Asia. Indeed, the most pressing geopolitical issue in Europe in the immediate aftermath of the Cold War—the continuing civil war in the Balkans—originally elicited little American response. During the 1992 presidential campaign, Clinton had argued that the Bush administration's failure to act in the Balkans amounted to an abdication of U.S. responsibilities in Europe. But when he got to office, he found that forceful action in the Balkans was at least as difficult as doing nothing. Many members of Congress no longer felt that much was at stake in Europe, and conventional political wisdom, particularly after the 1993 debacle in Somalia, held that the American people did not want to take risks in the Balkans for humanitarian purposes.

The American reluctance to take foreign policy risks or exercise assertive leadership over the alliance was perhaps most apparent in the spring of 1993, when Clinton, having resolved to lift the Bosnian arms embargo and initiate air strikes against the Bosnian Serbs, sent Secretary of State Warren Christopher on a marathon trip to six European capitals to rally European support. When Christopher failed to do so—or even, according to his critics, to try very hard—momentum within the U.S. government for the policy flagged. Then U.S. policy moved away from the notion of air strikes and toward the European approach of establishing (but not really enforcing) "safe havens," delaying forceful action for another two years. The Christopher mission would later come to be seen—especially among Republican critics, but also for many in the Clinton administration itself—as a model of how not to lead: by allowing the desire for allied support to create delays and indecision in the alliance.

The problems in the Balkans were exacerbated by the fact that Europeans had also misread the new era; they thought they could handle the situation alone and did not need U.S. leadership on the model of the Cold War. According to Foreign Minister Jacques Poos of Luxembourg, who held the European Community's rotating presidency in 1991, the Yugoslavia crisis signaled "the hour of Europe, not the hour of the Americans." With the Cold War over, the Europeans were going to use their developing institutions to play a more autonomous foreign policy role.

As it turned out, the Europeans proved incapable of handling the Yugoslav crisis without American leadership. European disarray and American disengagement had in very short order allowed a running sore to emerge in the heart of Europe, leaving over 200,000 dead. The threat that unrest might spread throughout southeastern Europe threatened to undo many of the gains of the Cold War and clearly implicated American, as well as European, security interests. NATO itself was seen to be at stake, and the Americans realized that even if they did not want to intervene, they would be obliged to rescue European peacekeepers if the Europeans were forced to withdraw.

Such prospects concentrated the minds of many Americans who had previously viewed the Balkans as a peripheral theater, while simultaneously encouraging Europeans—now somewhat bolstered by the May 1995 election of the more interventionist Jacques Chirac in France—to take a more assertive stand. In the summer of 1995, Washington finally decided to take the lead, and set about convincing the European allies, who were reluctant to intervene, of the necessity for forceful and concerted action. By using NATO as the mechanism for this engagement, the Americans demonstrated that NATO would continue to be their vehicle for U.S. involvement in Europe.

The experience in Bosnia provided several lessons both for U.S. and European policymakers. It made clear to Europeans that whatever their eventual aspirations for managing their own security, they were a long way from either possessing the internal consensus or the military capacity to act without U.S. leadership. It also disabused American policymakers of short-lived notions that Europe no longer mattered or that the United States could afford to ignore European developments. In other words, despite the disappearance of the Soviet threat, the fundamental dynamics of the Atlantic alliance had not completely changed. The United States still had to lead.

The Clinton administration learned from its early mistakes, and over time began to exercise more assertive leadership of the alliance. After much early hesitation, in 1995 it charted a clear course for the enlargement of NATO, which in July 1997 extended invitations to Poland, Hungary, and the Czech Republic. Clinton also aggressively pushed, particularly during his second term, for an expansion of NATO's missions to include new threats like terrorism, weapons of mass destruction, and "out of area" crises, as well as for the development of European defense capabilities better equipped to deal with these new challenges.

In the run-up to NATO's 50th anniversary summit held in Washington in April 1999, the administration called for a new "Strategic Concept" for the alliance that would recognize these new missions, and it put forward a Defense Capabilities Initiative designed to make European militaries more rapidly deployable and better able to work with American forces. The administration believed in the concept, coined by Senator Richard Lugar in the early 1990s, that NATO's future was "out of area" or "out of business." The Balkans may have given the alliance a new lease on life so long as that conflict persisted, but the long-term future of the alliance would depend on Americans and Europeans agreeing to work together to meet growing challenges beyond Europe's borders.

Foreshadowing some of the transatlantic debates that would erupt in the early 2000s, many Europeans were reluctant to embrace the new agenda. They were not persuaded that the new challenges could be best met with military power and were concerned that an increasingly powerful and unconstrained America might abuse its growing military might. These debates were particularly pointed in the negotiations over the new strategic concept. Ultimately, the allies did agree to emphasize the new threats, at least on paper, but they could not hide their enduring differences about the role of the UN in authorizing the use of force. The European allies, led by France, insisted on acknowledging the importance of the UN, while the Americans refused to make Security Council authorization an absolute requirement for military action.

U.S.-European differences—and the Clinton administration's approach to managing them—also came to the fore in the Kosovo crisis in the fall of 1998. When the crisis erupted following Serbia's expulsion of hundreds of thousands of ethnic Albanians from the troubled province, the United States took a much firmer stance than most Europeans. The Clinton administration also demonstrated more decisive leadership than it had for the first several years of the Bosnia debacle. Still, even while it wanted to lead, the administration remained strongly averse to undertaking military action without significant prior consultation and international approval. Clinton expended enormous efforts to win UN support for a tough line against Serbia. He managed in September 1999 to win passage of Resolution 1199, which declared the situation a "threat to international peace and security" and demanded specific actions by the Belgrade regime.

When a specific UN mandate for the use of force proved impossible because of Russia's threat to veto, Clinton then sought a mandate from the 19 democracies of the NATO alliance. Administration foreign policy officials and the President himself expended enormous efforts to convince reluctant NATO members—particularly Germany, Italy, and Greece—to support an alliance consensus. Even the most reluctant of the allies eventually acquiesced, not because their populace or even their leaders agreed on the need to go to war against Serbia, but mostly because of their commitment to the concept of the alliance. The result was not exactly diplomatic harmony, but it was nonetheless a successful military operation backed by a unified NATO. And as soon as the war was over, Clinton went right back to the UN, agreeing to its political control over Kosovo while NATO kept the peace.

The Clinton administration's conclusion was that for all the difficulties inherent in fighting as an alliance, the advantages were considerable. As Secretary of Defense William Cohen put it, when challenged by skeptical members of Congress about the desirability of going to such lengths to win consensus from difficult Europeans, "Let me state categorically, without strong continued cohesion in the alliance, this operation couldn't have gone forward. And so the notion somehow, that the United States could have carried out this mission unilaterally is simply not true. We could not have done it." NATO Supreme Allied Commander Wesley Clark also reached the conclusion that the strategic benefits of alliance outweighed the costs in terms of operational effectiveness. "NATO wasn't an obstacle to victory in Kosovo," he later wrote, "it was the reason for our victory."

Seeds of Dissent

The Clinton administration's commitment to alliance consensus and adherence to multilateral norms, of course, were not without limits, particularly given the growing hostility toward such norms in the Republican-controlled Congress. Indeed, in the latter part of the Clinton administration, Congressional opposition to compromises with allies and multilateral constraints reached a level unseen since before World War II. For example, Congress was unwilling to fully support U.S. deployments to the Balkans, stonewalled on paying U.S. dues to the United Nations, attempted to punish European companies doing business in Iran, Libya, and Cuba (through the Helms-Burton and Iran-Libya Sanctions Acts), and rejected the Comprehensive Nuclear Test Ban Treaty. Republican opposition also ensured that the Clinton administration opposed popular international efforts to create an International Criminal Court (ICC), though Clinton did sign the ICC treaty after the 2000 presidential election. All of these positions foreshadowed some of the clashes that would emerge between the Bush administration and the European allies after the election of 2000.

The influence of the Republican Congress, moreover, was not the only factor pushing the Clinton administration toward more assertive leadership—or even unilateralism. Growing U.S. power during the 1990s, and the absence of an enemy, were inevitably affecting Democrats as well. That power naturally led strategists and policymakers from across the political spectrum to contemplate the many possible uses of American power and to implicitly question the constraints of alliance interaction that had prevailed during the Cold War.

The effect of this power on U.S. foreign policy thinking would grow dramatically under the Bush administration, and it was certainly given a major boost by the vivid demonstration of new threats on September 11, 2001. But the process started under Clinton, whose National Security Strategy in 1995 announced that America would use "decisive and, if necessary, unilateral" force when vital American interests were at stake. Clinton understood the importance of the alliance and wanted to win allied support for any given foreign policy action. But already he was caught between the desire to preserve the alliance and the unique global responsibilities and enormous military power of the United States.

Nowhere did the temptations and responsibilities of power have a greater effect on the Clinton administration—or lead to greater tensions with Europeans—than over the issue of how to deal with the threat from what the Americans called "rogue," or "backlash," states— specifically Iran, Iraq, Cuba, North Korea, and Libya. Where the Europeans tilted toward engagement—using dialogue, trade and investment, and the enticement of full membership in the international community—to promote gradual political change, the U.S. approach increasingly emphasized coercion (in the form of economic sanctions, direct support to opposition forces, and even the threat of direct military action).

On one level, these were merely differences in emphasis. Nearly everyone touted the importance of transatlantic cooperation, and neither side believed in relying exclusively on either coercion or engagement. Moreover, there was a wide range of opinions within both the United States and Europe on the appropriate policies toward rogue states. The Republican-controlled U.S. Congress, for instance, took a very hard line on Iran and Libya, whereas the American business community opposed the growing use of economic sanctions, and the Clinton administration was often caught in the middle. In Europe, there was a general consensus on the relative virtues of engagement over confrontation, but each country had its own place on the spectrum, with Britain taking a much tougher line on Iraq than France, for example. But while these complexities must be acknowledged, the striking feature of the Clinton years was the increasing frequency with which policy disagreements over rogue states took place along U.S.-European lines.

These differences first became a serious issue in transatlantic relations as a result of efforts by the United States to enforce sanctions against Cuba, Iran, and Libya. Europe had long ignored unilateral U.S. sanctions against Cuba and took essentially the same approach when the United States unilaterally cut off trade with and investment in Iran in 1995. The United States had long complained that European willingness to circumvent U.S. sanctions elevated cynical commercial interests over common security concerns. The Americans did not, however, seek to prevent European firms from doing business in Iran or Cuba.

But in a world of dominant American power, and with the perception of a growing threat from rogue regimes, the U.S. Congress was increasingly unwilling to accept what many Americans viewed as "free-riding" on American efforts to provide the public good of international security. In an effort to force conformity with U.S. policy, Congress passed the Cuban Liberty and Democratic Solidarity Act (known as the Helms-Burton Act, after its Congressional sponsors) and the Iran-Libya Sanctions Act (ILSA) in 1996, asserting the right to impose sanctions on any company anywhere investing in Cuba or investing more than $40 million in the Iranian or Libyan energy sectors. European governments unanimously denounced the very principle of secondary boycotts and refused to abide by them, leading to a succession of transatlantic crises over whether the United States would follow through on the threats contained in Helms-Burton and ILSA.

Ironically, while Iran, Libya, and Cuba generated transatlantic frictions throughout the 1990s, the issue of Iraq was at first much less contentious. Iraq's blatant aggression against Kuwait in 1990, as well as careful diplomacy by the first Bush administration, helped create an unusually broad consensus on the need to isolate and disarm Saddam Hussein's regime. That consensus began to break down in the mid-1990s, however. Both Americans and Europeans tended to agree that the policy of sanctions and forceful containment had failed to remove the threat that Saddam's regime posed, but they disagreed sharply about what to do about that problem.

By 1996 many Europeans, most vocally the French, felt that sanctions would never achieve Saddam's overthrow or his full compliance with UN resolutions. Saddam had demonstrated a continuing ability to live with—and even prosper personally and politically from—the sanctions regime, which was perceived as a cause of suffering among the Iraqi people and stirring anti-Western resentment in the Arab world. The only long-term solution, they argued, was to gradually reintegrate Iraq into the international community through trade, investment, and diplomatic links. While acknowledging that Saddam was a dictator and a danger, they felt that his military capacity had been so decimated during the 1991 Gulf War and by the ensuing sanctions that there was little risk to international security in gradually engaging Iraq economically.

Many Americans agreed that the containment policy was not working well, but the position of both the Clinton administration and its Republican critics was that engagement with Iraq would be worse. Saddam's regime, in their view, was intent on challenging Western interests in the Gulf and on disrupting the status quo. Under such circumstances, relaxed scrutiny on his weapons programs, or increased trade and investment links, would only give him the money and space he needed to rearm. Thus, the main debate within the United States was not over whether to maintain or abandon the policy of containment. Rather, it was over whether to try to reinvigorate that policy through cooperation with Europe and with Iraq's neighbors, or whether to replace it with a more proactive policy to overthrow Saddam Hussein.

In the event, Saddam's periodic provocations and partial cooperation with the UN weapons inspectors had the effect of exposing U.S.-European differences. In September 1996, Iraqi troops intervened in an intra-Kurdish dispute in the part of effectively autonomous northern

Iraq that had been protected by U.S., U.K., and French air power since the 1991 Gulf War. The U.S. response—cruise missile strikes against air defense targets in other parts of Iraq and expansion of the southern no-fly zone almost to Baghdad—had little effect on the stability of Saddam's regime. But the American military actions did inspire the first public breakdown in the transatlantic consensus on Iraq. France denounced the air strikes and shortly thereafter withdrew from participation in the northern no-fly zone, claiming that Washington and London had moved the operation beyond its original humanitarian purpose.

In mid-1997 the Iraqis stepped up their challenge to the UN inspections and began systematic efforts to harass UN inspectors. The United States responded both by threatening force against Iraq if it did not comply with its obligations and by attempting to rally support in the UN Security Council for a tougher approach. That approach called for modification of the containment regime to more directly target Saddam's rule—often called "smart sanctions"—to reduce perceived Iraqi suffering, and to make more credible the threat of force by granting it firm international legitimacy.

From June 1997 through November 1998 the U.S. government worked assiduously to remake the containment regime and to recreate a consensus on Iraq within the UN Security Council. Three times during that period, the United States also threatened to use military force against Iraq. The first time, in November 1997, Russian Foreign Minister Yevgeny Primakov mediated a last minute compromise that was supposed to allow unfettered inspections of Iraq's weapons program, but the compromise quickly broke down. Three months later the United States accepted a replacement deal, brokered by UN Secretary General Kofi Annan, that obliged Iraq to provide UN weapons inspectors with "immediate, unconditional, and unrestricted access" to suspected weapons sites, though it effectively exempted eight vast "presidential sites" from the inspection regime. That deal also broke down, however, and in November 1998 the United States and Britain prepared to attack Iraq, stopping only at the last minute—with U.S. and British warplanes already in the air—when Iraqi Deputy Prime Minister Tariq Aziz on live television acceded to U.S. demands to stop obstructing inspectors.

In December 1998, Iraq's continuing obstruction of the weapons inspectors finally led to the departure of the UN inspection mission from Iraq. Having failed to achieve consensus in the UN, the United States and Britain launched Operation Desert Fox—four days of air and missile strikes against targets deemed crucial to Saddam Hussein's grip on power, and the largest attack against Iraq since the 1991 Gulf War. The air strikes failed to bring down Saddam's regime, but they shattered even the pretense of international consensus on the issue of Iraq. France, Russia, and China all condemned the attacks, and France withdrew from participation in the southern no-fly zone, its last military contribution to the containment of Iraq.

Even after this public and fundamental disagreement on Iraq, the United States and its partners continued to seek UN Security Council consensus on the issue. In difficult negotiations throughout most of 1999, the Clinton administration accepted a new compromise on how to deal with Iraq, expressed in December 1999 by UNSC Resolution 1284. The resolution established a new inspection regime, modified the sanctions to allow a greater range of goods to be imported, and affirmed the principle that the remaining sanctions would be lifted if UN inspectors accepted that Iraq had met its obligations. Unfortunately, the new consensus established in the negotiations for Resolution 1284 was shattered before it was even officially articulated when the French, Russians, and Chinese all abstained on the vote.

In essence, the basic differences within the Security Council had not been resolved. For its part, the United States was highly skeptical of the Security Council's willingness to enforce its mandates and highly dubious of Iraq's intentions to abide by them. Many Americans believed that the French, Russians, and others were purposefully undermining containment both because of the commercial opportunities in Iraq and because they felt that Iraq did not pose a security threat. Russia and France, for their part, doubted the American willingness to live with Saddam Hussein's regime under any circumstances. In their view, the goal of regime change impeded the process of establishing peaceful coexistence with Iraq because it removed any incentive Saddam Hussein might have had to moderate his behavior. As a result, no UN Security Council resolution had ever authorized the goal of regime change.

By the late 1990s the other Security Council members had substantial grounds for believing that this was U.S. policy. Already in March 1997, Secretary of State Madeleine Albright had stated that the United States would maintain sanctions on Iraq no matter what Saddam did, arguing that the evidence was "overwhelming that Saddam Hussein's intentions will never be peaceful." In October 1998, Congress, with strong bipartisan support, further forced the issue by passing the Iraq Liberation Act, which established that "it should be the policy of the United States to support efforts to remove the regime headed by Saddam Hussein from power in Iraq." Clinton signed that legislation, and in December 1998, at the end of Operation Desert Fox, openly advocated regime change, stating that "[so] long as Saddam remains in power he will remain a threat to his people, his region, and the world."

In sum, by the end of the Clinton presidency, the failure to agree on Iraq had become one of the most divisive issues in the Atlantic alliance. The clashes at the UN created a legacy of bitterness and betrayal that seriously damaged both sides' belief in the other's good faith as well as the belief that the UN could effectively cope with problems like Iraq. This legacy would have an important impact on the split over Iraq that would emerge in 2002.

Nonetheless, it was also clear from the Clinton administration's efforts to reach compromise that it still believed that allied support in the UN was essential for managing the Iraqi problem. In three successive crises in 1997 and 1998, the United States was unwilling to use force in Iraq without broad international support. Even after Clinton did use force in December 1998, the administration never abandoned the search for consensus at the UN.

While that process certainly proved cumbersome and incapable of permanently solving the security problems that Iraq posed, it had managed to keep Saddam contained for nearly 10 years. More important, all of the alternatives seemed worse. Full-scale invasion was a domestic political impossibility and an international liability, internal overthrow was a proven failure, and unilateral containment punished American companies rather than the Iraqi regime. The notion of abandoning the search for consensus was thus never seriously considered by the Clinton administration. Indeed, before September 11 the Bush administration did not actively pursue any of these alternatives and essentially continued the Clinton policy of seeking a reinvigorated "smart sanctions" regime at the UN, albeit with a new negotiating style.

A History of Discord

The history of alliance relations prior to the Bush administration contains several lessons. On one hand, the fact that the allies have always been at odds, sometimes as severely as they were over Iraq in 2002–2003, is comforting to those who believe the alliance has a future. A generation before Robert Kagan concluded that Europeans were from Venus (and Americans from Mars), other Americans were already arguing that Europeans were "relatively rich and ungrateful introverts." And decades before Germany's failure to support an American invasion of Iraq led to calls to remove U.S. troops from Germany, other Americans were predicting that the failure of their European allies to support U.S. policy in the Persian Gulf would lead to the removal of U.S. troops from Europe. The long history of transatlantic crises and the track record of overcoming those crises suggests that the United States and Europe have learned to manage some very serious stresses in their alliance—and provides hope that they can do so again.

At the same time, the history also shows why future cooperation will be more difficult. It was the Cold War that was responsible for the formation of the alliance in the first place and for its survival at least through its early crises. While alliance norms of consultation and compromise on issues of European strategy and security were extensive throughout the Cold War, those norms never applied very well to "out-of-area" issues, which are precisely the set of issues that pose the greatest challenges today.

Despite the end of the Cold War, the Clinton administration continued to believe in the value of allied support and made considerable efforts to persuade allies to adapt the Atlantic alliance to better deal with new types of threats from regions beyond Europe. Despite growing American power and freedom of maneuver to confront new threats, Clinton was convinced that the United States should do everything possible to ensure agreement among European allies before resorting to unilateral action, not only on issues like the Balkans, which directly affected those allies, but even on global issues like the Middle East.

That degree of commitment to alliance consensus would change significantly with the arrival of George W. Bush to the White House, and then again, even more so, after the September 11 terrorist attacks. In retrospect, the final Clinton years were the calm before the storm, and clouds were gathering on the Atlantic horizon. It was under George W. Bush that the storm would strike.

Chapter

2

Bush and Europe: The Growing Divide

As he took office in January 2001, George W. Bush's views on foreign affairs, and by extension, those of his administration, were not well known. Contrary to the now common notion that the Bush team was distinctly hawkish and unilateralist from the start, some core principles of foreign policy, particularly on when and how to use American military power, remained undecided when Bush entered office. The Bush campaign had avoided taking strong positions on foreign policy subjects that tended to divide Republicans, and many believed that Bush would follow in his father's footsteps in pursuing a prudent, multilateral foreign policy.

During the campaign, the focus of Bush's foreign policy speeches was on criticizing Clinton's policy. He did so using language and ideas that specifically avoided the controversial issue of when and how to use force. For those who feared imperial overstretch, Bush promised a "humble" foreign policy that concentrated on "enduring national interests"—a contrast with Clinton's alleged inconsistencies. He cautioned against too much foreign intervention or using U.S. troops for nation-building, warning against the notion that "our military is the answer to every difficult foreign policy situation—a substitute for strategy." At the same time, Bush declared his belief in the power of American confidence, moral clarity, and leadership to secure U.S. interests. His "distinctly American internationalism" presented an explicit contrast to Clinton's alleged lack of principles and excessive willingness to compromise with allies.

Reflecting this divide, the new Bush administration seemed structured to provide an undecided President with varied advice on foreign policy. Bush appointed people to the top positions at the Defense Department, who had a reputation for hawkish, even unilateralist, views, such as Donald Rumsfeld and Paul Wolfowitz. But his closest foreign policy adviser, Condoleezza Rice, was a protégé of his father's pragmatic National Security Adviser, Brent Scowcroft. Even more prominently, as Secretary of State, Bush appointed Colin Powell, the scourge of the hawkish wing of the Republican party. Powell was famous (or infamous, to some) for his reluctance to use force and for his insistence, borne of his painful experience in Vietnam, that military force when applied should be directed at securing identifiable and indisputable national interests.

Bush himself summed up this balance on appointing Rumsfeld Secretary of Defense in December 2000: "General Powell's a strong figure, and Dick Cheney's no shrinking violet. But neither is Don Rumsfeld . . . nor Condi Rice. I view the four as being able to complement each other. There's going to be disagreements. I hope there is disagreement, because I know the disagreement will be based upon solid thought." As a result, the administration's only sacred foreign policy principles on entering office seemed to be a commitment to national missile defense and a strong desire to distance itself from the policy of its predecessor.

Despite this very real balance, however, it would be wrong to conclude that prior to September 11 the Bush administration did not develop any new understanding of how foreign policy works in a world defined by U.S. power. In his first few months in office, Bush began to demonstrate this understanding, particularly in his dealings with European allies. Where Bill Clinton had engaged in protracted diplomacy and sometimes reached difficult compromises with European allies over such issues as missile defense, the International Criminal Court, the Kyoto Accords, and even Iran and Iraq, Bush clearly had little patience with European views. Many in the administration, moreover, saw Europeans as unwilling to recognize the importance of force in international relations and all too ready to appease dictators and weapons proliferators rather than confront them.

A Vision of Decisive Leadership

In retrospect, it's clear that changing circumstances led the administration to repudiate the previous administration's approach to transatlantic relations and to seek to assert American power more vigorously. In the new team's view, the Clinton administration had too often followed a model of diplomacy—symbolized by Warren Christopher's Balkan trip—that unwisely sought to achieve allied, and especially transatlantic, consensus before making important foreign policy decisions. That model, they believed, belonged to a bygone era. The increased relative power of the United States and its unique military capacity meant that breaking from these norms of cooperation and consultation—even on issues of intense salience for both sides—was now possible.

The growing divide in U.S.-European threat perceptions, as well as the agonizing and seemingly endless U.S.-European diplomacy over such issues as the Balkans, Iraq, and the Middle East peace process, argued that a new approach to alliance relations was necessary. The Bush administration's well-noted desire to distance itself from both the positions and the methods of its predecessor implied that a new approach was desirable from a domestic political perspective as well. In fact, over the years, the Clinton administration had come to take a much tougher-minded view of leadership. But the Bush team felt that even the late 1990s version of Clinton's foreign policy was far too deferential to allied sensibilities and that major changes were required.

The new administration's vision was that important U.S. foreign policy goals could only be realized through decisive U.S. leadership and, if necessary, unilateral action. Such leadership entailed staking out firm positions and then demonstrating a capacity, and an implacable will, to follow through on policies regardless of the opposition they might generate. The administration was convinced that U.S. allies and partners would eventually follow the American lead while simultaneously allowing the United States to maintain its freedom of action.

Robert Kagan articulated the theory as early as 1998, writing that "to be effective, multilateralism must be preceded by unilateralism. In the toughest situations, the most effective multilateral response comes when the strongest power decides to act, with or without the others, and then asks its partners whether they will join." Former CIA Director James Woolsey, another strong supporter of the Bush administration's foreign policy and leadership style, agreed: "My experience in a number of different jobs in government in this area has been that when the United States acts decisively and goes to its friends and allies and says, 'We're going to do this, and we want you with us,' we get a lot better response than if we start with the lowest denominator of a large group of countries and say, 'Gee, what do you think we ought to do?'"

This "if you build it, they will come" doctrine expresses the belief that the United States is a unique country not just in terms of the power it possesses, but also in its moral authority for using that power. It does not rule out acting in coalitions, but it does rely on the credible threat that the United States will act alone to make opposition to U.S. plans seem futile. This vision of U.S. leadership depends on the U.S. military and diplomatic capacity to act unilaterally, though it does not expect to have to do so, since others will eventually follow. And if allies are not comfortable with American power and leadership, the thinking goes— that's their problem, not America's. As William Kristol put it: "We need to err on the side of being strong. . . . And if people want to say we're an imperial power, fine." Writer Max Boot agrees: "Resentment comes with the territory."

This basic vision of how to conduct foreign policy has been widely shared throughout the Bush administration since its inception. While there have certainly been differences within the administration on the degree to which allied views should be taken into account, these disagreements have often been exaggerated. Even Secretary of State Colin Powell, identified as the member of the cabinet with the most multilateral instincts, has explained the process this way:

[Where] we have a principled position, what we will do is explain that principled position to our friends, try to see if we can find compromises, so we can join consensus. But where we can't join consensus, because of our own beliefs, or because we believe a particular issue and the direction it's going with others does not serve the purpose intended by that action, the United States will stick to its principled position. . . . The President is that kind of leader. He speaks clearly, he speaks directly, and he makes sure people know what he believes in. And then he tries to persuade others that is the correct position. When it does not work, then we will take the position we believe is correct, and I hope the Europeans are left with a better understanding of the way in which we want to do business.

The view that allies can best be won over through decisive American leadership naturally leads to a negative view of the utility of multilateral forums and international organizations. Indeed, such organizations, including the United Nations and even NATO, are based on the opposite premise: that no nation has either the inherent strength or the special moral authority to decide important international issues without the consent of other states. The specific purpose of many such organizations, especially the United Nations, is to provide a forum for its members in which state power can express itself peacefully and governments can reach compromise and, eventually, consensus through discussion.

The Bush administration's objection is not just that this process is often lengthy, inefficient, and frustrating, but also that, because of changes in the nature of threats and relative power, the current rules of the system unduly constrain the United States. According to Vice President Dick Cheney, the institutions and alliances "built to deal with the conflicts of the twentieth century ... may not be the right strategies and policies and institutions to deal with the kind of threat we face now." The United Nations in particular, Cheney believed, had "proven incapable of meeting the challenge we face in the twenty-first century of rogue states armed with deadly weapons, possibly sharing them with terrorists." Indeed, Cheney argued that subordinating U.S. national security interests to the need for international consensus was "a prescription for perpetual disunity and obstructionism." When presented with imminent threats, waiting for allies could even be dangerous.

The administration's view of the foreign policy process and its reluctance to engage in the messy business of international negotiation in multilateral forums are the common threads that unite Bush foreign policy before and after September 11. In terms of U.S. foreign policy the administration showed remarkable consistency even prior to the terrorist attacks, rejecting a variety of different foreign entanglements that for better or for worse would certainly have ensnared its predecessors. For instance, the Bush administration abandoned its predecessors' efforts to secure Senate ratification for the Comprehensive Test Ban Treaty (CTBT), which had already been signed by 161 countries and ratified by 71, including Russia and every state in the European Union. And the U.S. government refused to consider signing on to a United Nations agreement to limit traffic in small arms, or to verification protocols to the Biological Weapons Convention, a Nixon-era treaty that had long been criticized by arms control experts as ineffective specifically because it lacked any verification or enforcement mechanisms. Further, the Bush administration withdrew President Clinton's signature from the treaty establishing the International Criminal Court and, through bilateral agreements, began a highly coercive campaign to ensure that no U.S. citizen could ever be subject to the court's jurisdiction. And where Clinton had spent years trying to find a compromise position with allies on the issue of national missile defense, Bush simply made clear his intention to modify, and if necessary unilaterally to abrogate, the 1972 ABM treaty so the United States could deploy a national missile defense system.

Perhaps most significantly, however, at least from Europe's point of view, was the U.S. withdrawal from the Kyoto Protocol on global warming. U.S. objections to the treaty predated the Bush administration and derived from serious flaws in the treaty, which most observers agreed deserved addressing. Nonetheless, the treaty represented the only advances in a more than decade-long effort to confront an issue that poses, in the overwhelming view of European public opinion, a massive long-term threat to the environment.

Negotiations to meet those objections were proceeding, albeit with great difficulty, when the President's advisers suddenly let European diplomats know that "the Kyoto agreement is dead." President Bush abandoned all efforts to reach a compromise, promising a solely U.S. plan in the unspecified future to deal with the threat of global warming. Only hours before the first trip of his presidency to Europe, Bush reiterated his rejection of the treaty in a Rose Garden ceremony, declaring that an internal administration review had led to the definitive conclusion that "the Kyoto Protocol was fatally flawed in fundamental ways." The message to the European allies he was about to meet was abundantly clear: Washington had decided there would be no revival of the Kyoto pact, and the decision was final.

In retrospect, the manner in which the U.S. government withdrew from the process of international negotiation on global warming signaled more than just a repudiation of Kyoto. The harsh diplomatic style of the rejection contrasted sharply even with a similar rejection by the Reagan administration of the UN Convention on the Law of the Sea in 1982, when that administration also decided to reject a treaty that its predecessors had supported. But unlike the Kyoto rejection, before doing so the Reagan administration sent a special envoy—ironically, Donald Rumsfeld—to consult with allied governments and convince them not to sign or ratify the treaty. While that position hardly endeared him to European publics, Reagan's willingness to conform to established practices of consultation meant that criticism focused on the U.S. objections to the treaty itself, rather than on its potential to cause a breakdown in the alliance.

The Bush administration did not, of course, systematically avoid working with allies both bilaterally and even within multilateral forums. On specific issues, most notably in its efforts to end North Korean nuclear proliferation, the administration used and even preferred a multilateral approach that proactively sought the support of like-minded allies. Bush's strong support for NATO's further enlargement to seven new members, and his willingness in 2002–2003 to work extensively with Europeans on a new "Road Map" for the Middle East, also showed a willingness to engage with allies when doing so required little compromise. And in Europe, from the start of his term, Bush deliberately sought to develop special relationships with those countries—like Britain, Spain, Italy, Poland, and others—

whose leaders he felt would be sympathetic to American policies and goals.

Bush's efforts with the allies, however—as one senior administration official put it—could best be described as "multilateralism à la carte." He was willing to use multilateral forums when they presented the most convenient path to accomplishing some specific U.S. foreign policy goal. But much of the administration never seemed to believe that U.S. commitment to international institutions and allied relationships had a long-term value that justified U.S. engagement when unilateral action—or actions with the support of certain individual countries—would be more expedient in the short term. The sum total of Bush's actions in his adminstration's first two years sent the clear signal that this type of deeper commitment simply did not exist.

The Growing Divide

In many ways the emerging transatlantic disputes were a product of the presidency of George W. Bush, who came to power after one of the most closely fought and bizarrely concluded elections of all time. At the same time, Bush's election—as well as his policies and the transatlantic disputes to which they contributed—were themselves products of far-reaching structural changes that were affecting both sides of the Atlantic. It was not just the end of the Cold War and the removal of a common enemy that weakened the glue that once held the alliance together. It was that throughout the 1990s, internal and external developments were changing the domestic politics and worldviews—and consequently the foreign policies—of America and Europe in ways that tended to threaten the very basis of the alliance that they had once taken for granted.

One of the most important factors was the steady rise in U.S. power, and particularly military power, relative to Europe and all other states. The emergence of the United States as the sole superpower began with the decline of the Soviet Union in the 1980s and accelerated on the back of the booming American economy and technological base in the 1990s. By the time of the Bush presidency, more by chance than by design, the United States had become the strongest power the world had ever known, with an unprecedented ability to affect, essentially unassisted, developments around the globe.

This spectacular growth in power inevitably contributed to changes in American thinking about foreign policy and the emergence of differences with Europe. It is only natural to expect that a country with the technological, military, and diplomatic resources of the United States is inclined to try to "fix" problems—whether they be Balkan crises, missile threats, or rogue states—whereas countries with fewer such resources at their disposal try to "manage" them. America's vast military power, technological prowess, and history of unparalleled accomplishment have left Americans with a sense of "can do" optimism about the world that contrasts starkly with the relative pessimism—some would say "realism"—that comes from the more complicated historical experiences of Europe's much older nation states. These differences in political culture have long existed, but they widened significantly over the past decade, and they explain a lot about why American and European opinion was divided over what to do about Iraq.

Another important expression of this widening transatlantic cultural gap has been a slow but certain change in the way that the United States and Europe see the use of force. Beginning with the Gulf War in 1991, the U.S. military began to demonstrate just how devastating the combination of incomparable military power and cutting-edge innovation could be. A series of military victories—in the Gulf, Bosnia, Kosovo, and Afghanistan—each a more impressive demonstration of American military virtuosity than the last, slowly convinced both civilian policymakers and the public that U.S. military dominance now gave the nation a unique and unprecedented tool.

Based on this experience, U.S. policymakers slowly concluded that the use of force is a more viable option than ever before, and military deployments have accelerated markedly. In the 1980s the U.S. military conducted 19 foreign operations to 14 different countries; in the 1990s, it conducted 108 such operations to 53 different countries. While this increased pace reflected in part the greater flexibility accorded to the United States by the demise of the Soviet Union, it also increasingly reflected a belief that U.S. military power had become more effective and more applicable to foreign policy problems.

Postwar Europe has developed very different views about power and the use of force. With a collective population of 377 million and a GDP of some $8.5 trillion, the member states of the European Union certainly have the potential to develop military power comparable to that of the United States, but at least for now they have chosen not to. Collectively, NATO Europe spends about 45 percent of what the United States does on defense. But even that disparity understates the difference. The process through which Europe produces military power means that this money is spent less efficiently than in the United States, contributing to relative American military dominance. As a result, though Europe has some 1.5 million men and women in its ground forces, it would be hard pressed to deploy and sustain more than 6 percent of them abroad. In comparison, the United States can deploy and sustain some 62 percent of its ground forces.

Europe's lack of interest in developing military power is in part a perverse consequence of the American protectorate established by the United States through NATO during the Cold War. With the partial exception of the British and French, whose past experiences and permanent seats on the UN Security Council left them with enduring global ambitions and military roles, U.S. leadership of NATO largely absolved the Europeans from having to think much about international security beyond Europe's shores. Global military strategy was something primarily for the United States, while Europeans could focus on the difficult task of building their unprecedented zone of internal peace and prosperity.

But this disparity in military power is also partly a result of Europe's experience with war during the first half of the twentieth century and peace and integration during the second half. Those contrasting experiences have left most Europeans convinced that dialogue and development are more effective paths to security than military strength—a conviction that Europeans, understandably but sometimes naively, seek to project on other parts of the world. As British diplomat and author Robert Cooper has written, "Europe may have chosen to neglect power politics because it is militarily weak; but it is also true that it is militarily weak because it has chosen to abandon power politics."

Within the European "zone of peace," the EU has largely achieved its goal of escaping power politics. It has put a definitive end to the long rivalry between France and Germany, cemented the democratic transition in Spain, Greece, and Portugal, and preempted renewed ethnic conflict and border disputes in post-Soviet Eastern Europe with the enticement of EU (and NATO) membership.

These historic successes were achieved not through force, or even through traditional diplomacy—indeed the EU does not have an army and arguably does not have a foreign policy. Rather, in the European view, they were achieved through a softer form of power, in which pooled sovereignty, political and economic integration, and increasing wealth focused national energies on creating a Europe that was peaceful, prosperous, and stable. Immense challenges remain: completing the European internal market, integrating nearly 75 million citizens of formerly communist countries, and spreading democracy to Central and Eastern Europe, not to mention Russia, Turkey, and North Africa. In the face of these challenges, Europeans have little stomach for following the U.S. lead in spending more than $400 billion on defense or for invading and occupying large sections of the Middle East.

Europe's internal focus means that Europeans will often not pro-vide the material support for American priorities that, in the U.S. view, should concern statesmen in Europe as much as those in the United States. Americans have often complained that this lack of support rep-resents parochialism or free-riding—in essence, an inability to think globally and therefore strategically. Particularly in comparison to the Bush administration's activism in foreign affairs, Europe's status quo bias often seems both reactive and reactionary. But this perception misses the point: For Europeans whose strategic challenge for a centu-ry had been to overcome the deadly divisions on their own continent, European unification *is* a global strategy. That strategy asserts that a Europe that is "whole and free" can serve as a starting point for spread-ing stability and prosperity to other regions—first in the regions bor-dering the European Union, and eventually beyond.

Reacting to 9/11

The systematic divisions between the United States and Europe on world affairs thus began before 9/11, and even before the arrival of the Bush administration. But the terrorist attacks on New York and Washington vastly accelerated those trends and expanded the gap between the American and European approaches.

Initially, the attacks seemed to have brought Europe and the United States closer together, ushering in a new period of transatlantic coop-eration based, as before, on a common threat. The European allies immediately invoked NATO's Article V security guarantee and sup-ported a UN Security Council resolution that gave Washington broad international legitimacy for responding to the attacks. In turn, many thought the United States would become more multilateral. According to former President George H. W. Bush, "just as Pearl Harbor awakened this country from the notion that we could somehow avoid the call to duty and defend freedom in Europe and Asia in World War II, so too should this most recent surprise attack erase the concept in some quarters that America can somehow go it alone in the fight against terrorism or in anything else for that matter."

In retrospect, however, while the outpouring of human sympathy surrounding that event was sincere, it is now also clear that the terrorist attacks exacerbated rather than attenuated the trends that were dividing the alliance. While Europeans and Americans both now fully recognized the danger of Islamic terrorism, each chose to establish broad strategies for dealing with the terrorist threat that played to their respective strengths and fit into their conceptual understandings of how the post–Cold War world works.

For the United States, long insulated from international violence, the September 11 attacks were simply so massive that they had to be regarded as, in the words of President Bush, "an act of war against our country." The fact that those attacks were the most deadly terrorist strikes in history, and that they took place on U.S. soil against U.S. targets rather than in Europe, no doubt also made a difference. But the United States, with the geographical blessing of friendly neighbors, and the fact that it had hardly been attacked in its history, already had a lower tolerance for vulnerability than a Europe that, in a sense, had gotten used to terrorist attacks over a period of decades. This lower threshold for vulnerability, combined with greater American power and resources, leads Americans to be far more ready than Europeans to aggressively confront the threats they perceive.

Europeans, in comparison, have a long and painful experience with the phenomenon of terrorism—in Northern Ireland, the Basque region of Spain, with extreme left movements in Italy and Germany, and with Islamist terrorism throughout Europe, but particularly in France. Governments and societies in Europe have internalized the notion that terrorism, given its roots in deep social alienation and its tenacious resistance to purely repressive means, can never be completely eradicated.

Moreover, prior to 9/11, Europe's strategic priorities were not global military issues, but political and economic integration, enlargement to the East, and the completion of monetary union—in other words, in consolidating the gains of the end of the Cold War. The terrorist attacks in New York and Washington did not change that. In that sense, the divisions that have occurred are not so much a result of Europe changing or moving away from the United States as of a Europe reluctant to join America in its strategic revolution.

After the initial shock of the attacks wore off, the relationship started to deteriorate again. Serious differences emerged over how to fight the war on terrorism—or even whether it should be seen as a war—and over the American aversion to constructing a permanent antiterrorist alliance. European commentators denounced the Bush administration's use of the word "war" and its accompanying semantic baggage as not only inaccurate but actually counterproductive because, as British historian Sir Michael Howard put it, talk of war "arouses an expectation and a demand for military action against some easily identifiable adversary . . . leading to decisive results." Rather than fight wars, the United States, in this view, should adapt itself to living with vulnerability and to managing rather than solving the problem of terrorism, as Europe has long done. While U.S. power might defeat specific terrorist groups through offensive military action, terrorism itself would continue until the root social and political causes had been addressed— a long-term project under the best of circumstances, and certainly not one that could be accomplished by military means.

Rather than availing itself of permanent bodies such as the UN or NATO, which offered a degree of legitimacy and burden-sharing in return for some consultation, the United States instead preferred to operate on an ad hoc basis. In Secretary of Defense Donald Rumsfeld's formulation, "the mission needs to define the coalition, and we ought not to think that a coalition should define the mission." This, Europeans pointed out, was the very opposite of NATO's founding principle. Former NATO Secretary General Javier Solana, now the EU's foreign policy chief, responded that "the alliance should determine the mission and not vice versa," and complained that NATO had "invoked its most sacred covenant" and yet was totally ignored by American war planners.

The Bush administration, however, was in little mood to listen. The September 11 attacks did not create the recognition of American pre-eminence any more than they spawned the new vision of leadership that rested on that preeminence. Policy in this broad sense did not change. But the politics changed completely. Emboldened by enormous American power, inspired by its preexisting concept of alliance leadership, and angered by the 9/11 attack, the administration saw no advantages, and plenty of downsides, to involving European allies in the U.S. decision-making process.

Rather, Bush was ready to respond to the challenges that 9/11 revealed and to the political opportunity of the moment by elaborating a more precise and more overt version of his vision of U.S. leadership. For an administration already convinced that hard problems required decisive U.S. leadership, 9/11 confirmed that international affairs were now far too dangerous for the American people to accept anything less. If Europeans did not agree with the way America decided to respond to the new challenges, that was unfortunate, but it was their problem, and the United States would not risk its safety to accommodate dissenting views.

In the wake of the attacks, the U.S. government became much more willing to assert openly categorical imperatives, to directly deploy U.S. military power against enemies, and to insist upon compliance and cooperation from allies without prior consultation. Confident in American power, the administration lost no time declaring that the war against terror must not be impeded by either the ambitions of enemies or the indecision of allies. In a speech on September 20, 2001, before a joint session of Congress, President Bush laid down the gauntlet:

"Every nation, in every region, now has a decision to make. Either you are with us, or you are with the terrorists. . . . [This] country will define our times, not be defined by them. As long as the United States of America is determined and strong, this will not be an age of terror; this will be an age of liberty." Consistent with this message, and to the dismay of many allies, Washington did not engage in any significant multilateral consultations before moving against the Taliban in Afghanistan in October 2001. Multilateral support would have been easy for the United States to secure in this case—the Taliban had few sympathizers even before September 11. Indeed, significant approval and assistance was offered without the United States even needing to ask for it. Already on September 12, NATO, for the first time in its history, invoked its Article V treaty commitment of mutual defense on the initiative of NATO Secretary General Lord Robertson without an explicit American request (and despite the Pentagon's misgivings). Similarly, the UN Security Council, at France's initiative, passed Resolution 1383 on September 12, offering the United States any assistance necessary.

Despite this rapid show of support, the Bush administration decided that it did not want to risk future delays or diminish U.S. control by accepting too much international assistance. Indeed, on September 26, at the first high-level briefing provided by Washington to NATO defense ministers after September 11, Deputy Secretary of Defense Paul Wolfowitz ruled out using any international or NATO structures. He also made clear that Washington was not planning to rely heavily on European forces either, instead noting that the effort "would be made up of many different coalitions in different parts of the world." When Secretary of Defense Rumsfeld was later asked whether NATO might be involved in military action against Iraq, his response was revealing: "I can't imagine it . . . it hasn't crossed my mind."

This position reflected a longstanding mind-set in the Pentagon and among many Republican strategists that allied support would not add any appreciable military value to the U.S. effort. Such thinking was a natural outgrowth of the near universal view that preeminent U.S. power alone could ensure victory in the military phase of operations. It was reinforced by what many Americans saw as a key "lesson" of Kosovo. Whereas many in Europe saw the Kosovo air campaign as excessively dominated by the United States, most Americans—particularly within the military—saw just the opposite: excessive European meddling, with French politicians and European lawyers interfering with efficient targeting and bombing runs, and compromising operational security.

This time, the Bush team determined, would be different. NATO was not used in Afghanistan, and in fact—in ironic contrast to previous conflicts like the Gulf War, Bosnia, and Kosovo—the United States actually faced a situation in which the NATO allies were offering more troops and equipment than the Pentagon, for military and political reasons, wanted to use. The United States accepted some symbolic foreign assistance; in particular, NATO frigates patrolled the Eastern Mediterranean and NATO AWACS (early warning aircraft) patrolled U.S. airspace in order to free up U.S. assets for deployment. But in so doing, Washington refused to cede any degree of control or even any right of consultation. Assistance offered under even an implicit notion that participation conferred some such rights was refused.

For U.S. policymakers, the manner in which Operation Enduring Freedom in Afghanistan unfolded, confirmed, and indeed reinforced the wisdom of this approach to coalition management. Despite very strong initial support, allied confidence weakened easily under the stress of operations. When, after only three weeks of military operations, U.S. operational momentum stalled before Mazar-e-Sharif, European commentators began to question U.S. strategies, tactics, and even, obliquely, U.S. motives. They implied that the United States—like the British and Soviet Empires before it—had bitten off more in Afghanistan than even a superpower could chew. European governments—with what the U.S. administration saw as typical pessimism—began to hint that the United States had moved too quickly and foresworn the necessary allied and internal support.

The structure of the coalition in Afghanistan, however, meant that U.S. operations were invulnerable to allied interference. U.S. officials simply ignored such complaints in a manner that would not have been possible under, say, NATO auspices. U.S. military forces, aided primarily by local Afghan allies, pushed ahead according to the original plan. Contrary to many dire predictions, resistance crumbled suddenly under the weight of American military power. The critics were silenced, and all allied governments—those that had participated, those that had criticized, and those that had equivocated—rushed to offer troops and aid for postwar reconstruction.

The lesson for many Americans was clear: Europeans will whine and complain about *any* military operation, but victory will obviate such complaints and the Europeans will jump on the bandwagon. The process through which the coalition was created would not matter in the end. Because preeminent U.S. military power alone could produce a victory, there was little reason to endure the trials and tribulations of multilateral negotiations. In the end, all that is necessary to achieve support is to be clear, to be consistent, to win, and to be America.

Emboldened by this demonstrable vindication of the "if you build it, they will come" doctrine, the administration began to advance its vision of American leadership ever more assertively. In December 2001, Bush ended months of speculation and debate and announced that the United States would withdraw from the 1972 Anti-Ballistic Missile Treaty with Russia. Bush had campaigned on the need to build a national missile defense system, but had previously resisted pressure to make any final decision with regard to the ABM Treaty. Many within the United States and Europe viewed the treaty as a cornerstone of strategic stability whose relevance persisted into the post–Cold War era.

Even among supporters of national missile defense, many believed that a unilateral U.S. modification or withdrawal from the treaty would damage relations with the Russians and the Europeans more than was necessary or worthwhile. The Russians, sensing U.S. and European division on this question, were unwilling to cheaply concede one of their final bargaining chips.

After September 11 and Afghanistan, such considerations seemed remote, almost quaint, in U.S. policy circles. Those within the administration who had always advocated that there could be no real consequences for unilateral withdrawal now held the upper hand. The administration plowed ahead and abandoned the treaty. Criticism was vociferous in both the United States and Europe, but short lived and without political consequence for the administration. Just as Afghanistan had proven how effective the U.S. military could be if force were applied with consistency and purpose, the experience with the ABM Treaty seemed to prove that with determined U.S. leadership, allied sensitivities could easily be overcome.

Toward the Clash

The experiences of the months after September 11 served to confirm the Bush administration in its view that the Cold War norms of alliance relations no longer applied. The real turning point, however, was President Bush's January 29, 2002, State of the Union address, in which he denounced an "axis of evil" that included Iraq, Iran, and North Korea, and warned that the United States would not "permit the world's most dangerous regimes to threaten us with the world's most destructive weapons." By seeking weapons of mass destruction, these regimes posed "a grave threat and a growing danger" because they "could provide these arms to terrorists [and] attack our allies or attempt to blackmail the United States." But behind that important headline lay another message intended to put U.S. allies on notice:

My hope is that all nations will heed our call, and eliminate the terrorist parasites who threaten their countries and our own. . . . But some governments will be timid in the face of terror. And make no mistake about it: if they do not act, America will. . . . America will do what is necessary to ensure our nation's security. We will be deliberate, yet time is not on our side. I will not wait on events, while dangers gather. I will not stand by, as peril draws closer and closer. The United States of America will not permit the world's most dangerous regimes to threaten us with the world's most dangerous weapons.

The language implied a strategic doctrine of preventive war that in fact would emerge later in the year. By focusing on military issues like the need for a missile shield and large increases in defense spending (the administration had just proposed a $48 billion increase), and speaking in Manichaean terms of good and evil, Bush confirmed many Europeans' worst fears. European observers also noticed that while undemocratic countries like Pakistan were singled out for praise for cracking down on terror, the NATO allies that had shown total solidarity with the United States and were leading the Afghanistan security force did not merit mention. The implication was clear: If the President deemed force necessary to deal with a threat to the security of the United States, no nation or alliance should or could stand in the way.

European reaction was swift and scathing. French Foreign Minister Hubert Védrine called the speech "simplistic," EU Commissioner for External Affairs Chris Patten warned that even a superpower could not do everything alone, and German Foreign Minister Joschka Fischer complained that alliance partners should not be treated like "satellites." French Prime Minister Lionel Jospin remarked that "the problems of the world cannot be reduced simply to the struggle against terrorism, however vital that struggle may be." But what most worried Europeans was the implicit message in the speech that Bush was bent on attacking Iraq. It was hard to imagine that Bush would so boldly announce that he would "not wait on events" if he did not intend on taking action before his next State of the Union address, a year later.

Bush's articulation of the doctrine of military preemption in a speech at West Point, New York, in June 2002 only confirmed the European view that the Bush administration had a simplistic approach to foreign policy that reduced everything to the military aspects of the war on terrorism. Speaking to the graduation ceremony of West Point cadets, Bush described a "threat with no precedent" that "required new thinking." He said, "Deterrence means nothing against shadowy terrorist networks with no nation or citizens to defend. Containment is not possible when unbalanced dictators with weapons of mass destruction can deliver those weapons on missiles or secretly provide them to terrorist allies. We cannot defend America and our friends by hoping for the best. . . . If we wait for threats to fully materialize, we will have waited too long." Bush thus promised to "take the battle to the enemy, disrupt his plans, and confront the worst threats before they emerge." Lest anyone not get the message, Bush insisted that "in the world we have entered, the only path to safety is the path of action. And this nation will act."

The speech implied that the United States had both a right and a duty to take preemptive action, not only in the face of an imminent threat, but even, if Washington so decided, of a potential threat. By September 2002 the doctrine implied in the State of the Union and West Point speeches was elaborated and given official status in the National Security Strategy of the United States. The language of the NSS did not differ radically from similar documents issued during the Clinton administration, which also emphasized America's readiness to act alone if necessary. In fact the Bush document said much more about the value of cooperating with allies than it did about the potential need for military preemption. But the Bush strategy had a far greater impact and sent a message very different from the Clinton documents, which had largely passed unnoticed. In the context of a looming debate about invading Iraq, and in the wake of two major presidential speeches about the need to act against growing threats, the Bush NSS was seen as a completely open-ended document intended to provide blanket authority for the unilateral use of U.S. military power. Understandably, audiences concluded that the new Bush doctrine would soon be applied to Iraq.

Various short- and long-term factors had thus come together to create a political environment in which the once radical notions in the State of the Union address, the National Security Strategy document, and the break with previous patterns of transatlantic diplomacy were possible and even relatively uncontroversial—at least within the U.S. domestic debate. While September 11 is central to understanding why the U.S. government moved away from traditional diplomatic practices in this regard, it was not the genesis of that change. From a long-term perspective, the increasing power of the United States, particularly in the military realm, created the environment in which such a policy was possible. Simultaneously, Europe's preoccupation with its internal issues, and its related unwillingness to develop deployable military power, lessened the perceived value of placating European opinion in ways that would have been given much higher priority in the past.

In the more immediate term, the experience before the Iraq crisis lent credence to the idea that if America built it, they would indeed come. Time and again, pessimists at home and abroad had predicted that the U.S. military or American diplomacy was overreaching—on the Kyoto Protocol, the International Criminal Court, Afghanistan, and the ABM Treaty, among others. Time and again, clarity, consistency, and American power had rendered the original objections of other nations to American policies essentially meaningless, at least from the perspective of the U.S. government.

On some issues, such as Kyoto and the ICC, important U.S. allies in Europe did not formally adopt the U.S. position and maintained their official policies in opposition to the U.S. view. But this opposition was without effect for the United States as far as any diplomatic, political, or economic measure that seemed relevant to the Bush administration was concerned. There was no credible threat of sanction against the United States, and no refusal to cooperate on other subjects. Indeed, on other issues, such as the ABM Treaty and Afghanistan, originally doubtful or even hostile allies in Europe eventually followed the U.S. lead. In all cases, overwhelming U.S. power combined with consistent U.S. purpose seemed to have guaranteed that other nations would come to understand that their interest lay in assisting the United States or, at worst, stepping aside. According to Secretary of Defense Rumsfeld, such a course might, "at the outset . . . seem lonesome," and indeed subject to fierce criticism and debate among the chattering classes on both sides of the Atlantic, but what ultimately mattered was "doing the right thing." In any case, in the face of a new type of threat that required firm and timely action, there was no other choice.

This approach to American leadership had considerable merit, and its success on the issues mentioned was not illusory. But it inevitably posed real problems for the relationship with Europe. On the most general level, it underestimated the degree to which resentment against this policy and against the United States might accumulate over time and across issues in a manner that could eventually make U.S. goals more difficult to achieve. On any given day, the nations of Europe and their publics were either too divided on these issues or too preoccupied with internal problems of integration and demography to take serious stands against the United States. But as a whole they were not so inherently weak that they had to simply accept American policies.

Under such circumstances it is not surprising that the Americans and Europeans often failed to agree or, more important, to resolve disagreements even before the crisis over Iraq. An America imbued with a sense of unprecedented power—and after September 11, unprecedented vulnerability—concluded that the global status quo was no longer acceptable, and that it was within Washington's power to change it. Most Europeans—divided among themselves, internally preoccupied, and worried about the consequences of upsetting what they perceived to be a broadly favorable status quo—were not inclined to follow the American lead. The transatlantic relationship only needed the right issue to deteriorate rapidly into serious crisis. And Iraq was precisely the right issue.

PART II

THE
IRAQ CRISIS

Chapter

3

THE SOURCES
OF
DISAGREEMENT

It would be wrong to caricature the positions of "Americans" and "Europeans" in the Iraq debate. In fact, there was a range of positions on both sides. The *New York Times* editorial page, former National Security Adviser Brent Scowcroft, and Senator Edward Kennedy, for example, all opposed the war, while British Prime Minister Tony Blair, Spain's José Maria Aznar, and French politicians like Bernard Kouchner and Pierre Lellouche supported the Bush administration's position. Throughout 2002, public opinion polls showed that some 50 to 60 percent of Americans supported an invasion of Iraq, but that support fell to just 35 to 40 percent for a war without UN support, a figure much closer to the levels seen in Europe. If President Bush had not decided to devote the bully pulpit of the presidency to the case for invading Iraq, it's unlikely that a majority of the American public would have ended up clamoring for him to do so.

It was, nonetheless, possible to speak broadly about predominant views on each side of the Atlantic, views that would end up hardening into real differences as time went on. Certainly, there was no European equivalent of the American neoconservatives—men and women determined to put their country's military power to good use to try to transform the world. By the time the war was actually fought, over 70 percent of Americans supported it, compared with nearly 80 percent of Europeans opposed to it. After months of aggressive diplomacy and the outbreak of war, the transatlantic gap over Iraq that had existed before September 11 had developed into a chasm.

Many Americans were as puzzled by the depth of European opposition to the war as Europeans were by the relative lack of opposition in the United States. Americans asked why Europeans could not see that Saddam Hussein was a brutal dictator who had defied UN Security Council resolutions for over a decade and was bent on developing weapons of mass destruction. Didn't Europeans recognize that the perpetuation of the status quo—sanctions on Iraq, no-fly zones, and the presence of Western troops in Saudi Arabia—was itself a cause of terrorism and anti-Western feeling in the world? Yes, Europeans responded, we recognize that Iraq is a problem, but didn't Americans fail to see that using force was not the answer? And that an invasion of Iraq could lead to a long-term occupation that would actually provoke more terrorism from a resentful and destabilized Arab world?

There is a range of explanations for these divergent positions, but some of those most often heard were not compelling. Indeed, it was the constant drumbeat of mutual accusations—often expressed by strong proponents or opponents of war deliberately to discredit the views of the other side—that to a large degree contributed to the growing gap between American and European views on Iraq. Instead of trying to close that gap, many on both sides of the Atlantic seemed determin-ed to widen it. The efforts by American proponents of war to cast European opposition as the product of mercantile interests, combined with anti-Americanism, was mirrored by European efforts to suggest that the Americans were solely driven by a desire to expand U.S. power and by the thirst for foreign oil.

False Premises

One commonly suggested explanation for French and German policy, for example, suggests that it was driven primarily by commercial interests. As former CIA Director James Woolsey explained it: "I think a lot of the French interest is economic, they have a lot of deals with Saddam Hussein, oil deals and others." Fox News anchor Tony Snow was even more categorical, explaining that whereas "Americans on the left and right believe morals matter and that foreign policy should not serve merely economic and territorial aims, the German and French positions . . . proceed from expediency. Germany has supplied the hardware for much of Saddam's biochemical weapons program, and the French position on Iraq is all about oil." Even Secretary of State Colin Powell, less inclined to disparage allies' motives, attributed at least part of French policy to "various commercial relationships" between France and Iraq.

These explanations were incomplete at best. While both France and Germany once had significant trading relationships with Iraq, by the early 2000s the 12 years of sanctions on that country had reduced business interests to a minimum.

From 1997 through 2002, French exports to Iraq averaged approx-imately $388 million per year—less than 0.3 percent of overall exports and around 0.02 percent of France's GDP. French imports from Iraq during that period averaged around $850 million, or 0.2 percent of overall exports and 0.05 percent of French GDP. These were hardly levels likely to have a major impact on French foreign policy, even if the French business community had much political clout.

For Germany, the Iraqi trade share was even smaller; export and import percentages for 2002 were 0.001 and 0.062 percent, respectively. Moreover, nearly 100 percent of the imports from Iraq were from purchases of oil, which could have been purchased at the same price from any of a number of other suppliers. The United States in the early 2000s was importing nearly $6 billion in Iraqi oil per year—six times as much as France—an amount that does not seem to have given Washington an interest in the maintenance of the Saddam regime.

French oil companies, it was true, did have potentially lucrative oil agreements with the Iraqi regime, which were probably a factor in France's efforts during the 1990s to work toward lifting the sanctions on Iraq. But officials in Paris also understood that as long as sanctions remained—and in the post–September 11 environment, no one could seriously believe that the United States would fail to veto the lifting of UN financial controls on Saddam—those deals would never be realized. Neither the French government nor French oil companies, in fact, ever believed they would conclude deals with Saddam Hussein's regime while the UN sanctions regime remained in place. The same was true for the approximately $5 billion in Iraqi debt to France stemming from decades-old business deals—it was highly unlikely that the debts would be paid as long as Saddam was in power.

The bottom line is that if commercial interests and cynicism were really the main factors driving policy, the best strategy for France and Germany would have been to strongly back the U.S. threat of force, join the coalition, and insist on a share of the spoils. With the United States by the end of 2002 desperate to win UN backing for the invasion, it is likely that France could have successfully cut a deal that would have included debt repayment and a significant stake for French companies in Iraqi oil development—a far better economic outcome than the one France ended up with.

It was also overly simplistic to ascribe European public opposition—and French and German policy—to "anti-American" motivations, as was often done in the United States. To be sure, anti-Americanism is a longstanding factor in parts of Europe, and it had been growing steadily since Bush's election. Europeans' negative image of Bush as the "toxic Texan" and resentment of many of his policies during his first year in office no doubt contributed to opposition on Iraq. But even if Bush's negative image is considered "anti-Americanism," it is not a convincing explanation for why France and Germany opposed U.S. policy in Iraq while other governments in Europe supported it.

Consider that only 17 months prior to the Iraq war, when the United States used force in Afghanistan, France and Germany strongly supported the action, which was backed by 73 and 65 percent of their respective populations. A Social Democratic/Green majority in the German Bundestag supported sending 3900 German combat troops to fight alongside the Americans, and a Socialist-Communist-Green coalition in France authorized the sending of French troops. Clearly, the degree of European support for or opposition to U.S. policy had something to do with what that policy was, as opposed to a systematic opposition to whatever the United States does.

Attributing European opposition to French and German anti-Americanism also failed to account for the fact that large majorities of the population in traditionally "pro-American" European countries— 84 percent in Britain, 82 percent in Hungary, 80 percent in the Netherlands, 79 percent in Denmark, 75 percent in Poland, and over 90 percent in Turkey—also opposed U.S. policy in Iraq. The difference was that their governments, for a range of reasons, believed it was nonetheless important to support the United States.

It is true, of course, that for certain countries—most prominently France and Russia, and increasingly Germany—the debate about Iraq was also a question of world order and a test of how an increasingly powerful United States would accommodate allied views following September 11. The Franco-German response was not "anti-Americanism" in the sense of reflexive and unremitting hostility to whatever the United States does, but a refusal to accept U.S. leadership simply because America is the sole superpower, as well as a desire to underscore Europe's own right to be a key player in world affairs.

Rightly or wrongly, the vast majority of European public opinion, as well as most European politicians, preferred containment to regime change in Iraq. The difference among European states was simply that most leaders were willing to back the war anyway because they accepted the reality, the necessity, and even the advantages of U.S. leadership. French, German, and Russian leaders, on the other hand, were not prepared to allow decisions about global war and peace to be decided unilaterally in Washington, especially when presented by the Bush administration as part of a doctrine of military preemption that could set precedents for other regions and states. Europe's internal divisions over Iraq, in this sense, had much more to do with different countries' attitudes toward the United States than with different views of what to do about Iraq.

Some commonly offered European explanations for American policy toward Iraq were equally misguided. One often heard the accusation, for example, particularly among peace protesters in European capitals, that the driving force behind U.S. policy was Iraqi oil. According to a December 2002 poll, 76 percent of respondents in Russia, 75 percent in France, 54 percent in Germany, and 44 percent in Britain said that America wanted to invade Iraq because "the U.S. wants to control Iraqi oil." The German newsweekly *Der Spiegel* also argued, in a January 2003 cover story, that "blood for oil" was "what it was really about" in Iraq.

Oil was obviously a relevant factor in the sense that it made the Gulf a strategic region for the United States and the West. And oil was also relevant because if Iraq could eventually develop into a stable source of energy supplies, U.S. dependence on Saudi Arabia would be reduced (though a reduction in Saudi income could pose its own problems for American interests if it led to instability there). But as a sole or even primary explanation for why the United States wanted to invade Iraq, the oil argument was no better—indeed, it was considerably worse—than the argument that France's main consideration was its own commercial interests.

Generously assuming that Iraq's oil production could within a few years be increased to something near 3 million barrels per day, the revenue generated from that production (assuming an average oil price of $25 per barrel and production costs of $5 per barrel), would come to around $22 billion per year. Unless the United States was willing to appropriate this money and deny it to the Iraqi people, running huge political risks, nearly all of this income would have to be used by the 23 million people of Iraq, which had few other sources of revenue. And given the immense potential costs and risks of war and reconstruction in Iraq—up to $70 billion for the war itself; $50 to $70 billion to restore oil production facilities; and up to $250 billion more for security, reconstruction, and humanitarian needs over the next 10 years—it is difficult to see how this would be anything close to an economic bargain for the United States.

Some U.S. officials might have optimistically believed that Iraqi oil would ensure that an Iraq war would not be a major economic burden on the United States. But even if they vastly overestimated potential for early Iraqi oil production and vastly underestimated the cost and difficulty of reconstruction—which many of them did—they could not have believed that invading Iraq would be in the economic interest of the United States, at least for a very long time.

It is possible, of course, that the economic interest in war was not to serve the country as a whole, but rather, to benefit the U.S. energy industry, to which the U.S. President and Vice President had close links. But this explanation also seems implausible. While Bush clearly had sympathies and relationships with the energy sector, and some of his environmental policies were favorable to the oil industry, other administration policies directly undercut oil interests. The ban on trade and investment with Iran and Libya, for example, a policy Cheney had spoken forcefully against while he was the chief executive officer of the giant oil services company Halliburton, continues to handicap U.S. companies in those important markets, yet the Bush administration has not proposed relaxing them. Similarly, Bush has by some accounts headed the most pro-Israel administration in history, despite the difficulty that image presents for U.S. oil companies in the Arab world. In this context, given the immense cost of war and reconstruction, as well as the huge risks involved, it seems unlikely that President Bush concluded that the best way to help his friends in that industry was to send hundreds of thousands of American troops to fight a war halfway around the world.

The European charge that Bush was going after Iraq primarily for "domestic political reasons" was also wrong. True, Bush's experience as a wartime President enormously boosted his popularity and served to reinvent the "accidental president" as a firm, decisive leader capable of rallying the nation in times of crisis. Bush's political advisers were obviously aware of this effect and exploited the long-held Republican political advantage on national security issues in the fall 2002 Congressional elections, just as they planned to exploit it in future elections. "We can go to the country on this issue," asserted White House political adviser Karl Rove before the Republican National Committee on January 18, 2002, "because they trust the Republican Party to do a better job of protecting and strengthening America's military might and thereby protecting America."

Taking political advantage of a war, however, is very different from launching one solely or even primarily for political gain. Indeed, the idea of invading Iraq mainly to reap political gain overlooks the enormous political risks—American lives lost, the potential for a long and costly unilateral occupation, possible Iraqi WMD use, or the provocation of further major terrorist attacks—for a popular President who had more to lose than to gain. Those political risks would persist well after the war was won in a military sense. By the time he announced his intention to invade Iraq, Bush had already launched and won the war in Afghanistan and initiated a wide-ranging "war on terrorism." Choosing not to invade Iraq would undoubtedly have disappointed some of the President's right-wing base. But an administration led by Bush, Cheney, Rumsfeld, and Attorney General John Ashcroft, fresh from a victory in Afghanistan and winning high popularity ratings for its foreign policy in general, would not have run serious political risks by failing to launch a war against Iraq.

Explaining Allied Differences

There are better explanations for the U.S.-Europe split on Iraq than these clichés, which were often wielded more in the service of winning intellectual or political debates than to understand each side's motives—not all of which were as dishonorable as was often implied.

The first and most basic transatlantic difference was that, especially after the shock of September 11, 2001, Americans genuinely perceived a threat from Iraq, and Europeans genuinely did not. To link support for invading Iraq to September 11 is not to suggest that Iraq was behind those attacks, which it almost certainly was not. It is worth noting, however, that many Americans, apparently at least initially including the President, *believed* that Iraq had something to do with them. According to a Gallup poll taken as the Iraq debate was reaching a fever pitch in August 2002, for example, 53 percent of Americans said they believed Saddam Hussein was "personally involved in the September 11 attacks." According to a January 2003 poll, 50 percent of Americans were under the impression that there was a least one Iraqi hijacker involved in the September 11 attacks and 86 percent said they thought Saddam was involved more generally in supporting terrorist groups that had plans to attack the United States.

Even for Americans who did not believe Iraq was involved in 9/11, the attacks had a huge psychological impact on a population that had not felt as insecure since the Cuban Missile Crisis some 40 years before. The unprecedented attacks on U.S. soil—along with the anthrax attacks along the East Coast, which killed five people and terrorized the population—demonstrated the immense destruction that enemies of the United States could inflict on American cities. If terrorists got their hands on nuclear or biological weapons, which Saddam had for years been trying to develop, it did not take much imagination to see that they could potentially kill hundreds of thousands of Americans.

As noted earlier, Europeans felt enormous sympathy for the stricken Americans after the terrorist attacks on September 11, but they did not suddenly conclude that they were living in a different world. For Americans, September 11 changed the world; for Europeans, it changed America. Henceforth, Americans tended to see the world almost exclusively through the prism of international terrorism, whereas Europeans were still focused on the consequences of the end of the Cold War.

The September 11 attacks also played a major role in convincing U.S. policymakers that the status quo in the Middle East was no longer tolerable and that regime change in Iraq could be the first step toward long-term change. For decades the United States and other Western governments had tolerated repressive government throughout the Arab world as long as those governments were willing to sell oil at reasonable prices to the West, act as strategic allies of the United States, and not threaten the Middle East regional order. The long-term costs of this policy became apparent, however, when events revealed that the combination of the repressive regimes and American support for them had led to the sort of alienation, resentment, and hatred for the West that fueled terrorism and al Qaeda. Resentment of the specific status quo in Iraq, moreover—sanctions and economic deprivation, no-fly zones, periodic air strikes, and the enduringly brutal rule of Saddam Hussein—also seemed to be part of what was motivating the terrorists. Thus, even if Iraq were not directly involved in 9/11, it was seen to be at least a factor in the terrorism that had struck the United States. Such a situation, the administration concluded, could no longer be tolerated.

The proximate factor of the September 11 attacks only exacerbated some of the more longstanding differences in American and European perceptions and strategic culture that had led to differences on Iraq for some time.

Due to their long history of relative invulnerability—a product of friendly neighbors and protective oceans—and unprecedented relative power in the world, Americans had developed a much lower tolerance for threats than their European counterparts. This had of course been true for decades—it was evident in the Cold War debates of the 1970s and 1980s, for example, as Americans increasingly sought alternatives to mutually assured nuclear destruction with the Soviet Union, while Europeans were reconciled to living with it. And it grew tremendously with the rise of U.S. relative power in the 1990s, which gave America the means to eliminate the threats that it could not comfortably tolerate. During that decade, America's unwillingness to live with threats became clear through its determination to take forceful action against "rogue states" such as Iran and Iraq, and the willingness to spend tens of billions of dollars in an effort to protect Americans from the unlikely event of a ballistic missile attack. On Iraq, Americans were thus willing to put their faith in their technology and military prowess to remove the threat, whereas Europeans seemed much more comfortable with accepting, containing, and trying to deter that threat.

Another reason Europeans were more averse to war in Iraq was that most of them are, for a range of reasons, more averse to war in general. Having experienced military conflict on their continent within living memory, Europeans felt more attuned to its horrific consequences than Americans, and their threshold for deciding when war as a last resort becomes necessary was consequently higher. This obviously applied more to a country like Germany than to less pacifist Britain or France, but general antiwar feeling was widespread throughout the continent. American anxieties about war had of course also been high in the two decades following Vietnam, but low-casualty and successful wars in Iraq, Bosnia, Kosovo, and Afghanistan in the 1990s left Americans far more ready to accept military force as a useful part of their foreign policy tool kit.

Further, Europeans are more antiwar because, as Robert Kagan and others have pointed out, their lack of available military power leads them to look for peaceful solutions to problems. The U.S. ability to use military force, in comparison, tends to make Americans more ready to contemplate doing so. As Kagan argues: "A man armed only with a knife may decide that a bear prowling the forest is a tolerable danger, inasmuch as the alternative—hunting the bear only with a knife—is actually riskier than lying low and hoping the bear never attacks. The same man armed with a rifle, however, will likely make a different calculation of what constitutes a tolerable risk." After 50 years of integration and of overcoming past enmity, Europeans have come to place more faith in diplomacy and cooperation than Americans, whose lessons of the Cold War include a greater respect for the need to threaten or use military force.

And then there's the fact that both Americans and Europeans believed—rightly—that a nuclear, biological, or chemical threat from Iraq would primarily be an American problem, not a European one. If Saddam's Iraq were to develop nuclear weapons and decide to launch an attack on Kuwait, Saudi Arabia, or Jordan, American forces—not European forces—would have been expected to take the lead in containing that threat. Similarly, for all the talk of "the West" being the target of Islamic terrorism—and it is certainly true that Europeans had been targets in the past and could be targets in the future—the United States was (and probably remains) target number one.

The United States, after all, was the symbol of Western "repression" of the Islamic world, the country with troops in Saudi Arabia and elsewhere in the region, the lead actor in maintaining sanctions and no-fly zones in Iraq, the country that bombed Afghanistan, and Israel's most resolute ally. In the absence of Europe's own "September 11," Europeans will probably remain less worried about the even more remote possibility that WMDs developed in Iraq might find their way into the wrong hands.

For all these reasons, the Middle East status quo was a greater problem for Americans than for Europeans, and it was seen as such.

Diverging American and European historical perspectives also influenced the Iraq debate. Many Americans—either oblivious to the historical record of trying to govern Iraq or convinced that the new circumstances were different—were confident that Iraq could be conquered, stabilized, and even democratized. Imbued with the experience of creating democracy in Japan and Germany after World War II, and with a sense of American power and exceptionalism, many Americans argued that if Saddam Hussein were removed, democracy could flourish in the Middle East. Prominent neoconservatives like Kagan and William Kristol, for example, argued that a "devastating knockout blow against Saddam Hussein, followed by an American-sponsored effort to rebuild Iraq and put it on a path toward democratic governance, would have a seismic impact on the Arab world—for the better." Democratic foreign policy experts Ronald Asmus and Kenneth Pollack were more realistic about the challenge and potential costs of coping with a post-Saddam Iraq but still called for a "full-scale invasion" and expressed confidence in the possibility of establishing a "more democratic successor regime." After a range of highly successful foreign policy initiatives since the early 1980s, often opposed by Europeans—especially the military interventions in Bosnia, Kosovo, and Afghanistan in the 1990s and 2001—many Americans had concluded that Europeans had lost the will to act for good in the world. As a senior Bush administration official told the British journalist Martin Walker in November 2002: "The Europeans . . . have been wrong on just about every major international issue for the past 20 years."

In contrast, many European countries—particularly France and the UK, the Mandatory Powers for Iraq, Syria, Lebanon, and Palestine after World War I—saw little reason to infer from that history that Iraq could be stabilized and democratized. France and Britain both knew what it was like trying to rule foreign societies from abroad and trying to set up stable structures so that the locals could rule themselves.

France, for example, lost tens of thousands of soldiers while trying (and failing) to govern Indochina from 1945 to 1954, and tens of thousands more in Algeria from 1954 to 1962 (several times that many locals also died in the process). After French forces left, neither place was stable or at peace. These experiences must have played some role in influencing French President Jacques Chirac, who fought in the Algerian war as a young man. After several decades on the international stage, Chirac considered himself something of an authority on the Middle East, and when he considered postwar Iraq, he would have been inclined to think more about Lebanon or Algeria than Germany or Japan. French Ambassador Jean-David Levitte explained France's pessimism on this score in a *New York Times* opinion piece in February 2003: "We see Iraq as a very complex country, with many different ethnic groups, a tradition of violence, and no experience of democracy. You can't create democracy with bombs—in Iraq, it would require time, a strong presence, and a strong commitment."

Britain's colonial experience was less bloody, but the departure from India and a number of places in the Middle East—including Iraq—hardly left the British with more optimism that outsiders can ensure democracy or stability in places that have no history of either. Indeed, historians liked to point out that the British after World

War I, like the Americans today, expected to be greeted as liberators in Iraq and elsewhere in the Middle East—and were proved very wrong. The statement British General Francis Maude made upon entering Baghdad in March 1917—"Our armies do not come into your cities and lands as conquerors or enemies, but as liberators"— was in fact strikingly similar to statements made by George W. Bush and other American leaders in 2003. Many British citizens were well aware that the British experiment with Iraq's liberation concluded with a coup d'état in 1958, when the Iraqi prime minister was chopped up into pieces.

Thus, even if they supported the goal of removing Saddam's dictatorial regime, both the British and the French harbored real doubts that Iraq's ethnically divided population, resentful Shiite majority, artificial borders, and unequally allocated natural resources lent themselves to future stability. They feared that disorder in Iraq could prove disastrous for the entire Arab world—even worse than the brutal dictatorship of Saddam Hussein.

The differing assessment of how likely it was that a post-Saddam Iraq could be stabilized led to almost opposite assessments of how an Iraq invasion would affect the war on terrorism.

In the United States, invading Iraq was perceived to be—and certainly sold as—part of that campaign. Saddam's Iraq, Bush administration officials alleged, was intimately involved with global terrorism, and in any case, the failure of the United States to stand by or liberate oppressed Muslims in the Middle East was a cause of resentment that helped fuel the terrorist scourge.

Most Europeans, on the other hand, saw no link between Saddam Hussein's regime and al Qaeda—and indeed saw cooperation between the secular Ba'athists and the religiously fanatic al Qaeda as implausible in the extreme. Instead they believed that a U.S.-led invasion of an Arab country—with its consequent civilian casualties and likely need for a long-term occupation—would more likely be a recruitment tool for al Qaeda than a blow against terrorism. "People in France and more broadly in Europe," wrote French Ambassador Levitte, "fear that a military intervention could fuel extremism and encourage al Qaeda recruitment." Osama bin Laden's February 11, 2003, audio tape calling on Iraqis to rise up and attack the country's invaders, cited by Secretary of State Colin Powell as proof of al Qaeda's ties with Iraq, demonstrated the opposite to most Europeans: the terrorists' desire to try to incite the Iraqi people and the entire Arab world to oppose an American presence in the region. As French President Chirac put it in an interview with *Time* magazine in February 2003, war in Iraq would risk creating "a large number of little bin Ladens."

Finally, no one should ignore how domestic situations influenced leaders in the United States and Europe, and how that shaped the public debate. In Europe, leaders had to be conscious of the restiveness among their poorly integrated and very large Muslim populations—including 4 to 6 million in France, over 3 million in Germany, and 1.5 million in Britain—and worried that an invasion of the Arab heartland could provoke unrest. High civilian casualties or a lengthy and difficult Western occupation of Iraq, the leaders of these countries feared, could radicalize Muslim populations that had already proven themselves potential breeding grounds for al Qaeda. In late 2001 and early 2002, clashes between Israelis and Palestinians spilled over into Europe itself, and in France and Belgium led to minor clashes between Muslim and Jewish populations, as well as acts of anti-Semitic violence and vandalism. The Europeans thus feared the potential domestic implications of an Iraq war with possibly high Arab civilian casualties or a long Western occupation leading to Arab resentment.

In the United States, domestic politics pushed in the opposite direction. Influential Jewish and other pro-Israel groups were worried about the threat Saddam Hussein posed to Israel and tended to favor action, even if that meant using force to topple Saddam. Indeed, whereas Europeans argued passionately that the U.S. priority on Iraq was misplaced and that Washington would do better to focus more on the Israel-Palestine problem, some Americans argued that an Iraq war could actually contribute to Israel-Palestinian peace. As former Secretary of State Henry Kissinger put it in August 2002: "It is not true that the road to Baghdad leads through Jerusalem. Much more likely, the road to Jerusalem will lead through Baghdad." Bush himself argued just prior to the start of the war that:

> . . . success in Iraq could . . . begin a new stage for Middle Eastern peace, and set in motion progress toward a truly democratic Palestinian state. The passing of Saddam Hussein's regime will deprive terrorist networks of a wealthy patron that pays for terrorist training, and offers rewards to families of suicide bombers. And other regimes will be given a clear warning that support for terror will not be tolerated. Without this outside support for terrorism, Palestinians who are working for reform and long for democracy will be in a better position to choose new leaders.

It was a seductive theory to American supporters of Israel, who had become persuaded that the old approach of negotiating with Yasser Arafat—pursued by the Clinton administration for eight years and at the highest levels—no longer offered any hope of success.

An Avoidable Crisis

The differences between Americans and Europeans on what to do about Iraq were real—the products of history, political culture, and the two sides' respective strategic situations. Those different perspectives had led to tensions on the issue for over a decade, and it was thus not surprising that they exploded into crisis when the United States decided to dramatically change the status quo by invading Iraq.

The transatlantic crisis over Iraq, however, was not inevitable. It resulted in part from the structural gaps that divided Americans and Europeans, but just as much from the often regrettable decisions made in capitals on either side of the Atlantic and by Saddam Hussein in Iraq. As we show in the following two chapters, the transatlantic split over Iraq was as much the result of diplomatic mistakes, personality clashes, unfortunate timing, faulty analysis, and bad luck as it was a product of an unavoidable march toward transatlantic divorce.

Chapter

4

TOWARD
CRISIS

The story of how the United States and Europe came to clash over Iraq goes back many years; deep transatlantic differences on the issue were apparent since at least the mid-1990s. But the turning point toward crisis came, as on so much else, with September 11, 2001.

Before the attacks on America, hard-liners within the Bush administration had not yet convinced the administration as a whole that Iraq constituted an imminent threat to U.S. national security or that it required urgent action in the face of strong international opposition. In January 2000, for example, Bush's chief foreign policy adviser on the campaign, Condoleezza Rice, had effectively rejected the notion of using the American military to overthrow rogue regimes, asserting in a *Foreign Affairs* article that regimes like those in Iraq and North Korea were "living on borrowed time, so there need be no sense of panic about them. Rather, the first line of defense should be a clear and classical statement of deterrence—if they do acquire WMDs, their weapons will be unusable because any attempt to use them will bring national obliteration."

Similarly, in his January 2001 confirmation hearings, Secretary of State–designate Colin Powell expressed skepticism that Iraq constituted a serious threat: "[As] long as we are able to control the major source of money going into Iraq, we can keep them in the rather broken condition they are in now . . . it is fundamentally a broken, weak country." Reflecting the administration's internal divisions, the Iraq "policy review" launched soon after inauguration was bogged down in bureaucratic wrangling, with advocates of regime change failing to win the case for early action. As late as the summer of 2001, the policy priority was still on improving the sanctions regime on Iraq, and the review was not expected to conclude until at least September.

That schedule changed with 9/11 and the anthrax attacks along the East Coast of the United States that followed it—seen as a vivid demonstration of what weapons of mass destruction in the wrong hands could do. After that, the balance between proponents of overthrowing Saddam and skeptics within the administration tipped, and the argument in favor of doing something about Iraq—as well as the viability of selling the idea politically—tipped with it. The risk of a WMD attack on the United States, however remote, was simply no longer acceptable, and the administration, backed by a population more fearful for its security than it had been for decades, resolved to do whatever it took to eliminate the threat.

The Bush administration did not decide immediately and irrevocably after September 11 to go to war against Iraq, as many opponents of war in Europe later seemed to believe. But there can be little doubt that 9/11 pushed the debate strongly in that direction. In the immediate aftermath of the attacks, proponents of regime change felt they had a more compelling case and saw a window of opportunity to make it.

On September 13, 2001, for example, Deputy Secretary of Defense Paul Wolfowitz publicly argued that the campaign against terrorism would be not only about capturing terrorists, but about "removing the sanctuaries, removing the support systems, ending states who sponsor terrorism," which was widely interpreted to be a reference to Iraq. A few days later, at a National Security Council meeting at Camp David, Wolfowitz made the case for attacking Iraq as part of the war on terrorism, provoking a discussion about Iraq that included Secretary of Defense Rumsfeld, National Security Adviser Rice, and President Bush himself. Bush, however, while suspicious of Iraqi involvement and sympathetic to arguments that Saddam would eventually have to be removed, decided against a near-term attack.

By the end of the weekend's deliberations on how to respond to the terrorist attacks, Bush had made it clear that Iraq would not be part of the initial response and that the focus should be on Afghanistan and al Qaeda. "I believe Iraq was involved," Bush told the NSC meeting on September 17, "but I'm not going to strike them now. I don't have the evidence at this point." Three days later Bush told visiting British Prime Minister Tony Blair that he agreed with Blair that "the job in hand is al Qaeda and the Taliban. Iraq, we keep for another day."

Over the following months, Bush stuck to his decision not to "strike them now." But he also began to make it increasingly clear that he did not intend to live with the status quo in Iraq forever. There does not seem to have been any single day on which the President or his senior advisers formally decided on war, but the momentum toward a policy of confronting Iraq grew steadily over the course of the winter and spring of 2002.

In January 2002, with the war in Afghanistan won, the President hinted at a new phase in the war on terror. His State of the Union address denouncing an "axis of evil" was a clear shot across the bow of the Iraqi regime and a signal to all that he saw a direct link between the problem of rogue regimes and the problem of terrorism. The warning that "the United States of America will not permit the world's most dangerous regimes to threaten us with the world's most destructive weapons" could only be read—and was read—as a warning to and about Iraq. Similarly, the President's June 2002 West Point speech outlining the doctrine of military preemption only made military action against Iraq seem more likely and more imminent.

Bush's arguments that containment was "not possible" with dictators who have weapons of mass destruction and that "the only path to safety was the path of action" were unmistakable signals that the United States was determined to act. And it did not take much of a logical leap to figure out just whom the Americans were going to act against. The new agenda, as one senior official later put it, was "not whether Iraq, but how."

Debating Iraq

The President's West Point speech contributed to a growing domestic and international debate that summer both about whether to attack Iraq and about the need to gain UN support for such an operation. On July 31-August 1, 2002, the Senate Foreign Relations Committee, under the chairmanship of Democrat Joseph Biden, Jr., had held hearings on Iraq. Many of the witnesses—and many of the senators themselves—warned of the possible risks and costs of going to war. Only two weeks later, on August 15, the first President Bush's National Security Adviser, Brent Scowcroft, published a *Wall Street Journal* op-ed article entitled "Don't Attack Saddam." Scowcroft warned that an attack on Iraq could undermine the war on terrorism and have other unpredictable consequences. His status as a close friend and adviser to the father of the President and as mentor of National Security Adviser Condoleezza Rice gave particular weight to his arguments.

Ten days later another close adviser to the first President Bush—former Secretary of State James A. Baker III—weighed in. Baker did not argue against an invasion of Iraq, but he did make the case for seeking a UN Security Council resolution before taking any action and warned that either way there could be high costs and risks. Former Secretary of State Henry Kissinger came out in favor of regime change but warned that winning international legitimacy for action would be essential, while another former Secretary of State, Lawrence Eagleberger, argued that war in Iraq was not worth the risks. On August 23, the former commander of U.S. forces in the Gulf, General Anthony Zinni, argued that "attacking Iraq now will cause a lot of problems," and that the Middle East peace process and war on terrorism should be higher priorities. Zinni argued that regime change would mean that the United States would "inherit the country of Iraq," which would be difficult to hold together, and suggested that Generals Scowcroft, Powell, and Schwarzkopf all "see this the same way." All these debates seemed to be having an effect on U.S. public opinion, as support for using force against Iraq fell from averages of between 67 and 78 percent of Americans who had "strongly" or "somewhat strongly" supported "having U.S. forces take military action against Iraq to force Saddam Hussein from power" since September 11, 2001, to 56 percent by the end of August 2002.

Within the administration, a debate was also raging, though less about whether to confront Iraq and more about how best to secure domestic and international support for action. Some advisers, primarily in the Pentagon and the Office of the Vice President, argued that no new UN Security Council resolutions were needed, and that the very process of pursuing one would risk getting the United States bogged down at the UN. Assertive and decisive U.S. leadership, in this view, was the best method of securing support, both at home and abroad. Secretary of State Powell, however, favored working through the UN. He used the opportunity of a private dinner with President Bush and National Security Adviser Rice on August 5 to present "the upside of making an aggressive approach at the UN, and the downside of not doing it."

A week later, on August 12, Cheney, Rice, Rumsfeld, Powell, and their top aides met at the White House to discuss how Bush should use his already scheduled speech to the UN General Assembly on September 12, 2002. The administration's original idea was for Bush to speak generally about democratic values, but the foreign policy team decided—reportedly at the suggestion of Cheney—that the UN speech would be a good opportunity to challenge the UN to "live up to its heritage." Four days later Rice flew to join President Bush at his ranch in Crawford, Texas, where she chaired a meeting with the other principals on Iraq by videoconference. Powell again made the case for seeking a tough new UN resolution and more intrusive weapons inspections, and the group unanimously agreed with that plan. An internal administration debate continued, however, over the question of precisely what Bush should say at the UN. The hard-liners in the Pentagon and Vice President's office argued that Bush should simply declare that the United States had existing legal authority to attack Iraq based on Iraq's material breach of past UN Security Council resolutions, while Powell and others at the State Department argued for giving UN weapons inspections a realistic chance to work. Two groups within the administration thus began to draft separate texts, and would end up competing to persuade the President right up until the time of the speech on September 12.

In part as a response to the growing public debate in Washington, Europe's Iraq debate was also heating up. In Germany, Chancellor Gerhard Schröder launched his reelection campaign on August 5—a few days after the Senate Foreign Relations Committee hearings—with a public declaration that Germany would not provide any troops or money for an attack on Iraq. Trailing in opinion polls, Schröder had decided to try to win back public support through a tough antiwar stand. "We're not available for adventures, and the time of checkbook diplomacy is over once and for all," Schröder announced to cheers from his Social Democratic faithful and the dismay of the Bush administration. In Britain, a large number of those within Prime Minister Tony Blair's own Labor Party were questioning the case for military action, and polls showed the public strongly opposed to war. And in France, officials said that only the Security Council could authorize the use of force against Iraq, and called for the reintroduction of UN weapons inspectors, not the use of force to change the regime.

On August 26, 2002, in a speech before the Veterans of Foreign Wars in Nashville, Tennessee, Vice President Cheney entered the debate with the most powerful case yet put forth both for regime change in Iraq and against a UN-based approach. Cheney repeated Bush's West Point argument that "old doctrines of security do not apply," and said, "'Containment' was not possible when dictators obtain weapons of mass destruction and are prepared to share them with terrorists who intend to inflict catastrophic casualties on the United States." He also expressed considerable certainty that Saddam possessed weapons of mass destruction: "Simply stated, there is no doubt that Saddam Hussein now has weapons of mass destruction. There is no doubt he is amassing them to use against our friends, against our allies, and against us. Many of us," the Vice President asserted, "are convinced that Saddam will acquire nuclear weapons fairly soon."

Perhaps most important, from the European perspective, Cheney made clear that he had no confidence that containment bolstered by renewed weapons inspections could work. In his view, this approach had been tried and had definitively failed: "A return of inspectors would provide no assurance whatsoever of [Saddam's] compliance with UN resolutions. On the contrary, there is a great danger that it would provide false comfort that Saddam was somehow back in his box." Given Cheney's perceived importance within the administration, this harsh speech was widely seen in Europe as a sign that the White House was saying that the debate was over and it was time to accept the reality that the United States was going to use force against Iraq.

Europe Reacts

The Cheney speech set off a flurry of reactions in Europe, as each ally now had to decide how to deal with what it perceived to be the new reality in Washington. In Germany, where the headline of the mass circulation paper *Bild Zeitung* screamed "Krieg!"—War!—after the Cheney speech, Chancellor Schröder had already decided to use opposition to war in Iraq as an electoral issue and to come out against German participation in a potential conflict. The Cheney speech played right into his hands. Stepping up the pace and tone of his antiwar statements, the unpopular Schröder saw his poll numbers increase. At campaign rallies, he discovered that his only effective applause line was when he denounced the idea of war on Iraq. On August 30, Schröder announced that Germany would withdraw its biological and chemical detection equipment from Kuwait if the Americans attacked Iraq. Earlier in the year he had told a German journalist that he knew that any German chancellor who withdrew such equipment would "not be welcome in the United States in the next 20 or 30 years." But now, with his political back against the wall, he was proposing to do just that.

A few days later, asked by the *New York Times* whether he thought Cheney was speaking for President Bush, Schröder responded that he was "not qualified to say." He did say that "the problem" was "that [Bush] has or seems to have committed himself so strongly that it is hard to imagine how he can climb down." Moreover, the chancellor continued, "it is just not good enough if I learn from the American press about a speech which clearly states: We are going to do it, no matter what the world or our allies think. That is no way to treat others."

But it was not only the American style that bothered the German chancellor; he had strong problems with the substance as well. Arguing that an attack on Iraq could disrupt the international coalition against terror and bring uncertainty to the entire Middle East, Schröder used the same interview to announce a change in his stated policy of backing the possible use of force in Iraq only under a UN Security Council mandate. Instead, he asserted, the arguments "against an intervention are so important that I would also be against such an intervention if—for whatever reasons and in whatever form—the Security Council of the United Nations were to say 'Yes,' which I cannot imagine happening in the present situation." On September 12, while Bush was at the UN seeking support on Iraq, Schröder was asserting on the campaign trail that "we need more peace, not more war. And that's why under my leadership Germany will not participate."

Schröder's opposition to the war and refusal to allow any German participation in it, a key part of his electoral campaign, persisted right up until the September 22 election itself. That opposition, moreover, arguably contributed to the narrow victory of his Social Democrat–led coalition (with the Green party), 306 seats to 295, over the potential bloc led by the Christian Democratic Union. Two days before the election, Schröder's justice minister, Herta Däubler-Gmelin, took the criticism of the United States and its policies one step further by accusing Bush of using the possible war to "divert attention from his domestic problems." The minister went on: "It's a classic tactic. It's one that Hitler also used."

The comparison of Bush to Hitler set off a furious reaction in Washington, where White House spokesman Ari Fleischer called it "outrageous" and Condoleezza Rice said it had "poisoned" Germany's relationship with the United States. Schröder immediately wrote to Bush to distance himself from the remark and to hint that Däubler-Gmelin would not be reappointed to a cabinet post (which she was not). But the letter seemed to the White House to be more a denial than an apology:

> I would hereby like to let you know how very much I regret that, through the alleged remarks of the German Justice Minister, an impression was left that deeply wounded your feelings. The Minister has assured me that she did not make these

alleged statements. She has also stated this publicly. I would like to assure you that there is no place at my cabinet table for anyone who connects the American President with a criminal. The White House spokesman has correctly noted the special and close relationship between the German and American people.

To the extent that this was a disavowal, it was not nearly enough for the White House, which had expected a clear apology from Schröder and the immediate dismissal of Däubler-Gmelin. Bush felt that Schröder had not only tolerated the atmosphere that made the justice minister's comments possible, but had even encouraged it. White House officials called his letter to the President insulting: "Schröder effectively said he was sorry that Bush chose to get angry about comments that Däubler-Gmelin didn't really make."

The spat over the Hitler remark was a symbol of a much larger problem in German-American relations. Indeed, it was telling that relations between the two countries had deteriorated to the point where the leader of traditionally Atlanticist Germany would see an advantage in running an election campaign against the United States. In response to American criticism of Schröder's unilateral decision to oppose the war, Germans argued that Schröder was simply putting Bush's method of decision making right back at him: Listen to what your ally has to say, but then act in your own interest regardless of what the ally thinks. The Bush administration, however, took the view that the United States was endowed by its history and its power with privileges and responsibilities very different from those of Germany.

Bush, in fact, would not forgive Schröder for campaigning against the war and the United States. According to senior administration officials, Schröder had told Bush after a long and friendly dinner in January 2002 that he "understood" that Bush might have to go to war in Iraq, and he advised Bush only to do so quickly and decisively. Again in Berlin in May 2002, U.S. officials say, Schröder pledged not to run his election campaign against a possible U.S. war in Iraq. When Schröder ended up doing so, Bush—who aides say "believes the character of a person is known by whether he keeps his word"—felt betrayed and did not hesitate in private conversations to call Schröder a "liar." Bush refused to congratulate Schröder on his election victory, and later, throughout the entire Iraq crisis, spoke to him only once on the phone, in an awkward, strained conversation.

A few days after the election Rumsfeld joined Rice in calling U.S.-German relations "poisoned" and allegedly snubbed his German counterpart Peter Struck at a NATO ministerial meeting in Warsaw—calling him "that person" and leaving the meeting just before the German was to speak. Rumsfeld denied any snub, but did comment afterward that his advice to Germany would be: "If you're in a hole, stop digging." Months later, in May 2003, Rice was still arguing that the relationship between Mr. Bush and Mr. Schröder "will never again be as it was and as it should be." Washington was making efforts to improve relations with Germany, but "we are doing it around the Chancellor, whom we prefer to bypass." Rice also commented that Bush felt that German Foreign Minister Fischer's "background and career do not suit the profile of the statesman."

The feelings of betrayal were mutual. Schröder denied having misled Bush in May 2002, and he had no intention of apologizing for his antiwar stance. With Schröder at his side during his May 2002 Berlin visit, Bush had pledged publicly and privately that he "had no war plans on his desk" and that he would consult Germany on the decision to go to war. In retrospect, Schröder felt he was not in fact consulted, and Germans believed that Bush misled them about his true intentions.

After the Cheney speech, the French also took stock of where U.S. policy seemed to be headed. Long among the most strongly opposed to regime change in Iraq, the French had spent the previous spring and summer focusing on the issue of renewing the containment of Iraq by revising the economic sanctions regime. The apparent message from

Washington that Bush was moving toward the use of force, however, obliged the French to decide what they would do if Bush carried out his threat. Chirac was still opposed to war, but he also realized that categorical opposition similar to Germany's would only lead the United States to act without even making an attempt to revive the UN weapons inspections process—thus marginalizing the UN Security Council, France's preferred international forum. To prevent this scenario, Paris decided in late August to pursue a new course that allowed for the threat of force in the name of ensuring Iraqi compliance.

On August 27, Foreign Minister Dominique de Villepin marked a change in the tone if not the substance of French policy in a speech to a gathering of all of France's ambassadors in Paris. De Villepin stressed the importance of nonproliferation and denounced an Iraqi regime that "for years has defied the international rules defined by the UN Security Council, holds its people hostage, and threatens security, especially that of its neighbors." He went on: "We Europeans know all too well the price of weakness in dealing with dictators to close our eyes and remain passive. We must thus maintain as firmly as possible our demand of an unconditional return of UN inspectors." The statement was not exactly a threat of force against Iraq, and de Villepin stressed that "the steps to be taken must be decided by the international community, according to a collective process." This meant that "no military action could be conducted without a decision of the Security Council." Still, de Villepin's speech called Saddam's defiance "unacceptable" and insisted that "all must face up to their responsibilities." According to French diplomats at the time and later, the speech was meant to signal France's acceptance of the threat to use force, so long as the ultimate decision to do so remained in the Security Council's hands.

Two weeks later Chirac granted an interview to the *New York Times* in which he also left the door open to French support for a threat to use force in Iraq. Chirac repeated his opposition to "unilateral actions" and said he wanted to hear directly from Bush about U.S. policy. But like de

Villepin, he also condemned the Iraqi regime "for all the reasons we know, for all the dangers that it puts on the region and the tragedy it constitutes for the Iraqi people who are being held hostage by it." Saddam, according to Chirac, was "especially dangerous to his own people, who are living under extraordinarily difficult circumstances." The French leader distanced himself from Schröder's "categorical" position, which he said was linked to the German election, and noted that France had special responsibilities as a permanent member of the Security Council.

Chirac also revealed a proposal for two separate Security Council resolutions that would soon become a key element of the French position. "There must be a Security Council decision concerning the return of the inspectors," he said. If the inspectors were not allowed to return, "then there should be a second Security Council resolution to say if there should be or not an intervention." Asked specifically about military solutions, he answered that "nothing is impossible, if it's decided by the international community on the basis of indisputable proof." Chirac claimed that such proof for the moment did not exist, but still held out the possibility that France might actually come around and support war in Iraq.

The new tone from Paris, as qualified as it was, would prove critical in convincing many Americans that in the right circumstances France might ultimately be willing to support the use of force. Former UN Ambassador Richard Holbrooke was among many who predicted that France would "undoubtedly play its normal role as a difficult and contentious ally, but in the end, it will not stop the concerted will of America and Britain." This assumption, shared by many in the administration, helped to persuade Bush that going back to the UN for a new resolution would not be futile, which may have been one of the reasons for the change of rhetoric in Paris in the first place.

The British also reacted to Cheney, albeit from a different starting point. While the British public and much of the governing Labor party were deeply opposed to war, the UK government, and Prime Minister Tony Blair in particular, had long taken a hawkish approach to Iraq. Blair had supported all previous U.S. military actions against Iraq, including Operation Desert Fox in 1998 and the more recent intensi-fied enforcement of the no-fly zones in northern Iraq, in which British forces played an active part. Indeed, Blair had long taken a clear moral stand on defending human rights and confronting dictators with his determination to stand up to Serbian ruler Slobodan Milosevic during the Kosovo conflict. He articulated a doctrine of military intervention then, in the name of upholding international values and rules, and took the lead in advocating the use of ground forces if necessary to ensure victory. Singling out Milosevic and Saddam Hussein as "dangerous and ruthless men," Blair denounced the "evil" of ethnic cleansing and insist-ed that "evil dictators" must be challenged early lest doing so prove even more costly later on.

According to people close to him, Blair, like Bush and many other Americans, concluded from the September 11 attacks that the potential linkage between terrorism and weapons of mass destruction was the strategic issue of our time and required decisive action. According to British journalist Hugo Young, Blair has even claimed that if Bush had held back from intervening in Iraq, he would have pushed him in that direction.

The British government thus had no problem with Cheney's threat of military force against Iraq. Already in March 2002, Foreign Secretary Jack Straw had warned of "consequences" if Saddam continued to refuse weapons inspections. But the British public, and most of the Labor party in particular, were strongly opposed to war, and even more opposed to the specter of Britain coming to the rescue of the unilater-alism of George W. Bush. Blair thus felt that the only way to win domestic support was to get UN approval for a forceful stance. For months, in fact, UK officials had been pressing the Americans to go back to the UN for any new authorization of a threat to use force, a message Blair's top security adviser, David Manning, was sent to Washington to reiterate in July 2002. Straw had made the same case to Powell on numerous occasions.

With Cheney's speech suggesting that the message might not be getting through, Blair himself flew to see Bush at Camp David on September 7, to stress how critically important it was for the United States to go back to the UN. He did not say that Britain's support for possible war was contingent on a new UN resolution ("Blair would never say that," one of the Prime Minister's advisers asserted), but he made clear how politically difficult it would be for him without a new resolution. What Blair didn't realize before arriving in Washington was that Bush, persuaded by Powell, had already decided to take his case to the UN; Blair found himself pushing on an open door.

Persuaded by Powell and the British to take his case to the UN— and encouraged by a new French position that seemed to hold out promise that a tough new resolution could be agreed upon—Bush on September 12 challenged the UN to enforce its own resolutions. "All the world now faces a test," he said, "and the United Nations a difficult and defining moment. Are Security Council resolutions to be honored and enforced, or cast aside without consequence? Will the United Nations serve the purpose of its founding, or will it be irrelevant?" Bush made clear that the United States reserved the right to act alone if the UN failed: "The Security Council resolutions will be enforced—the just demands of peace and security will be met—or action will be un-avoidable. And a regime that has lost its legitimacy will also lose its power." But, in a statement that some of his hard-line advisers tried to take out of the speech at the last minute, he also accepted the need to work with the international community: "We will work with the UN Security Council for the necessary resolutions." Europeans were deeply relieved, and saw hope that the United States was finally accept-ing a multilateral approach and the possibility of a peaceful resolution of the crisis.

Negotiating 1441

Bush's decision to seek a new UN resolution on Iraq set off what would turn out to be eight weeks of tortuous negotiations in New York. Essentially, the American objective, mostly shared by Britain, was to craft a resolution such that anything short of full compliance would lead nearly automatically to an authorization to use force to change the Iraqi regime. As one administration official had put it, "If we find anything in what they give us that is not true, that is the trigger. If they delay, obstruct, or lie about anything they disclosed, then this will trigger action."

France, on the other hand, backed by Russia and China, had a different goal. After all of the scorn heaped on the potential efficacy of UN weapons inspections by some of Bush's top advisers, the French and others were skeptical that the United States would be willing to take yes for an answer even if Iraq were to disarm. Thus they sought a resolution that would demand Iraqi disarmament, and were willing to support more intrusive and comprehensive inspections and the threat of force to achieve that goal. But they also insisted on avoiding any automatic triggers for military action and on leaving final control over any decision to act in the hands of the Security Council.

The latter point was critical for France for two reasons. First, the French felt that to disarm Iraq without war meant that Saddam Hussein had to believe he could give up his weapons and still survive in power. And given the oft-stated U.S. goal of regime change, it was unlikely Saddam would believe as much if the United States alone could legitimately decide on war. More broadly, the French wanted to uphold the principle of "putting the Security Council in the center of international life and not permitting a nation—whatever nation it may be—to do what it wants, where it wants."

Within days of Bush's speech, an interagency team of U.S. officials (working with their UK counterparts) had prepared a tough draft resolution replete with rigorous demands on Iraq. As one U.S. official commented: "It had everything but the kitchen sink in it." First floated on September 26, the draft declared that Iraq was still, and had been for a number of years, in "material breach" of its obligations, especially through its failure to cooperate with UN weapons inspectors. It required Iraq to provide the Security Council with a complete declaration of all its chemical, biological, and nuclear programs, as well as the locations of the work and research in these areas, within 30 days. Iraq had to provide UN weapons inspectors with immediate and unrestricted access to any sites in Iraq that the inspectors wished to visit—including the "presidential sites" that had been excluded in a 1998 deal with UN Secretary General Kofi Annan. The text, moreover, allowed any permanent member of the Security Council to order inspectors to visit certain sites, and authorized its representatives—including armed troops—to accompany the inspectors to the sites. The draft foresaw intelligence sharing between the inspectors and members of the Security Council, unlimited interviews with Iraqi scientists who may have worked on weapons programs, and the right to take those scientists and their families outside of Iraq to ensure that they felt free to talk. Finally, the draft resolution made clear that Iraq's failure to comply with the resolution would constitute further material breach and authorize members of the Security Council to use "all necessary means" to restore international peace and security—UN code words for the use of military force.

Told by his advisers that such a resolution was "totally unsellable in New York," Bush called Chirac on September 27 and also dispatched Undersecretary of State for Policy Marc Grossman to Paris and Moscow, accompanied by the Political Director of the UK Foreign Office, Peter Ricketts.

France, as the administration expected, opposed the proposed U.S. text, and French diplomats spent the next three weeks working to eliminate all those elements they believed could be used as a pretext for war. The French argued, for example, that as a practical matter, it was unrealistic to expect Iraq to allow all of its scientists and their extended families to leave the country. They felt that armed inspections would be unnecessarily provocative and could possibly lead to an accidental conflict. And they believed the phrase "all necessary means" gave too much of a blank check to the United States. Most important for France was to keep control over the decision-making process in the Security Council, where it not only had a veto and a key voice in the debate, but where the voices of other countries opposed to war would count, making American military action more difficult politically.

Thus, France continued to insist on a process that would require two resolutions, as Chirac had proposed in early September: one resolution to set the demands on Iraq, and a second to determine what to do about noncompliance. In the French view, without a second resolution, the Security Council risked abdicating its responsibilities for international peace and security.

Early on in the process, the French told the Americans that if Washington accepted the need for a second resolution before military action, France would accept a "close link" between the two. But the French were never willing to accept automatic authorization of force in case of noncompliance. The Americans refused, insisting that to be credible, the Council had to threaten to use force, not threaten to discuss the matter further.

The Americans and British formally presented their draft on October 2, but France and other Council members—especially Russia—continued to oppose it. By mid-October, with negotiations at a stalemate, France was claiming that a majority of Security Council members supported its view and began to threaten to put its own text to a vote if the United States did not take its views into account. Washington, now fearing that a failed attempt to get a UN resolution would be worse, in political terms, than not to have tried in the first place, began to seek compromise language that did not violate U.S. requirements but would still be acceptable to the French.

In the preparation of a draft formally circulated on October 23, the French and Americans took two major steps toward consensus. Washington agreed to drop the sensitive reference to "all necessary means" in exchange for French willingness to state that the failure to comply with the resolution would have "serious consequences." The latter formulation did not have the same power as "all necessary means," but the Americans felt it was clear enough, especially taken together with the assertion that Iraq was already in "material breach."

The second and even more important compromise involved the United States agreeing that in case of violations of the resolution, the Security Council would "convene immediately . . . in order to consider the situation." This formulation gave something to both sides: The French could claim that Washington had agreed to come back to the Security Council before acting, thus preserving the ultimate authority of the Council, while the Americans could, and did, insist that no further vote would be required to enforce the resolution.

Over the next two weeks, Powell, de Villepin, Straw, and Russian Foreign Minister Igor Ivanov engaged heavily (and directly) with each other and with the rest of the Council to try to reach consensus. At the suggestion of British UN Ambassador Jeremy Greenstock, the negotiators added a statement that the new resolution provided a "final opportunity" for Iraq to comply. The phrase pleased the French because it reaffirmed the commitment to allow Iraq the opportunity to avoid war, and it satisfied the Americans because it made clear that there would be no further chances to do so.

The concluding stage of the negotiation took place in a phone call between Bush and Chirac on November 7, when the two Presidents agreed on two final word changes, which were tiny in size but in fact quite important to the French. The first was to state that a violation of the resolution would result in the Council taking action to "secure" peace, rather than to "restore" peace, which the French believed implied less automatic action. The second and more important change was to replace the word "or" with "and" in the part of operational paragraph four, which dealt with how alleged violations of the resolution would be handled. The new language stated that such violations would be handled in accordance with paragraphs 11 *and* 12—the former directing UNMOVIC to report violations immediately to the Security Council, the latter committing the Security Council to convene to consider the situation. This language reinforced the French argument that action was for the Council, not the Americans, to decide. The Americans did not share that interpretation but went along with the language as a means to close the deal, arguing that other aspects of the text—such as the reference to "serious consequences" in the event of Iraqi noncompliance—gave them the right to act without further Council approval. When the Russians agreed to the same text later in the day, all the key pieces for agreement were in place. On November 8, after France and the United States helped persuade Syria that a unified Security Council ensured the best chance for a resolution of the crisis without war, Resolution 1441 passed by a unanimous vote of 15-0.

In the final text of 1441, neither the French nor the Americans got everything they wanted, but both were satisfied. France knew it had accepted tough new demands on Iraq with a high threshold for compliance, but it also felt it had avoided a resolution that could have been used by the United States as a technical pretext for war even if Iraq were to disarm. The French knew that if Saddam blatantly violated the new resolution—which they understood was a real possibility—they would be expected to support military action. But they also held out the hope that the new requirements could actually bring about significant disarmament without war. France insisted that the new resolution made the UN inspectors—not any individual member of the Security Council—the arbiters of any disputes within the Security Council about whether Iraq was complying or not. Thus, Paris was confident that if Iraq took reasonable steps toward disarmament, this mechanism would prevent the hawks in the U.S. administration from propelling the country to war.

The United States, however, was also satisfied, because it had won support for a very tough new set of conditions on Iraq that it felt certain the Baghdad regime would never meet. The final version of Resolution 1441 stated that Iraq "has been and remains in material breach" of previous resolutions passed under Chapter VII of the UN charter, which governs the use of military force. The resolution required Iraq to submit a "currently accurate, full, and complete" declaration of all its chemical, biological, and nuclear programs, and obliged Iraq to provide unconditional access to UN weapons inspectors to verify the declaration, including interviews with Iraqi scientists. The resolution noted that false statements or omissions in the weapons declaration and failure "at any time" to "cooperate immediately, unconditionally, and actively" would constitute further material breach. The resolution thus gave Iraq a "final opportunity" to comply with its disarmament obligations, and it reminded the regime that it would face "serious consequences" if it continued to violate those obligations.

While some of the most enthusiastic American proponents of using force against Iraq denounced the new UN resolution as an American sellout to France, most observers tended to agree with former UN Ambassador Richard Holbrooke that it was "one of the best resolutions ever crafted in the UN." By placing such demanding conditions on Iraq and lining up the international community behind a credible threat of force, the resolution provided the best opportunity yet to finally convince Saddam Hussein to comply with his obligations. And there was, in fact, good reason to believe that Saddam would either so blatantly violate the terms of the resolution that the Security Council would unite against him or that a credible threat of force would convince him to actually cooperate, and a war could be put off.

The apparent unity achieved in Resolution 1441, however, was illusory. The resolution was a worthwhile effort to reconcile different views about what to do about Iraq, and it provided a useful mechanism for dealing with the scenarios of either blatant noncompliance or full compliance. It also "worked" in the sense of getting weapons inspectors back into Iraq—and even into Saddam's palaces—a goal that had eluded the international community for nearly four years.

The resolution failed, however, to establish an agreed mechanism if members of the Security Council disagreed over whether Saddam's actions constituted compliance. In legal terms, in fact, Resolution 1441 consisted of two contradictory resolutions in one. One reasonable interpretation of the text provided for the near automatic use of force in the event of noncompliance, and another equally arguable view of the text held that force could only be used when inspectors had reported back to the Security Council for a further decision. In the French view, if members of the Security Council disagreed on the interpretation of the resolution, it would be up to the weapons inspectors, and the Security Council as a whole, to decide what to do. In the U.S. view, however, that decision had already been made, and Washington had all the authority it needed to take action. In other words, key members of the Security Council not only did not agree on the interpretation of the resolution, but disagreed about the mechanism for resolving such differences.

In the event, Saddam Hussein's response to 1441 revealed this divide within the international community. He cooperated enough to convince France and a number of other members of the Security Council that war was not necessary, while simultaneously convincing Washington and London that war was the only remaining option. It was at that point that the ambiguities of 1441—and the strategic differences that they were designed to hide—would come out.

Chapter

5

THE
TRANSATLANTIC
SPLIT

That the transatlantic allies—primarily the United States and France—were going to diverge over Iraq began to become clear a month after Resolution 1441 was passed, when, on December 7, 2002, Iraq submitted its weapons declaration—12,000 pages of mostly old and incomplete data. The declaration denied that Iraq possessed any weapons of mass destruction programs or precursor agents, and failed to account for the chemical and biological warfare materials that UN inspectors had previously documented.

For the Americans, this was a clear sign that Iraq was not going to comply with the resolution. After taking some time to translate and evaluate the text, the American judgment, in the words of Secretary of State Colin Powell, was that the document was "anything but currently accurate, full or complete." It "totally failed" to meet Resolution 1441's requirements, and its material omissions constituted "another material breach." U.S. Ambassador to the United Nations John Negroponte declared on the same day that "Iraq has spurned its last opportunity to comply with its disarmament obligations." For senior Bush administration officials—and indeed for the President himself—Iraq's failure to be more forthcoming meant that force would almost certainly have to be used, whether all the allies supported it or not.

The French had a somewhat different view—not of the quality of the Iraqi document, but of what to do about it. Like the Americans, French experts deemed the Iraqi declaration incomplete. It "added little that was new," the French Permanent Representative to the United Nations said, and thus "left doubts open about Iraq's pursuit of prohibited weapons." But the French view was that Iraq's failure to clarify unresolved issues about its weapons programs only made it more important to move forward with inspections, in order to verify if the Iraqis in fact had such programs. Consistent with their interpretation of 1441, the French insisted that only the Security Council as a whole, and not individual member states, could declare Iraq to be in "further material breach."

The French also insisted that, according to operational paragraph 4 of the resolution, further material breach only occurred when there were "false statements or omissions in the declarations submitted by Iraq *and* failure by Iraq at any time to comply with and cooperate fully in the implementation" of the resolution. In other words, the incomplete declaration by itself was not to be considered a sufficient breach of Iraq's obligations under 1441 to justify an immediate war.

Other members of the Security Council—including the British—concurred with this interpretation, and did not support the American declaration of material breach. British Ambassador to Washington Christopher Meyer later recalled "having a very strong exchange with Scooter Libby, the vice president's chief of staff, about this. [He] felt that . . . Saddam Hussein [had] transgressed over the last 12 years, that a further declaration, which was a lying declaration, should itself be a reason for war. But we said, 'No, that won't run. It won't wash in the Security Council.'"

Faced with little support for an immediate military response, and against the advice of some administration officials, Bush decided to hold off on military action. According to U.S. officials, the Pentagon was not yet ready to act in any case, and Bush concluded there was no point in publicly announcing a path to war before the military was ready to wage one. The British, moreover, had promised the French, Russians, and Chinese that they would not support military action without at least giving Iraq a chance to cooperate with the weapons inspectors. UK Defense Secretary Geoff Hoon acknowledged the French argument that "Resolution 1441 clearly states that it is not only gaps in the declaration but deliberate obstruction of the inspectors by Iraq" that would constitute material breach. Tony Blair also felt strongly that chief weapons inspector Hans Blix—who had great credibility in Europe—should be given time to report on Iraqi cooperation. Blair was personally convinced that the report would be a damning one, thus bolstering the case for action.

After all the threats that Washington would not tolerate the slightest violation of 1441, many Europeans hoped that the lack of immediate American military action meant that war could perhaps be avoided after all. Indeed, throughout December and as late as January 2003, many French, German, and even British officials still believed that sufficient cooperation by Iraq might forestall war. "War is looking less likely," Chirac's diplomatic adviser Maurice Gourdault-Montagne privately told a group of senior French officials in the Elysée presidential palace during the first week of January. That same week, according to German officials, the German Embassy in Washington was still convinced—based on assurances from senior American officials that the President had not taken a decision—that war could be avoided, a view shared at the time by Foreign Minister Fischer. In Britain, on January 5, Foreign Secretary Jack Straw publicly commented that with Iraqi cooperation, the odds in favor of a diplomatic solution had risen to 60-40. British strategist Lawrence Freedman agreed, saying there were "good grounds for supposing that [a war] may not happen. . . . Having decided to follow a multilateral path on this matter, [Bush] will now find it difficult to stray."

Over the course of January, however, many of these same European officials and analysts started to realize that war was practically inevitable—whether they liked it or not. The first sign came from the pace of U.S. military deployments to the region, which suggested that America was not going to wait to see how inspections and UN Security Council debates played out before deploying its fighting forces to Iraq. Already on January 3, Bush spoke to U.S. troops at Fort Hood, Texas, home of the army's 1st Cavalry Division, and announced that the United States was "ready." A U.S. military operation, he said, would be a noble one: "Should Saddam Hussein seal his fate by refusing to disarm, by ignoring the opinion of the world, you will be fighting not to conquer anybody, but to liberate people." Newspapers began reporting that military units were "shipping out of U.S. bases almost daily," and that the number of U.S. deployed troops could rise to 120,000 in the coming weeks. By mid-January some 140,000 troops, including elements of key fighting units like the 3rd and 4th Infantry Divisions, would receive deployment orders to Iraq.

The Europeans knew that proceeding with such a large and expensive deployment made it much more likely that the Americans would insist on using force before the summer, when the rising heat in the region would render military operations more difficult and risky. The deployment would cost billions of dollars, disrupt military family life across the country, and put U.S. credibility on the line, especially with the Gulf regimes that had made the difficult and domestically unpopular political commitment to host the American troops. The idea that troop deployment schedules or weather conditions could determine whether America would go to war was widely condemned, and in any case, U.S. officials denied that this was the case. But the reality was, the more troops that were sent to the region, the less likely it was that they would be recalled before being used to remove Saddam, lest renewed Iraqi noncompliance later on require the United States to begin the whole costly buildup process once again.

Thus, the accelerating American military deployment was interpreted across Europe as a sign of the growing inevitability of war, and led to accelerated efforts by the war's opponents to prevent it. On January 7, speaking to the French diplomatic corps, French President Chirac reiterated his insistence that Iraq fully comply with UN Resolution 1441 and reminded Iraq that it had been given a "final opportunity" to disarm. But Chirac also made clear that France would only support the use of force after an "explicit decision" by the Security Council "based on a report motivated by the inspectors"—in other words, not based on a U.S. decision alone. Just one day later, Foreign Minister de Villepin sent a letter to France's 14 UN Security Council partners calling for the "immediate transmission of available information" to the inspectors. If the Americans had proof that Iraq was not complying, he felt it was their obligation to supply that proof to the inspectors. De Villepin then traveled to Moscow, where he praised "exemplary" French-Russian cooperation and announced that Russian President Vladimir Putin would be visiting President Chirac in Paris the following month.

In a further attempt to gauge the American position and to make clear that France was not yet ready to support war, Chirac dispatched his diplomatic adviser, Maurice Gourdault-Montagne, to Washington on January 13–14. He had meetings with Condoleezza Rice, Deputy Secretary of Defense Paul Wolfowitz, and Deputy Secretary of State Richard Armitage, all of whom dismissed the French case that more time should be given to inspectors. Rice bluntly dismissed the

Frenchman's arguments, and Wolfowitz told him that the French position was "wishy-washy" and "irresponsible" at a time when everyone
was at risk from Iraq's weapons of mass destruction and their potential
to fall into the hands of terrorists. Even Chirac's office in the Elysée
Palace, Wolfowitz said, was not safe from a potential chemical attack.
Upon returning to Paris, Gourdault-Montagne told Chirac that he now
believed the United States would go to war "no matter what."

Despite the now unmistakable signals from Washington, France
still opposed the use of force on both legal and political-strategic
grounds.

Legally, Paris still argued that the conditions for using force in Iraq
had not yet been met. Iraq's weapons declaration was incomplete and
cooperation with inspectors was not perfect, but progress was being
made. In any case, the French insisted, only the Security Council could
authorize the use of force, and according to Resolution 1441, only a
report by the inspectors could serve as a trigger for action by the
Council. Where Washington now argued that the inspectors' scheduled
January 27 briefing should be their final report, France (and the inspectors) argued that previous UN resolutions calling for continued periodic reports still applied and would last at least through the summer.
In one senior French official's words, accepting that the January 27
report would be the basis for a decision on war or peace would be a
"complete change of the rules of the game."

But the more powerful factors behind French opposition to war
were political and strategic. Whatever the legal arguments, the reality
was that France's leaders preferred containment of Iraq to regime
change, and now—by their own admission, thanks to the American
military threats—containment seemed to be working. And it was also
more politically popular in Europe, where public opinion across the
continent wondered why the United States was planning to go to war
against Iraq just as it was finally welcoming weapons inspectors, but
doing little about North Korea, which was kicking such inspectors out.

When Gourdault-Montagne was asked by one of his American counterparts what France would do in case a "smoking gun" were found in
Iraq, he answered that France would "thank the President for restoring
the credibility of the UN." In other words, France would continue to
make the case for containment—rather than military force—whether
WMDs were found or not. Some in Paris were even prepared to admit
that the French legal case was weak but that did not matter. As one
senior French official involved in the negotiations later admitted in
private, "We accept that we lost the legal debate, but we thought we
could win the political debate."

The gradually diverging French and American policies were thus
bound to clash, and the venue for the clash—and the turning point in
the effort to reach consensus over Iraq—turned out to be a January 20
meeting on terrorism at UN Security Council headquarters in New
York. American and French officials offer differing versions of what
happened, but it's clear that de Villepin, at the start of the French
assumption of the rotating presidency of the Security Council in
January 2003, called for a ministerial-level Security Council meeting on
terrorism. The purpose was to underscore his belief that this, and not
Iraq, should be the Council's top priority. Secretary of State Powell was
skeptical about the need for such a meeting and did not want to risk a
debate about Iraq, so he told de Villepin that he did not want to attend.
January 20, moreover, was Martin Luther King Day in the United
States, and Powell, the first African-American Secretary of State, had
been planning to commemorate it by attending a church service that
day. De Villepin, however, called Powell—with whom he had a good
working relationship—and persuaded him to attend the meeting,
promising that Iraq would be kept off the agenda.

The night before the terrorism conference, Sunday, January 19, the
two men met in Powell's suite at the Waldorf-Astoria hotel and had a
private discussion about Iraq. If de Villepin had any doubts about the
report he had heard from Gourdault-Montagne that Washington was

bent on war, those doubts were removed by the comments of top administration officials on the Sunday television talk shows that aired the morning he and Powell were to meet. Rice, Rumsfeld, and Powell all argued that "time is running out," and Rice stressed that President Bush already had "all of the authority necessary to deal with this very serious problem." Echoing Cheney's arguments from August, Powell added that if Saddam was not serious about disarming, "then it doesn't make any difference how long the inspection goes on." The officials seemed to be preparing the public for action and letting their diplomatic partners know that the United States was determined to act.

De Villepin, nonetheless, made clear to Powell that France was not ready to support a war. He insisted that pursuing inspections, and not force, was the right way to deal with Iraq. Citing Hans Blix's view that Iraq's cooperation was "passive" but not "active," de Villepin told Powell that "you don't go to war over an adjective." Powell, however, responded with a warning to de Villepin not to "underestimate the resolve of the United States to settle this, without dragging it out." Like Rice and Wolfowitz the week before, in their meetings with Gourdault-Montagne, Powell rejected the French argument that UN resolutions provided for ongoing interim weapons inspections reports, and insisted instead that the January 27 report would be the one on which a decision on force would be made. De Villepin thought Powell, both on television and in person, was starting to sound like some of Bush's more hard-line advisers, and realized that the Americans were in fact planning to go to war.

At the UN meeting the next day, de Villepin stuck to his promise not to bring up Iraq, and did not even mention Iraq once in his presentation to the Council. German Foreign Minister Joschka Fischer did talk about Iraq, however, and warned that an attack on Baghdad would have "disastrous consequences for long-term regional stability [and] possible negative repercussions for the joint fight against terrorism." Other speakers, including Russian Foreign Minister Igor Ivanov, also brought up Iraq in their remarks. Ivanov warned against "unilateral steps that might threaten the unity of the entire [anti] terrorism coalition" and stressed that Russia was "strictly in favor of a political settlement of the situation revolving around Iraq."

Caught off guard by the debate, Powell felt obliged to respond when it was his turn to speak. He departed from his prepared text and implored his colleagues to take seriously their commitments in Resolution 1441. "We must not shrink from our duties and our responsibilities when the material [on Iraqi weapons programs] comes before us next week," he said, before using a variation of the phrase "must not shrink" three more times during his address.

After the Security Council session, several of the foreign ministers made brief informal statements to the press, but de Villepin, given France's role as rotating Council president, held a more formal press conference. He said little about Iraq in his opening statement, though he did warn that "if war is the only way to resolve this problem, we are going down a dead end." In response to questioning, however, de Villepin plunged into the Iraq debate. Asked about Iraq by a reporter, he asserted, in his usual animated and energetic way, that the United Nations should stay "on the path of cooperation. The other choice is to move forward out of impatience over a situation in Iraq to move toward military intervention. We believe that nothing today justifies military action." When asked in a follow-up question if that meant France would veto a new resolution authorizing force, he responded, "Believe me, in a matter of principles, we will go to the very end." It was the first time a French leader was so explicit about the possible use of a veto to block the United States.

The U.S. reaction to de Villepin's comments was harsh. The *Washington Post* described the event as the "diplomatic version of an ambush," a description State Department sources did not dispute. According to his close aides, Powell himself was furious. "Powell was very upset, because he felt that de Villepin had pulled a 'bait and switch' and acted in bad faith," said a senior State Department source.

Powell was angry not only because he had been promised that Iraq would not be the subject in New York, but also because he felt that de Villepin was betraying an early agreement to support force against Iraq if Saddam did not comply. During the negotiations over Resolution 1441, Powell says he told de Villepin: "Be sure about one thing. Don't vote for the first, unless you are prepared to vote for the second." Now de Villepin and France seemed to be refusing to implement the Security Council resolution on which they agreed. De Villepin, meanwhile, denied there was such an agreement, and also felt a sense of betrayal. He believed Powell was committed to standing up to the other U.S. cabinet officials who were bent on regime change, and now he was backing down.

Powell's sense that de Villepin had undercut him was no doubt genuine; he'd been the most prominent Bush administration proponent of taking the Iraq issue to the UN Security Council, and now that route was blocked because of the opposition of France. But Powell also had strong bureaucratic reasons to lash out at France. At home, Powell understood that whatever his personal preference might be, the United States was going to war. By January 20 the Pentagon had deployed over 100,000 troops to Iraq, and all the signs said the President was going to act, sooner rather than later. Powell, who had long experience in divided administrations dating back to the Reagan administration, knew that once such an important presidential decision was made, the Secretary of State had little choice but to get on board or resign—indeed, it was common practice to deny that there had even been a dispute within the administration. So Powell got on board.

As Powell's friend General Anthony Zinni observed, Powell seemed to have concluded that "we're going down this road and he wants to keep steering the train. The way to do that is not to be off to one side, but to be out front." Within days, Powell, who only weeks before was arguing that inspections needed time to get up and running, was sounding like the administration's hawks, and questioning the value of inspections: "The question isn't how much longer do you need for inspections to work. Inspections will not work."

French officials continue to deny that the January 20 meeting was a deliberate ambush. They point out that de Villepin was not the one to introduce Iraq into the debate and insist that he could hardly have avoided the subject when asked about it at the press conference. They resented U.S. press reporting that gave the impression that de Villepin had deliberately misled Powell about the purpose of the meeting. But French claims at the time and later that de Villepin did nothing but restate existing French policy, perhaps in a somewhat dramatic way, are unpersuasive. It had only been a week since Gourdault-Montagne was dressed down by U.S. officials and returned to Paris with the news that the Americans were determined to act. If de Villepin wanted to stop that action from appearing inevitable, he would have had to raise a red flag, and a high-profile press conference in New York—even if genuinely organized initially for a different purpose—must have seemed an irresistible opportunity to do so. And certainly, if de Villepin's strong antiwar message and implied veto threat had been a misunderstanding or taken out of context, there would have been ample time over the coming days for Paris to correct the impression.

It would quickly become clear, however, that Paris had no intention of doing so. De Villepin may not have set out to deliberately undercut Colin Powell, but there was now no hiding the fact that France had decided not to go along with an American war in Iraq.

The Franco-German Couple

Just two days after the clash in New York, Jacques Chirac met Gerhard Schröder in Paris for the long-scheduled celebration of the 40th anniversary of the Elysée Treaty. The treaty was a 1963 agreement between French President Charles de Gaulle and German Chancellor Konrad Adenauer to promote Franco-German friendship and foreign and security policy unity. If Paris were looking for an opportunity to clarify what de Villepin had said in New York, Chirac could have used this high profile occasion to reemphasize France's willingness under certain conditions to support war, and perhaps even to try to draw Germany toward a more moderate position. Indeed, many observers had expected, and many Germans had feared, that France would do just that. They expected Germany to be faced with the choice between continued isolation within Europe and a policy reversal, as France joined the U.S.-led coalition in order to maintain its world influence and reap some economic reward.

In the event, however, Chirac did the opposite. Meeting with Schröder in his Elysée office just before the anniversary celebrations, Chirac explained to Schröder that he remained unprepared to accept the inevitability of war, despite what the Americans were saying and doing. Schröder, still ostracized by the White House, and conscious of the German public's continued strong opposition to war, welcomed the French stance, and the meeting ended with Chirac concluding they were "in agreement."

At the press conference following the ceremony, Chirac made this agreement public and confirmed that France had no intention of backing down: "Germany and France have an identical judgment about this crisis that is essentially based on two ideas. The first is that the Security Council and only the Security Council can make the decisions, in conformity with the relevant resolutions that it has adopted. The second reality is that, for us, war is always an acknowledgment of defeat and always the worst solution, and therefore, everything must be done to prevent it." France and Germany now had a common antiwar position, and hopes for transatlantic agreement were fading.

Some saw the hardening French position on Iraq as part of a cynical deal between France and Germany. Columnist William Safire of the *New York Times*, for example, called the Franco-German agreement a "stunning power play" in which France would compensate Germany's support on European issues like agriculture and the European Constitutional Convention by "double crossing the United States at the United Nations." That view is too simple and overlooks the fact that both Chirac and Schröder were genuinely opposed to the war, a stance that had won them widespread domestic political support and helped transform their political fortunes. The agreements between France and Germany on agriculture and the constitution, moreover, were largely sealed in the fall of 2002; they need not have prevented Chirac from backing the Americans on Iraq in January 2003, and trying to persuade Germany to do the same.

It was true, however, that the new Franco-German solidarity was about more than opposition to the Iraq war itself. The evolving European political context was driving Chirac and Schröder—who had previously found little common political ground—together, and both saw an opportunity in the new situation to influence the future of Europe. Germany, for the first time in decades the *demandeur* in the bilateral relationship because of Schröder's weak political position and Berlin's frayed ties with Washington, now needed French assistance more than at any time since Schröder's election. France, in turn, saw an opportunity both to restore the balance in Franco-German relations and to reestablish Franco-German leadership of the European Union, which had been suffering as the Union expanded and formerly periph- eral members like Britain and Spain began to play greater roles. An agreement on Iraq, then, represented an opportunity for France to advance its vision of Europe at a time when EU expansion was forcing a redefinition of the very nature of the European project.

The Franco-German stance on Iraq was also an opportunity for Chirac and Schröder to isolate more Atlanticist leaders like Blair, Aznar, and Berlusconi vis-à-vis their antiwar publics. Chirac may have under- stood that he could not speak for "Europe" about Iraq, but he saw this as an opportunity to speak for "Europeans," and to make the British, Spanish, and Italian leaders pay a price for falling into line behind the

United States. In his rapprochement with Germany, then, Chirac did not have to choose between his position on Iraq and his desire to play a leadership role in Europe. Both pointed in the direction of opposing an American-led war.

Whatever its reasons, the clear Franco-German stand against war led to a greater backlash from Washington. Indeed, on January 22, the very day Chirac and Schröder were presenting their common position in Paris, Secretary of Defense Rumsfeld practically defined their two countries out of Europe at a Pentagon press briefing. When asked about "European" opposition to the war, Rumsfeld commented: "You're thinking of Europe as Germany and France. I don't. I think that's 'old Europe.' If you look at the entire NATO Europe today, the center of gravity is shifting to the East." Powell also expressed his impatience, taking issue with those (like France and Germany) who called for more time by insisting it was already clear that Iraq would not cooperate. "Frankly," Powell told Jim Lehrer on television, "there are some nations in the world who would like simply to turn away from this problem, pretend it isn't there." A few days later Rumsfeld compared Germany's Iraq policy to that of some of America's greatest adversaries: "There are three or four countries that have said they won't do anything; I believe Libya, Cuba, and Germany are ones that have indicated they won't help in any respect. . . ." It was a conscious slap at the Germans and a clear signal from Rumsfeld that the Bush administration was not prepared to give any ground.

Disputes Within Europe

As tensions between the United States and France and Germany deepened, so did the strains among the Europeans themselves. Long clear beneath the surface, they emerged in particularly stark daylight on the morning of January 30, when a joint letter of support for the United States from eight European governments appeared in the *Wall Street Journal* and several other newspapers across Europe. The letter, signed by leaders from Britain, Spain, Italy, Poland, Hungary, Denmark, Portugal, and the Czech Republic, expressed solidarity with the United States and underscored the shared values that constituted the "real bond" between the United States and Europe. It cited past American "bravery, generosity, and farsightedness" and pledged support for the United States in the effort to "rid the world of the danger posed by Saddam Hussein's weapons of mass destruction." It underlined the signatories' "backing for Resolution 1441" and their "wish to pursue the UN route."

In fact, the contents of the letter were not particularly controversial; officials from France and Germany later said that they had no objection to the language in the text. The timing and symbolism of the letter, however, were highly significant. The idea of such a letter originated with Michael Gonzalez, the deputy editorial page editor at the *Wall Street Journal Europe*, who did not believe that the Franco-German vision of Iraq or transatlantic relations was shared by other European leaders. Gonzalez thus contacted the office of Italian Prime Minister Silvio Berlusconi to propose that Berlusconi write an op-ed piece setting out his own, more Atlanticist, views. Berlusconi liked the idea, but wanted to associate it with other like-minded leaders, so he contacted Spanish Prime Minister José Maria Aznar, who in turn got in touch with Portuguese Prime Minister José Manuel Durao Barroso and Britain's Tony Blair.

The British initially showed little enthusiasm for the project, but when Aznar's diplomatic adviser Alberto Carnero produced what Downing Street officials considered to be a "good text," London got on board and encouraged the Spanish to reach out to other European leaders. Poland, Hungary, the Czech Republic, and Denmark all agreed to sign. Of the countries contacted, only the Dutch leaders declined to sign, not because they opposed the substance or the process, but because they were in the midst of an election. Blair also insisted that the piece be published not only in the *Wall Street Journal*, but in major newspapers in all the signatories' countries. The leaders from France, Germany, Belgium, and Luxembourg, who were opposed to the war, were not only not asked to sign, but were not even informed that the letter was being prepared.

The signatories of the "Letter of Eight," and particularly Blair, Aznar, and Berlusconi, saw it as a good opportunity to express support for the United States on Iraq at a sensitive time. At least as important, however, was the opportunity to make a statement about the future of Europe, contrasting their own Atlanticist vision with the vision being put forth by Paris and Berlin. Only a week before, after all, France and Germany had used the Elysée Treaty celebration to reclaim their European leadership position and to insist on their special role as the "motor" of European integration. "For 40 years," Chirac and Schröder had asserted, "each decisive step was taken in Europe thanks to the motor that Germany and France represent. . . . Experience shows that when Berlin and Paris agree, Europe can move forward; if there is disagreement, Europe marks time."

The assumption that France and Germany were the natural leaders of Europe had long caused resentment in Europe. Britain considered itself to be just as important to Europe's future as France and Germany were, especially in foreign policy. Spain, with a growing economy and ties to the vast Spanish speaking world, now saw itself as an up and coming European power that deserved to be treated as one of the "big guys." Italy resented never being treated as an equal despite its economic weight. And all the smaller countries felt that the Franco-German vision of the EU gave excessive weight to the larger countries. Blair, Berlusconi, and Aznar also felt that Chirac and Schröder were deliberately undermining them politically by portraying themselves as the true spokesmen of Europe's antiwar sentiment, while effectively labeling them lackeys of the United States. Here, then, was an opportunity to get a measure of revenge. They could make clear that the Franco-German vision of Europe was not the only one.

The idea of a public statement by eight European governments without consulting their EU partners was, of course, a distinct slap at the very notion of the common foreign policy that the EU was meant to be developing—and which even the signatories of the letter claimed to support. The rotating presidency of the EU, held at that time by Greece, was not informed about the letter, nor was European Commission President Romani Prodi or Javier Solana, the EU foreign policy high representative. Solana, who had spent the previous week painfully (and, he had thought, successfully) coaxing EU leaders into a common policy on Iraq, first heard about the publication on the radio, and was furious to have been cut out. The fact that the signatories were willing to proceed with such a divisive effort was thus a measure of the strength of their feeling about issues like the future of Europe and relations with the United States. Tony Blair told associates repeatedly that his goal was to have a united Europe that was pro-American, but that if that proved impossible, he would prefer a divided Europe that was partly pro-American to a united Europe lined up against the United States.

Not surprisingly, Washington—which contrary to widespread European suspicions had no role in the publication of the letter, although U.S. officials were aware of it—was delighted with it. Bush, who had from the beginning of his term pursued a deliberate strategy of maintaining close ties with conservative Atlanticist leaders in Europe like Aznar and Berlusconi, saw the letter as vindication of this approach. He wrote a personal note of thanks to Aznar, saying, "God bless you and Spain." The French and Germans, meanwhile, were furious. The Germans denounced the signatories for blatantly undermining the EU's Common Foreign and Security Policy. And French Foreign Minister de Villepin cancelled a trip to join Jack Straw for dinner at his official residence, citing a pretext of other pressing work. Even after the uproar, however, British and Spanish officials said they were so unhappy with the French and Germans by then that they had no regrets. They pointed out that neither Berlin nor Paris seemed to have any problems with their own unilateral statements about the war, which were unco-ordinated with the EU or others.

The intra-European tensions over Iraq and over how to deal with the United States also spilled over into relations between Western and Eastern Europe. The publication of the Letter of Eight irritated a num-ber of other countries in Central and Eastern Europe whose leaders agreed with the letter's message but were not asked to sign. In part-icular, a group of 10 new democracies—Albania, Bulgaria, Croatia, Estonia, Latvia, Lithuania, Macedonia, Slovakia, Slovenia, and Romania—known as the "Vilnius 10," after the Lithuanian city in which they launched their common bid to join NATO in May 2000, resented having been left out. At NATO's Prague summit in November 2002, seven of them had just been invited to join the alliance (all but Albania, Croatia, and Macedonia), and the entire group had issued a statement on transatlantic solidarity and Iraq that was similar in tone to the Letter of Eight from which they had nonetheless been excluded. With the ratification of their NATO accession still to come, these coun-tries were particularly keen to demonstrate, especially to the United States, their credentials as strong Atlantic allies committed to the alliance and its values.

The Vilnius 10 thus looked for an opportunity to issue their own statement of solidarity with the United States, and their ambassadors in Washington—who meet regularly to coordinate strategy—took the lead in drafting a new text in coordination with their capitals. They were assisted by Bruce Jackson, a former Pentagon official, Wall Street banker, and vice president of Lockheed Martin, who had developed close ties to the Central and East Europeans through his leadership of the United States Committee to Expand NATO during the 1990s. White House officials were aware of and supportive of the effort but did not want to get directly involved, so it was left to Jackson—who had close political ties to the Bush team and often advised the Central Europeans on relations with the United States—to help craft the message.

The Vilnius 10 text was issued on February 5. Like the Letter of Eight, it mainly stressed the signatories' solidarity with the United States and their determination to enforce the Security Council resolutions calling for Saddam Hussein's disarmament. As former communist states, many dominated by the Soviet Union, the leaders who signed it also insisted that their countries understood "the dangers posed by tyranny and the special responsibility of democracies to defend our shared values. The transatlantic community, of which we are a part, must stand together to face the threat posed by the nexus of terrorism and dictators with weapons of mass destruction." It was music to the Bush administration's ears, and its purpose was to make clear that NATO's newest members would be strong supporters of the United States. The message was that it was the French and German governments who were isolated, not the United States.

If the Letter of Eight irritated the French and Germans, the Vilnius 10 text was seen as a direct provocation, especially in Paris. Particularly irritating to the French was the fact that the letter began with a reference to Colin Powell's presentation of "compelling evidence" to the UN about Iraq's weapons of mass destruction, despite the fact that none of the signatories had actually seen that evidence—Powell would not make his presentation until the day after the text was finalized. In other words, the Vilnius 10 countries were confirming France's worst fears: that they were reflexively Atlanticist countries waiting to become Trojan horses for the Americans within the EU and challenge Franco-German leadership of Europe. According to his senior aides, Jacques Chirac was also deeply irritated with the notion that sovereign European countries, aspiring to EU membership, were taking instructions from an American "lobbyist" with ties to the Bush White House.

Chirac took the opportunity to express himself on the subject at a press conference following an EU summit in Brussels on February 17. Ironically, the summit had just issued a statement on Iraq that was meant to show that members had patched up their differences and agreed on a course of disarmament first and use of force as a last resort. Chirac's statement, however, made clear that the intra-European resentment had not disappeared. The EU candidates who signed the Vilnius 10 letter, Chirac asserted, had acted "a bit lightly." After all, joining the European Union required "a minimum of consideration for others, a minimum of policy coordination. If, when a difficult subject comes up, you start giving independent points of view that have not been coordinated with the group you want to join, well, that's not very responsible behavior." The Central Europeans, then, had "missed a good opportunity to keep quiet."

Chirac then went on to add the warning that the behavior of these candidates was not only wrong, but could cost them membership in the EU if they were not careful. "Beyond the somewhat amusing or childish aspects of the matter," Chirac said, it was:

> . . . dangerous. It should not be forgotten that a number of EU countries will have to ratify enlargement by referendum. And we already know that public opinion, as always when it's a matter of something new, have reservations about enlargement, not really seeing exactly what their interest is in approving it. Obviously, then, [what the Central Europeans have done] can only reinforce hostile public opinion sentiments among the 15 and especially those who will hold a referendum. Remember that all it takes is for one country not to ratify by referendum, for [enlargement] not to happen. Thus, I would say that these countries have been, let's be frank, both not very well brought up and rather unconscious about the dangers that too quick an alignment with the American position could have for them.

The statement was not only undiplomatic but will no doubt be remembered in Central Europe for a long time to come. It was also ironic, in that Chirac was furious with the Central Europeans for exactly the same offense that he was committing in the eyes of the Americans and British—disloyalty to those who saw themselves as the natural leaders of an alliance. (Chirac, no doubt, would contest the analogy, asserting that the EU has a mission and mechanism for forging a common foreign policy, while the transatlantic alliance does not.) But just as Blair and the others would say that they did not regret the Letter of Eight, Chirac also remained unrepentant. "I don't regret it," he said months later. "I should regret it, but I don't. When you decide to get together as a family, then at least when you take a different position from the rest of the family, you discuss it first. You warn people ahead of time. I learned about their position from the press. . . . That's just not acceptable." Many Central Europeans, to say nothing of the British, Spanish, and Italians, did not recall Chirac discussing all his own positions "with the family" before taking them, a pattern they saw as part of a double standard the French and Germans wanted to impose on the rest of the EU.

Chirac's outburst after the EU meeting was not the only opportunity for the family to squabble. Just a few days after publication of the Vilnius 10 letter, in fact, Americans and Europeans from "old" and "new" Europe alike had the opportunity to discuss their differences at the February 7–9 meeting of the Munich Conference on Security Policy. The normally staid event, which usually consisted of defense ministers giving set-piece speeches about their commitment to the NATO alliance, was instead marked by bitter debates between American representatives and their French and German counterparts, as well as among Europeans. U.S. Secretary of Defense Rumsfeld, encouraged by the signs of solidarity from the leaders of 18 European countries, warned the French and Germans that they would be isolated if they opposed a war in Iraq. Rumsfeld called on them to support a position that would help the United Nations move "from a path of ridicule to a path of responsibility." The Germans and French, however, were not persuaded. At one point German Foreign Minister Joschka Fischer turned to the American delegation and said, in English: "Excuse me, I am not convinced!"

Just as striking as the ongoing transatlantic spat was the debate among Europeans, both in the corridors of the event and during the plenary sessions. Portuguese Defense Minister Paulo Portas also assailed Fischer, warning him of the dangers of excessive pacifism, and reminding him that pacifists were "wrong in 1939 . . . wrong in the 1980s . . . and wrong on Milosevic," to which Fischer responded by questioning Portugal's contribution to Afghanistan and comparing it negatively to Germany's. At the same meeting, Bruce Jackson acknowledged to members of the press that he was indeed involved in the drafting of the Vilnius 10 letter, noting that "if France and Germany think they can run Europe or set up their own alliances, then so can we." U.S. Senator Joseph Lieberman, critical of both the Bush administration and the antiwar Europeans, commented that the allies seemed like a "dysfunctional family" in need of therapy.

NATO's Crisis of Credibility

So vitriolic had the Iraq dispute become by early February that it began to inflict collateral damage on even the most sacrosanct institution of the Atlantic alliance—NATO. Stung by the criticism that it had snubbed its NATO allies during the Afghanistan operation the previous year—and anxious to get European allies on board for a possible Iraq war—the United States already in November 2002 began to consider how NATO might be involved in a possible operation. On December 4, Deputy Secretary of Defense Paul Wolfowitz visited NATO headquarters to lay out four possible options. These included assistance to Turkey in the context of an Iraqi threat to Turkish territory (covered by NATO's Article V defense guarantee); technical support to allies involved in a war; an actual military role in a war; or a postwar role for the alliance. By mid-January the proposals had been refined and expanded, and Wolfowitz visited Brussels again to formally propose a list of possible tasks. These included sending AWACS surveillance planes and Patriot antimissile batteries to help defend Turkey; using NATO naval forces to help defend U.S. ships heading to the Persian Gulf through the Mediterranean Sea; enlisting NATO troops to guard U.S. and other bases in Europe and elsewhere; and substituting NATO forces for U.S. troops that might be redeployed from peacekeeping missions in the Balkans and elsewhere.

On the face of it, this was simply prudent contingency planning, and most of the NATO allies supported the preventive measures. Indeed, initially no ally objected to the planning taking place so long as it was not made public. In mid-January, however, word leaked to the press about possible NATO involvement, and France, Germany, Belgium, and Luxembourg insisted that such planning immediately stop. Leaders in those countries argued that taking action at NATO would be a premature acceptance of the notion that war was inevitable, a notion they vehemently wanted to forestall. On January 22, the day Chirac and Schröder were jointly pledging to oppose war in Iraq during the 40th anniversary celebrations of the Elysée Treaty, France and Germany formally blocked planning at NATO from taking place.

The Americans, however, did not want to take no for an answer. Eschewing the option of fulfilling the proposed tasks through bilateral deals with individual allies—and ignoring the fact that Turkey itself was lukewarm about a possible NATO role—the Americans pressed NATO to act, especially on the issue of Turkey's defense. Invoking the NATO Treaty's Article IV, which allows for consultations whenever one ally's security might be threatened, the Americans insisted that the alliance prepare to come to Turkey's defense in the event Iraq retaliated against Turkey during a possible war. This was seen in Washington as a good way to line up NATO support for an eventual conflict. To officials at the U.S. mission to NATO who wanted to see the alliance play a greater role, it was also a good way to "push the organization" lest its perceived relevance, already shaken by its exclusion from Afghanistan, fade further.

The dispute about NATO's potential role came to a head at a February 10 meeting of NATO ambassadors in Brussels, which led to angry exchanges and even shouting matches not normally heard at meetings of the North Atlantic Council. The meeting pitted representatives of France, Germany, and Belgium, all of whom argued that NATO planning was unnecessary and unnecessarily provocative, against representatives of other allies, led by those of the United States and Great Britain, who argued that the defense of an ally should not be ignored. According to one participant, after UK Ambassador to NATO Emyr Jones-Parry had sharply criticized the position of his French, German, and Belgian counterparts, he was told he "could not say things like that at NATO," to which he responded "I just did." But the opponents of a NATO role would not budge. As Belgian Foreign Minister Louis Michel put it, NATO planning to defend Turkey "would signify that we have already entered into the logic of war, that . . . any chance, any initiative to still resolve the conflict in a peaceful way was gone."

U.S. officials were furious—and also seized a good opportunity to castigate their opponents on the war. U.S. Ambassador to NATO Nicholas Burns called the French, German, and Belgian position at NATO "most unfortunate" and said that it created a "crisis of credibility" for the alliance. Other Americans, including the most senior officials, were less diplomatic: Secretary of State Colin Powell called French, German, and Belgian policy "inexcusable"; Defense Secretary Donald Rumsfeld said it was "shameful"; and former United States Ambassador to the United Nations Richard Holbrooke said it was "disgraceful." Congressman Tom Lantos, a Democrat from California, said that he was "particularly disgusted by the blind intransigence and utter ingratitude" of the French, Germans, and Belgians. Powell feared that the alliance was "breaking itself up because it will not meet its responsibilities."

In an attempt to break the deadlock, on February 12 the United States put forward a scaled-back proposal. The new plan maintained the call on NATO allies to provide AWACS, Patriot missiles, and chemical and biological weapons protection units to Turkey, but eliminated Washington's request that European forces replace allied forces that were guarding U.S. bases in Europe or those sent from their current posts to the Gulf. The Americans also began to up the ante by talking about other ways to proceed if collective agreement could not be reached. One of these was to use NATO's Defense Planning Committee, a body that France had withdrawn from in 1966, to plan for Turkey's defense; that would not eliminate the challenge of winning German and Belgian support, but it would at least marginalize France. The other option was to have the Supreme Allied Commander Europe (SACEUR) use his "delegated authority" to defend Turkey if no collective NATO decision were made. In a little noticed North Atlantic Council (NAC) decision of February 2000, NATO had decided that in time of crisis or war, SACEUR would have the authority to defend NATO territory and airspace. Washington, NATO Secretary General Robertson, and NATO SACEUR James Jones had already agreed to proceed on that basis if an agreement at the NAC could not be reached, and made it clear to the recalcitrant allies that they were prepared to do so.

Neither the scaled-back plan nor the threat to go around the NAC, however, was enough for Belgium and France, which continued to insist that a NATO decision to protect Turkey was an implicit acceptance of the case for war. A French government spokesman asserted: "We cannot, via a decision of NATO, give our implicit support to an armed intervention in Iraq and thus prejudge decisions which belong to the Security Council."

Germany, however, began to look for a way out of the crisis. Unlike France, Germany had depended so directly on NATO for so long that Berlin was increasingly uncomfortable about the damage that was being done to the alliance and to relations with Washington. With

Turkey now directly requesting support under NATO's Article IV consultation mechanism (previously, Washington was requesting help on Turkey's behalf), Berlin decided that it did not want to hold out any longer. On February 13, German diplomats told the French that they were prepared to accede to the scaled-back proposal at the Defense Planning Committee (DPC) by the weekend of February 15.

Belgium would remain a lone holdout for another 24 hours, but finally Brussels also gave in, and on February 16, NATO's 18 members of the DPC put two months of squabbling behind them and agreed to do collectively what most individual members had long agreed to do anyway.

The NATO dispute demonstrated just how tense Atlantic relations had become and showed how the differences over Iraq could spill over into other areas of supposed allied cooperation. And as on many other occasions, there was plenty of blame to go around. Knowing that several NATO members were not yet willing to proceed with NATO plans for Turkey's defense, the United States could easily have avoided the controversy and ensured that the defensive measures were taken on a bilateral basis. During the Cold War, Washington never made support for its out-of-area activities—such as the Korean or Vietnam wars—a litmus test of loyalty to the alliance as a whole. And given Washington's snubbing of NATO in Afghanistan little more than a year earlier, it was hard to argue that it pushed a NATO role this time out of devotion and loyalty to the alliance.

The Americans who denounced the German and French positions, moreover, overlooked the fact that Turkey itself was never particularly concerned about having NATO play a role, and that both France and Germany were prepared to do whatever was necessary to actually help Turkey, just not to have NATO do it. As a German official put it, "We promised to supply the Patriots to Turkey bilaterally and asked the United States please not to force us to be an obstruction within NATO. But the Bush administration was determined to make life difficult for

Schröder by having Germany vote yes to the deployment, thus undermining the chancellor's own position against the Iraq war. That was a really nasty bit of political game playing, and we viewed [it] as bullying, pure and simple." The French Defense Minister also insisted that "France would be one of the first at [Turkey's] side" if it were really under threat.

But if the American determination to involve NATO was a trap, the French and Germans certainly fell into it. Whatever the French and German pledges of bilateral support, it was difficult for Americans and other supporters of the alliance to understand how certain allies could fail to heed a request by another for contingency planning for a possible attack. Given that France itself had consistently said that the use of force remained an option, it was hard to argue that contingency planning in NATO would be anything other than an expression of solidarity and prudent preparation. No matter how much the French, Germans, and Belgians insisted that their solidarity with Turkey was complete, the way events transpired left an impression of allies unwilling to stand together in a time of need. It would have been much easier for those allies, and much healthier for the alliance, to have quietly accepted the American proposal in January while simultaneously emphasizing that their acceptance did not constitute approval of an attack on Iraq. Instead, the result was that Americans who were already skeptical about relying on NATO to pursue common transatlantic interests would now become even more reluctant to do so.

Losing the French

By early February the international community was deeply divided over Iraq. The United States and United Kingdom were increasingly determined to take action, and they had the support of Spain, Italy, Poland, and other allies. Unfortunately for them, however, the opposition to the war, especially from France, was not declining—it was growing. And France's determined opposition, in turn, emboldened others to believe that perhaps the war could still be stopped or the Americans denied legitimacy after all.

Many Americans would later come to conclude that Paris had never really taken the military option seriously and that Chirac, as columnist Thomas Friedman later wrote, "[never] intended to go to war against Saddam, under any circumstances." In fact, however, while it is impossible to know for sure, given the French president's near total control of such decisions in France, this was probably not the case. Chirac had been prepared to support war under certain conditions—including blatant Iraqi obstruction of weapons inspectors, refusal to destroy any illicit arms that were found, the discovery of a "smoking gun" too important to ignore, or an Iraqi military provocation. But during the winter of 2002–2003, developments in Iraq (greater cooperation on weapons inspections than France had expected), in Europe (strong and growing opposition to war), and at the Security Council (the reluctance of other important members to back the Americans), persuaded him that those conditions were not met.

As late as January 7, 2003, Chirac was still making contingency plans for participating in an eventual war, and warning his armed forces to "be ready for any eventuality" in the context of implementing Resolution 1441. Chirac had authorized his chief of staff, Henri Bentegeat, to send General Jean-Patrick Gaviard on a secret mission to Washington for discussions about a potential French contribution of some 15,000 troops, 100 airplanes, and use of significant naval assets, including an aircraft carrier group in case of French military participation in Iraq. And in Paris, officials had concluded that blatant Iraqi noncompliance—such as refusing inspectors access to weapons sites or refusing to destroy any prohibited weapons found—would mean that France would accept and support military action against Iraq.

Events on the ground during January and February 2003, however, were pushing the French—and with them, many other Europeans—in the opposite direction. First, not only had the inspectors found no "smoking gun"—which would have made French opposition difficult to sustain—but Saddam's cooperation was actually turning out to be better than France had initially expected. As de Villepin put it in his January 20 press conference, the UN weapons inspectors were now conducting some 300 inspections per month, and the process was "satisfactory." De Villepin concluded: "Already we know for a fact that Iraq's weapons of mass destruction programs are being largely blocked, even frozen. We must do everything possible to strengthen this process."

The French, in fact, had never expected full cooperation and were therefore not surprised when it did not materialize. In October 2002 a senior French official responsible for Iraq told a group of visiting Americans that he would consider 70 percent a reasonable—and acceptable—level of cooperation to expect. Thus, when Saddam actually agreed to let inspectors visit his palaces and other "sensitive sites" and to conduct interviews with at least some scientists, the French thought real progress was being made.

France's conviction that inspections were working reasonably well was only strengthened by the presentations made by weapons inspectors Hans Blix and Mohamed ElBaradei at the UN Security Council on February 14. Blix's first report to the Security Council, on January 27, had been quite harsh, concluding that Iraq "appears not to have come to a genuine acceptance, not even today, of the disarmament which was demanded of it." Now, three weeks later, Blix still had a number of unanswered questions, but was able to report that at least where the inspections process was concerned, "The situation has improved." Those inspections, he added, "are effectively helping to bridge the gap in knowledge that arose due to the absence of inspections between December 1998 and November 2002." In addition, Blix challenged a number of the allegations made by U.S. Secretary of State Powell in his UN presentation on February 5, asserting that he had no evidence that Iraqis had been tipped off about any of the inspections and claiming that some of the reported movement of munitions to which Powell had referred could have been "routine." ElBaradei also painted an improved picture, concluding that while a number of issues were still under investigation, the inspectors had "to date found no evidence of ongoing prohibited nuclear or nuclear-related activities in Iraq." France may have felt obliged to support a war if the inspectors were giving negative reports, but Paris was certainly not going to cut them off when they said they were making progress.

At the same time, in part as a consequence of Iraqi cooperation with the inspectors, world and European public opinion turned even more clearly against the war. In France itself, for example, those opposed to U.S. and allied military action rose from 65 percent in September 2002 to 77 percent by February 2003. In Britain, the percentage of those who approved of the way Bush was handling Iraq fell from 30 percent in September 2002 to 19 percent in January 2003, and the percentage that approved of Blair's handling of Iraq fell from 40 to 26 percent over the same period. And in Russia, opposition to military action in Iraq rose from 79 percent in November 2002 to 87 percent in March 2003.

European public opinion also began to express itself. The weekend of February 15, one day after the weapons inspectors spoke to the UN, saw some of the largest public protests in decades, with nearly one million people in London (the largest protest in British history), one to two million in Rome, and nearly one million in both Madrid and Barcelona. In Berlin there were 300,000 to 500,000, and in Paris some 100,000, the lower numbers in part due to more public satisfaction with their governments' antiwar stands. By mid-February, Chirac—an instinctive politician who harbored aspirations to be a leader of Europe—had concluded that the vast majority of French and European public opinion agreed with his strong opposition to the war and not with the support other European governments were giving it. Having so recently only barely survived his own elections in France, when he got 19 percent of the vote in the first round of the presidential race, the opportunity to lead a unified French public opinion, including the Muslim population, and European and world opinion, was too much to resist.

Finally, and critically important, was the interaction of the positions of all the countries opposed to the war. Russia, another permanent Security Council member, was not selling out to the United States for economic compensation, as many had predicted. China was keeping a low profile, but also making clear that it did not support the use of force. Germany, strongly opposed to the war and in any case ostracized by the White House, was unlikely to waver. Even Turkey, a major U.S. ally, was deeply opposed to war—polls there were showing 94 percent of the public against it—and still refusing to grant U.S. access to bases. Without Turkey, the French believed, an invasion of Iraq might not be possible. And finally there were the so-called "Undecided Six" on the Security Council—Chile, Mexico, Guinea, Cameroon, Angola, and Pakistan. Leaders of these countries were probably willing to support war if the permanent members of the Council were united, but they did not want to take such an unpopular decision so long as countries like France and Russia remained opposed. The applause de Villepin received at the end of his antiwar Security Council statement on February 14—only Nelson Mandela had ever been similarly applauded in the entire history of the UN—was hardly likely to persuade the French to back down. As former U.S. Assistant Secretary of State Martin Indyk later wrote, "If everyone else had been on board, the French wouldn't have dared to try to block the resolution. The reality is that the French were in respectable company: The Russians and the Chinese were also determined to veto. The Mexicans, Canadians, and Chileans—our closest friends in the hemisphere—were not with us."

Americans who were baffled by France's opposition to war even after it became clear that Bush was going to act—and that no one could stop him—thus missed the point. Actually stopping the war may well have been a French aim early in the process, but by mid-January even the French realized the war was almost inevitable. By then, however, opposing the war had become a matter of principle—and of politics. The French genuinely thought the war was a bad idea and worried that a Western occupation of Iraq could turn into a quagmire that would serve as a recruiting tool for al Qaeda. But equally important, they were simply not prepared to bow to American leadership when so much of the world disagreed with the policy of the United States. As Robert Kagan put it at the time, "The French expect to fail in their effort to prevent war, but they expect the war and its aftermath to bring disaster both for the United States and for those European leaders who have thrown in their lot with Bush. When the dust settles, the French believe their brave stance will be vindicated before the court of European public opinion."

The Failed "Second Resolution"

France's unwavering opposition to the war created problems for the Americans, who would have preferred a consensus for action. But the real challenge was for Britain's Tony Blair. In the face of hostility toward the war from his Labor party and public opinion, Blair had promised in December 2002 that he would only support a war with UN approval—or if "the spirit of the UN resolution was broken because an unreasonable veto was put down." With veto-wielding France now clearly determined to block his efforts at the UN, Blair's only hope was to isolate the French by winning the support of a majority of Security Council members for a new resolution authorizing the U.S.-led coalition to take action. If Blair could get the 9 out of 15 votes needed to pass a resolution, and could avoid a veto by Russia or China, France would be obliged either to go along or to veto alone, leaving the British with at least a "moral majority" at the UN.

The Americans had long claimed that no "second resolution" was necessary to authorize war—indeed, they had fought hard and successfully to avoid such a requirement in 1441. As late as January 31, despite a Blair visit to the White House designed to persuade President Bush to support returning to the UN, Bush was still publicly noncommittal. Queried at a press conference with Blair at his side, Bush would say only that "should the United Nations decide to pass a second resolution, it would be welcomed if it is yet another signal that we are intent upon disarming Saddam Hussein." But, the President insisted that "1441 gives us the authority to move without any second resolution, and Saddam Hussein must understand that if he does not disarm for the sake of peace, we, along with others, will go and disarm Saddam Hussein." It was not the ringing statement of support for a second resolution that Blair was looking for.

To maximize their chances of winning support, the British began to consider formally introducing a series of "benchmarks" or "disarmament tasks" into the new resolution that would concretely define what the Iraqi regime would have to do to avoid the use of force. This, the logic ran, would make it more difficult for the French and others to claim that Iraq was not in violation of UN demands. The benchmarks would include accounting for certain types of prohibited weapons and materials for prohibited weapons, and permitting full access to Iraqi scientists. But Washington, fearing that Saddam could comply with specific tasks but still retain an overall weapons of mass destruction capability, remained opposed to formally introducing the benchmarks into the proposed second resolution, at least for the time being.

With Blair facing a critical vote in Parliament that could determine not only whether Britain could support the use of force in Iraq, but even Blair's political future, the Americans decided in mid-February to support their embattled friend: The United States and Britain would table the second resolution in New York by the end of the month.

France, however, with support from Germany and Russia, remained hostile to the plan. Benchmarks or not, France remained unprepared to legitimize a war on Iraq, and it did not believe the

United States had the necessary votes to pass a new resolution authorizing war. At the same time, however, the French also wanted to avoid a situation that would oblige them to wield a veto in New York, which they had not done against a U.S.-supported resolution since 1956. It was an ironic twist. The Americans, who claimed they needed no second resolution, were now insisting on bringing one to a vote. At the same time, France, which had fought so hard to require such a resolution, now suggested that the United States and Britain avoid coming back to the Security Council.

The French and the Germans had been advising the Americans for almost a month not to go back to the UN. On February 21 the French ambassador to the United States, Jean-David Levitte, went to the White House to make the proposal formal. Levitte met with Deputy National Security Adviser Steven Hadley. Acting on direct instructions from the Elysée, Levitte told Hadley that going back to the UN would undermine Bush's argument that the United States already had the authorization it needed to use force in Iraq. France also believed, Levitte said, that the U.S. would fail to get nine votes in favor of the new resolution. This meant that even in the absence of a veto by France or Russia, the United States would be acting illegally, which would be worse than foregoing the resolution in the first place.

Thus, Levitte proposed a "gentlemen's agreement" in which the United States would avoid forcing France to give UN sanction to a war it did not support, and in exchange the French would "agree to disagree" about the justification for using force. The model Levitte suggested would be the "yellow light" that the United States and its NATO allies got from Russia before the Kosovo operation in 1999—no UN approval, but an agreement not to create a crisis. France would of course make clear its continued opposition to war and question its legality, but the proposed approach would avoid the huge rupture that would occur if the United States insisted on going back to the UN, where France would feel obliged to oppose it.

Hadley said he appreciated Levitte's arguments, but that it was too late. The United States did not need the second resolution, but Blair did, and the United States needed Blair. Contrary to what the French believed, moreover, Hadley said the White House was confident that it would win the nine votes. U.S. diplomats at the UN were reporting with cautious optimism that most of the undecided permanent members would ultimately vote with the United States. If they did, then the ball would be in France's court, and responsibility for a clash in New York would lie with Paris and not Washington. The United States was thus determined to go ahead, and an unseemly competition was engaged in to see which side really could win the nine votes. With Spain and Bulgaria clearly in the American-British camp, and with France, Germany, Russia, and China solidly against a second resolution, it would be the "undecided six" elected members of the Council— Angola, Cameroon, Chile, Guinea, Pakistan, and Mexico—that would be decisive.

The American and British effort to win Council members over to their side suffered an early setback on March 1, when the Turkish parliament voted to deny the United States permission to launch an attack on northern Iraq from Turkish soil. In fact, more members of the Turkish parliament voted in favor of a resolution to allow U.S. troops to use Turkish territory than voted against it (the vote was 264-250), but under Turkish parliamentary rules, the 19 abstentions counted as no votes, which meant that the resolution had failed. For opponents of the war, it was one more reason to stand firm in opposition. If the United States could not even win support from one of its closest strategic allies—the use of whose territory seemed to be a critical element in the war plan—perhaps there was a way to stop the war after all.

On March 5 the foreign ministers of France, Germany, and Russia met in Paris to try to do just that. Stressing what they claimed was Iraq's increasing cooperation with weapons inspectors following the destruction of some prohibited Al Samoud missiles that the inspectors had said violated UN resolutions, the three foreign ministers stated their opposition to war—and to a second resolution—in no uncertain terms. "We will not allow a proposed resolution to pass that authorizes the resort to force," a joint declaration stated. "Russia and France, as permanent members of the Security Council, will uphold all their responsibilities on this point." French Foreign Minister de Villepin was equally clear, insisting categorically that "there will be no second resolution opening the way for the Security Council to authorize the use of force."

But the Americans would not back down either, and the following day Bush publicly called de Villepin's bluff. At a press conference in the East Room of the White House, Bush insisted that the United States was going to push ahead with the second resolution no matter what. "[The resolution says Saddam Hussein] is in defiance of 1441. . . . And it's hard to believe anybody is saying he isn't in defiance of 1441, because 1441 said he must disarm. [. . .] No matter what the whip count is, we're calling for the vote." Doing so, Bush suggested, would oblige other countries to choose between U.S. leadership and Saddam Hussein: "We want to see people stand up and say what their opinion is about Saddam Hussein and the utility of the United Nations Security Council. And so, you bet. It's time for people to show their cards, to let the world know where they stand when it comes to Saddam."

With the undecided six still undecided—on March 8 their UN ambassadors met at a hotel in New York and agreed that they were not yet prepared to support the resolution—the French not only showed their cards, but played them. On March 9, Dominique de Villepin undertook an extraordinary trip to Angola, Guinea, and Cameroon to seek to persuade those countries not to support the resolution. In Yaounde, the Cameroonian capital, he repeated that France would "not let a new resolution pass that would open the way to war on Iraq" and that France would "assume its responsibilities as a permanent member of the Security Council."

The Americans and British would later characterize the de Villepin trip as the height of treachery, an example of France not only blocking the American plans on his own country's behalf, but lobbying other Security Council members to do the same. But the Americans and British were hardly passive either. In fact, Colin Powell later acknowledged that he was on the phone with the very capitals that de Villepin was visiting "before he landed at each stop. [I was] making sure he did not get three African votes." And London also played the influence game. British Foreign Office Minister Valerie Amos went to the same countries at de Villepin, Blair's diplomatic adviser, David Manning, traveled to Chile and Mexico, and Blair worked the phones with his undecided six counterparts.

Both sides were thus engaged in furious lobbying, but neither was having much luck. None of the undecided six wanted to risk its relationship with the United States by standing in the way of a war that Washington seemed almost certain to wage. But at the same time, with France and Russia threatening vetoes and the populations in the undecided countries still overwhelmingly hostile to war, they also did not want to end up in a position of supporting an unpopular Security Council resolution that was in any case going to be rejected. The enormous pressure felt by the undecided six from both sides was perhaps best expressed by a Slovak official not long after Slovakia's term on the Security Council ended in January 2003. Coming across a French official with whom he was well acquainted, the Slovak summed up his country's feelings by raising his eyes skyward and putting his hands together, saying, "Thank God we got off the Security Council in time."

Still under pressure to find a compromise that would make a second resolution possible, U.S. and British officials began in early March to show new openness to the formal introduction of benchmarks. Some of the undecided six representatives in New York were hinting that such a step might be enough to get them to support the new resolution. Over the weekend of March 8–9, British Ambassador to the UN

Jeremy Greenstock thus developed a list of five specific disarmament tests for introduction into the resolution. These required specific Iraqi progress in arranging unmonitored interviews of weapons scientists and technicians, and for Iraq to provide substantive information on alleged stores of VX nerve gas, outstanding stores of anthrax, prohibited ballistic missiles, and remotely piloted aircraft. He submitted his list to Blix's team, which approved the five benchmarks with only minor changes, and—at the suggestion of Deputy Executive Chairman Dimitrios Pericos—suggested adding a sixth point: getting Saddam to go on TV to announce that he had lied about the weapons. Such a requirement would truly test whether Saddam had fundamentally agreed to comply with disarmament demands or not. The British then added the six benchmarks to the proposed resolution, along with a new deadline for compliance of March 17. Many of the undecided six had been pushing for a later deadline—the Guineans suggested 45 days, for example—but such a delay would put off possible combat until the heat of the summer, which Greenstock knew would be a nonstarter for the Americans.

France's response, and what would prove to be the fatal blow to prospects for a second resolution, came almost immediately, in the form of a live, televised interview on March 10 with Jacques Chirac. The interview began with Chirac explaining France's opposition to war in Iraq in terms of its desire to "live in a multipolar world," an answer that irritated many Americans and British, who saw in it the confirmation that challenging American hegemony was the true driver behind French policy. But the decisive moment was when Chirac said that France would veto any new ultimatum to Iraq "whatever the circumstances, because France believes this evening that there is no reason to make war to reach the objective we have given ourselves, the disarmament of Iraq."

Chirac's assertion that he would block a new resolution "whatever the circumstances" was the last straw for the Americans and British, who portrayed it as the unreasonable position of a man determined to oppose war on Iraq no matter what. In fact, as was clear from the context of the discussion, Chirac's references to "whatever the circumstances" was a reference to the circumstances of the vote in New York—whether or not there were nine votes in favor—not what was happening on the ground in Iraq. Still, his comments made clear that he was not going to back down, and Washington and London were going to have to go to war without UN approval. Thus, American and British officials had a strong interest in emphasizing that they would be doing so only in the face of perfidious French opposition, rather than because they could not muster a majority on the Council. When Blair called Chirac later that week for a clarification of his remarks, Chirac explained that he was open to considering benchmarks and new deadlines for inspectors, but that he could not accept any ultimatum that referred to an "automatic" use of force.

With that, any remaining hopes for a second resolution were doomed. The undecided six wanted political cover and were not prepared to vote for a resolution that France was going to veto. And so long as France was not prepared to accept "automaticity," any other proposals for extending the deadline before military action would be rejected by the Americans. On March 11, Canada proposed giving Iraq a deadline of three weeks to "demonstrate conclusively" that it was implementing required disarmament tasks and "cooperating actively on real disarmament"—but the proposal was dismissed immediately by the White House as a "nonstarter." Three days later Chilean President Lagos came forward with his own proposal to grant Iraq three more weeks to fulfill a series of benchmarks similar to the six outlined by the United Kingdom. But this too was immediately rebuffed in Washington as a mere delaying tactic. White House press spokesman Ari Fleischer referred back to his reaction to the similar Canadian proposal of a few days before: "If it was a nonstarter then, it's a nonstarter now."

Analysts would later speculate about what might have happened had France agreed to the Canadian or Chilean proposals, accepting a degree of automaticity of military action in exchange for extending the deadline for military force by a few more weeks. Some British officials believe that Blair, in a difficult political situation at home, would have had to accept the proposal, thus obliging the Americans either to accept it as well or lose their valued British partner. Others speculated about what would have happened if Washington had gone along with the new proposals, hypothesizing that the result would have been an isolated France and a stronger case for war at the end of the process. But the answers to these questions will never be known. France refused to accept automaticity at the end of the process, and Washington was not prepared to risk delaying the war for several weeks, only to find itself back where it started—with France, Germany, and Russia still opposing the use of force and still advocating yet another "final" ultimatum.

By the time Chirac spoke of a possible 30- or 60-day deadline on March 16, Washington had already decided to act without putting the second resolution to a vote, and Bush was attending a prewar summit in the Azores with Blair, Aznar, and Portuguese Prime Minister Barroso. On March 17, Bush appeared on national television to announce a 48-hour ultimatum for Saddam Hussein to give up power or face an invasion, and two days later that invasion began with a massive bombardment of a bunker where the Iraqi leader was thought to be hiding. The battle over whether to invade Iraq was over, and the battle to remove the Iraqi regime had begun.

Chapter
6

THE
VICIOUS CIRCLE

The diplomatic disagreement over Iraq produced the worst transatlantic crisis in nearly 50 years. By the time the war began, relations between the United States and some leading European governments were so strained that the very future of the alliance was open to question. The degree of divergence across the Atlantic seemed to confirm arguments made well before the crisis that Europeans and Americans disagreed so significantly in their analysis of the world that they were fated to go their separate ways. And whatever goodwill and desire to cooperate may have still existed in the run-up to the crisis appeared to have been destroyed by the crisis itself.

There is no doubt that structural and cultural divergences pushed Americans and Europeans apart over Iraq. Americans' new sense of vulnerability, immense military power, and genuine belief in their ability to change the world led most of them to believe it necessary and possible to go to war. By contrast, Europeans' concerns for stability, aversion to war, and preoccupation with important matters closer to home led most of them to oppose doing so. In this context, serious policy disagreement over Iraq was probably inevitable. What was not inevitable, however, was that this legitimate disagreement over what all had to admit was a painfully difficult issue would degenerate into a crisis that threatened the very existence of the alliance itself.

The real story of the Iraq crisis was neither the simple American-British narrative about how the French and Germans betrayed them for commercial or some other nefarious reasons, nor the European argument that the Americans and their allies launched a war without justification or regard for its consequences. In fact it was the toxic interaction of the two sides' diplomatic approaches and the vicious circle they created that pushed the alliance to the brink. Hard-line, uncompromising, and undiplomatic advocates of war in America, utterly convinced that justice and prudence were on their side, only encouraged public opinion and several leaders in Europe to resist and resent American policy. That resistance and resentment, in turn, only strengthened the hard-liners in America and undermined those who claimed that they could successfully work with Europe and the rest of the international community, which completed the vicious circle.

Neither the Americans nor their European critics seemed to take into account the potential impact of their policies on the Atlantic alliance; indeed, some even seemed to want to undermine it. Serious mistakes and miscalculations, along with a number of contingent factors outside of anyone's hands, turned what might have been just another in a long line of transatlantic disputes into a clash of historic proportions.

Bad Moves and Bad Luck

Though in retrospect the transatlantic clash over Iraq certainly appeared to be the result of inexorable structural forces, a careful examination of that clash shows that it was not. Obviously, Americans and Europeans had disagreed for years about how to deal with Iraq, and the Bush administration certainly came to a different conclusion from some key European governments in the winter of 2002–2003. As late as January 2003, however, it was not only possible, but in fact it still seemed likely, that defiance by Saddam Hussein would rally the international community to support the use of force against Iraq in accordance with UN Security Resolution 1441. After all, Saddam had long demonstrated a remarkably consistent capacity to miscalculate opponents' reactions to his actions, and there was every reason to believe that this time, too, he would refuse to cooperate with UN Security Council demands, creating a pretext for war. It was also possible that the United States, having agreed to go to the United Nations and make disarmament its key objective, would agree to forego an immediate attack on Iraq.

That neither of these scenarios came to pass resulted from a combination of inexplicable Iraqi decisions and the unfortunate choices of the leaders who happened to be in power in the United States and Europe. Why Iraq, even when facing a credible military threat, never accounted for its prohibited weapons—especially if in fact those weapons no longer existed—may never be known. Whatever the reasons, Baghdad managed, whether deliberately or by accident, to calibrate its cooperation with UN disarmament demands to split the United States and Europe on the question of the necessity of war in Iraq. Under those circumstances, a U.S. administration that assumed for itself the right and duty to take unilateral national security decisions to defend America and its interests resolved to overthrow the Iraqi regime. Meanwhile, the personalities and political situations of the leaders in Germany, France, and Russia led them to challenge that right. The result was a diplomatic disaster.

Both sides made some real miscalculations. Bush administration officials, hewing to a theory of leadership that weaker allies would have little choice but to follow America's lead if the direction of U.S. policy were clearly spelled out, never believed that opponents in Europe would dare challenge U.S. power. They were thus surprised and appalled when France, Germany, and Russia—let alone Mexico, Chile, Cameroon, and others on the Security Council—did just that. The Americans, so convinced they were right about what to do in Iraq, vastly underestimated the resistance to war in Western Europe, in Turkey, and in the rest of the world. For their part, many Europeans—particularly the French—for too long did not believe that even the assertive, unilateralist Bush administration would, in the face of widespread public opposition, be able to go to war based mostly on alleged flaws in a highly technical Iraqi weapons declaration. They thus misread Bush as badly as some in Washington misread the French.

Another important miscalculation—which derived in part from the underestimation of opposition to war—was the British decision, with reluctant American support, to insist on seeking a "second resolution" authorizing military action against Iraq. There were, of course, real reasons for Blair to desire such a resolution, and even to believe that he could achieve one. Faced with strong domestic opposition to the war, Blair had always insisted that he would only act with international legitimacy and support, and acting without explicit UN support would have appeared to violate that pledge. Having been assured by Blair that he would get a second resolution, moreover, numerous members of Parliament from Blair's Labor party had repeatedly promised their antiwar constituents that they would only support a war backed by the UN, and were reluctant to break that pledge.

Ultimately, however, pursuing the new UN authorization turned out to be a misstep that significantly raised the stakes in the growing contest with France. Had Blair gone along with the United States' original preference to declare that they already had all the legal and moral authority to act—as even the French were by then urging them to do—much of the hostility that emerged in February and March 2003 could have been avoided. The United States and Britain would still have acted, and the French, Germans, and Russians would still have opposed the war, but the mutual resentments and accusations of acting in bad faith—both across the Atlantic and within the European Union—would have been much less fervent.

The combustible interaction of politicians on both sides also deeply exacerbated the transatlantic split. On the American side, the self-assured, moralistic, and often condescending attitude of much of the Bush administration—particularly Defense Secretary Donald Rumsfeld and Vice President Richard Cheney, but often the President himself—made many Europeans even more determined to resist American leadership. From the start, Americans, including the President, gave the impression that they considered the Iraq decision—and indeed all decisions about global peace and security—solely for them to make, and that Europeans had little choice but to follow their lead or get out of the way. This was an attitude almost designed to provoke opposition from those in Europe who were reluctant to accept unquestioningly the virtues of American leadership or the merits of a unipolar world.

Bush's deep personal unpopularity in Europe going into the conflict—his track record on issues ranging from the environment to the death penalty to missile defense—only made things worse. Europeans were being asked not only to support a war the wisdom of which they strongly questioned, but to give political backing to a leader whose priorities they did not share and whose vision of leadership seemed to offer them little in return for their support. A different American leadership may or may not have decided to confront Iraq in 2002, but it would almost certainly have placed a higher premium on international agreement—and faced less overall hostility—than the Bush administration did.

Europe's particular constellation of leaders and political circumstances also contributed to the severity of the clash. German Chancellor Gerhard Schröder's willingness to pander to voters (and divert their attention away from Germany's economic crisis) by launching a categorical antiwar campaign broke with a longstanding tradition of German Atlanticism and caused deep resentment in Washington. A pure and instinctive politician, Schröder differed greatly from his predecessor, Helmut Kohl, who thought in geopolitical terms and put a high premium on foreign policy and relations with the United States. And at the very time when the United States was forcing Iraq onto the global agenda, Schröder happened to be facing the fiercest electoral battle of his political life.

The Atlanticism Schröder seemed interested in promoting the year before—when he pledged "unlimited solidarity" with the Americans after 9/11 and forged a surprisingly good initial relationship with George W. Bush—was sacrificed on the altar of domestic political expediency. Had the United States delayed the launch of its campaign to rally domestic and international opinion for a showdown with Iraq until after the German election, there may have been no public clash with Germany. It does not appear, however, that the White House—or the Vice President's office—ever considered doing so. According to scholar Stephen Szabo, when asked whether Vice President Cheney had considered the potential impact on the German election of his tough Iraq speech in August 2002, a close confidant of Cheney's responded, "Why should he care about the reaction in Germany?"

The political leadership that happened to be in power in France also made the transatlantic clash far more severe than it needed to be. President Jacques Chirac was an assertive Gaullist who had long personal relationships with leaders in the Middle East and strong views about the region. As such, he was the perfect foil for a Bush administration that saw the United States as the natural leader of the free world. Chirac's foreign minister, Dominique de Villepin, was a part-time poet and an avowed admirer of Napoleon who had recently written a book glorifying the "hundred days"—the former Emperor's failed attempt to reconquer Europe after escaping from prison. De Villepin wrote that "not a day goes by without me inhaling the perfume of the discreet violet," the flower worn by those who sought to help Napoleon retake France, and he approvingly cited the former Emperor's motto, "Defeat or death, but glory in any case." This was not a worldview likely to find admirers among the foreign minister's more pragmatic (and prosaic) counterparts in the Bush administration.

And just as a different American leadership would probably have handled Iraq very differently than the way the Bush administration did, a different leadership in France would likely have pursued a less confrontational French policy. According to former French Foreign Minister Hubert Védrine, had the Socialists won the April–May 2002 elections, they would still have opposed the war, but it is unlikely that they would have launched such an all-out campaign to stop the United States.

In other words, the crisis that in some ways seemed to be the inevitable result of powerful centrifugal forces splitting the Atlantic alliance might have been far less severe—or even avoided altogether—under slightly different circumstances. If *either* Florida's famous butterfly ballot had not deprived Gore of that state's electoral votes *or* if fringe presidential candidate Christiane Taubira had not kept leading Socialist candidate Lionel Jospin out of the second round of the French presidential election by taking 2.3 percent of the vote, the diplomacy of 2002–2003 might have been significantly different. These were not exactly tectonic forces.

In Turkey, too, contingent factors played a major role. Turkey's opposition to the war, as already noted, played a significant role in bolstering others, in France, Germany, and elsewhere, who hoped to avoid a war. The irony, however, was that Turkey's opposition was also to a large degree accidental. The Turkish public was genuinely and deeply opposed to war, but the Islamist-oriented government that was elected in November 2002 nonetheless went to great lengths to support the United States. Faced with a U.S. request for access to Turkish territory for forces that would invade Iraq, the governing Justice and Development party supported that request and asked its members of parliament to do the same, which more than 70 percent of them did.

The powerful Turkish military, however, and the opposition Republican People's Party, did not want to implicate themselves in such an unpopular decision and decided to allow the ruling Islamists to take the heat for it, assuming—like most outside observers—that the measure was going to pass anyway. Even then, when the vote took place on March 1, 2003, more members of parliament actually voted for the resolution than voted against it, but the resolution failed. As noted in the previous chapter, according to Turkish parliamentary rules, the 19 abstentions were effectively counted as votes against the resolution. For several minutes after the vote, the parliament did not even realize that it had rejected the measure.

None of this is to say that there were not genuine divisions across the Atlantic. But it is clear that a large number of contingent factors came together to turn what might have otherwise been just one more major diplomatic challenge for the Atlantic alliance into a crisis that risked tearing it apart.

America's Role

Whatever the reasons for the transatlantic clash, what is certain is that both sides deeply resented the positions taken by the other, and accused their opponents of bad faith. The core of the European complaint against the United States was that the Bush administration decided unilaterally and early on—possibly from the beginning of the administration in January 2001—that it was going to invade Iraq, and that the whole process of seeking international support and allied involvement throughout 2002–2003 was not sincere.

The criticism is not entirely fair. While it does seem clear that Bush decided as early as the fall of 2001 that he was going to change the Iraqi regime one way or another, he also allowed for the possibility of fore-going an invasion if Saddam genuinely disarmed or was removed from power from within. Indeed, Bush prepared the ground politically for this outcome when, in an October 2002 speech (and on other occasions), he asserted that Iraq's effective disarmament would essentially constitute "regime change," since complying with UN Security Council resolutions "would also change the nature of the Iraqi regime itself."

By signing on to Resolution 1441 in November 2002, Bush ran a risk that Saddam would comply with the disarmament demands placed upon him, thereby undermining the legal and political basis for war. If Saddam had actually accounted for his past weapons programs, it would have been difficult for Bush to act, especially since Britain—America's closest ally, and key to the perceived legitimacy of an invasion—may not have been able to support military action in those circumstances. Only after Iraq's December 7 declaration clearly demonstrated that Saddam Hussein had no intention of adhering to Resolution 1441 did that caution disappear. And while it was true that Bush ended up launching a war without UN support in March 2003, the United States had a strong case that Iraq had failed to cooperate "immediately, unconditionally, and actively" with UN weapons inspectors as called for in the resolution. Opponents of war can argue that war was inadvisable in the spring of 2003, but it is hard for them to make the case that there were no legal grounds for it based on 1441 and past resolutions.

That said, the European complaint that the American decision-making process and diplomacy about Iraq violated reasonable alliance norms and expectations is valid. Bush's speech to the UN General

Assembly on September 12, 2002, appeared to recognize U.S. obligations to seek and to achieve some undefined degree of international legitimacy for regime change in Iraq. In particular, he committed the United States to seek UN support for a new resolution that would oblige Iraq to disarm. The problem, however, was that many American actions, statements, and policies prior to and following the speech suggested that the multilateral approach was pure form—it was not about collective decision making or even real consultations, but simply an effort to win legitimacy for decisions that had been and would be taken by Washington alone. After all, Bush had asserted that if the UN did not agree with him, he reserved the right to act alone or with like-minded partners. Even more important, in the weeks just before and after the speech, some of the President's top advisers expressed their absolute lack of faith in the main alternative to war that Bush proposed: a new containment regime backed up by reinforced inspections.

As the diplomatic process moved forward, there was little evidence that Bush was ever prepared to take allied views into account or to fundamentally change his own course if allies objected to it. The President's firm conviction, as asserted in his January 28, 2003, State of the Union address, was that "the course of this nation does not depend on others." He would decide if America felt threatened, and act accordingly. "When it comes to our security," Bush asserted in March 2003, "we really don't need anybody's permission." The hope and expectation, as Bush and his senior advisers had often asserted, was that U.S. determination would lead others to follow. But if they did not, then so be it. "At some point we may be the only ones left," the President conceded when referring to the war on terrorism. "That's okay with me. We are America."

The degree to which allied and other views actually counted to the administration was revealed in the way one senior administration official explained the role of other Security Council members to one of his counterparts, a foreign diplomat, in February 2003: "You are not going to decide whether there is war in Iraq or not. That decision is ours, and we have already made it. It is already final. The only question now is whether the Council will go along with it or not." The official's honesty was perhaps admirable, but the sentiment he expressed was unlikely to persuade allies that their role was anything more than that of a rubber stamp.

The most concrete proof that Bush had already made up his mind was the rapid and early deployment of large numbers of troops to Iraq. As even the French admitted, a military deployment to the region was a necessary component of reinforcing the credibility of the threat inherent in Resolution 1441. But the Pentagon's decision to deploy over 100,000 troops in early 2003, without any provisions for maintaining the deployment for more than a few months, put America's credibility at stake in a way that suggested Washington was deliberately closing off the nonmilitary option. By mid-January, military experts were warning that the troops could not be maintained in the desert all summer, while Middle East specialists were warning that they could not be withdrawn without a loss of credibility.

Donald Rumsfeld had a reputation as a master bureaucratic operator who successfully outmaneuvered opponents by creating facts on the ground. And there is every indication that the Pentagon's deployment strategy was part of a process designed not only to make a military option credible, but to make backing away from that option difficult. Even the timing of Bush's decision to go to the Security Council seemed part of an administration plan to go to war according to its own timetable in the winter of 2002–2003. By failing to go to the UN until mid-September 2002, Bush appeared to deliberately narrow the window of opportunity to test the proposition that Saddam could be disarmed through inspections backed by force. That might have been a good way to set up a war, but it was not likely to persuade critics that the stated U.S. goal—ensuring that Saddam had no weapons of mass destruction—was the actual goal.

The often changing—and often exaggerated—presentation of the American case for war also contributed to the impression that the Bush administration was selling a precooked policy, rather than genuinely allowing allies into the decision-making process. As they built the case for overthrowing Saddam, administration officials at various times emphasized weapons of mass destruction, terrorism, humanitarian concerns, regional security, the need to enforce UN Security Council resolutions, or the need to begin the democratic transformation of the Middle East. There was nothing inherently wrong with listing a range of considerations, and in fact all of these issues were real—indeed, this accumulation of factors bolstered the case for war. But by the winter of 2002–2003, the Bush administration did not act as if it were trying to make a case for a collective decision. Rather it was selling a product that it had already decided, on its own and for its own reasons, to produce.

The case that force had to be used to implement a series of UN Security Council resolutions dating back 12 years, for example, was strong one, but it was not particularly credible coming from an administration that had made clear its disdain for international organizations. It was hard to believe that preserving the sanctity of the UN was anywhere near the top of the Bush team's list of reasons to invade Iraq. Similarly, there were good humanitarian arguments in favor of an effort to liberate 25 million people from the grip of one of the world's most brutal regimes, but again, this seemed less than compelling coming from an administration that had expressed great skepticism about nation-building and humanitarian intervention. Even Paul Wolfowitz, one of the senior administration officials most strongly in favor of using American military power to do good in the world, acknowledged that improving the lives of Iraqi citizens was by itself "not a reason to put American kids' lives at risk."

Another potentially compelling case for war would have been a demonstration either that Saddam Hussein was involved in the

September 11, 2001, terrorist attacks or that his regime had links to al Qaeda. Despite allegations and tremendous efforts to prove such links, however, the administration consistently failed to do so. Rumsfeld, for example, frequently asserted the existence of al Qaeda fighters in Iraq. He suggested that the Islamic extremist group Ansar al-Islam was further proof of Saddam's complicity with Islamic terrorism, despite the fact that the group operated in the northern part of the country controlled not by Saddam but nominally, at least, by Kurdish allies of the United States. Vice President Cheney also often alleged a Saddam–al Qaeda link and repeatedly suggested that Iraq might have had a role in 9/11.

Bush was more circumspect, but he never hesitated to invoke 9/11 as a way of making his case for invading Iraq, beginning many of his major speeches with a reference to the terrorist attacks, and frequently mentioning them in association with the case for getting rid of Saddam Hussein. Even the cautious Secretary of State Colin Powell often asserted a Saddam–al Qaeda link in making the case for war. Powell even suggested that an Osama bin Laden audio tape calling on his followers to resist an American attack on Iraq was a sign of bin Laden being "in partnership with Iraq"—even though bin Laden denounced Saddam and his regime as "infidels" in the very same tape. The problem with these unproven allegations was not just that no other country believed them, but the impression they give that the Americans were willing to do or say anything to win their case for war. This only made things worse for an administration that was already deeply unpopular in Europe and unlikely to receive the benefit of the doubt.

The administration's inability to agree internally on the primary justification for regime change in Iraq led it to settle—"for reasons that have a lot to do with the U.S. government bureaucracy," Wolfowitz said—on weapons of mass destruction. This decision made a lot of sense, since destroying Iraq's WMDs was the key demand of numerous UN Security Council resolutions. By most accounts, Saddam was so addicted to such weapons that he would be unlikely to give them up, thus creating a strong legal and political case for war.

The problem, however, was that once the renewed inspections process began to suggest that Iraq's weapons programs might not be as developed as the Americans had claimed, the WMD case for war weakened dramatically. The Bush administration continued to assert that it had evidence of large Iraqi prohibited weapons programs and even stocks of weapons. But it was never able to provide solid proof to allies who were not inclined to take such assertions at face value, especially given the administration's apparent determination to use the WMD risk as a pretext to wage war for a range of other reasons. As James Rubin put it, "much of the world believed that Washington was so determined to overthrow Saddam that it would never take yes for an answer—even if the Iraqi leader did comply with international ultimatums."

In making its case to the American people and the world, administration officials dispensed with all the caveats that, it later turned out, were in the intelligence assessments they had received. In August 2002, for example, Cheney expressed his conviction that "Saddam will acquire nuclear weapons fairly soon," and asserted that there was "no doubt that Saddam Hussein now has weapons of mass destruction." Two weeks later Bush told the United Nations that Iraq was likely to possess stockpiles of VX, mustard gas, and other chemical agents, and that it was expanding and improving facilities capable of producing such agents. He also warned that Iraq had made several attempts to buy high-strength aluminum tubes to enrich uranium for a nuclear weapon, and that if it acquired fissile material it "would be able to build a nuclear weapon within a year." In October, Bush made the unqualified assertion that Iraq "possesses and produces chemical and biological weapons" and that it was "seeking nuclear weapons." He warned that we had to act on this "clear evidence" lest the "final proof . . . come in the form of a mushroom cloud."

The assertions continued the following year, even as weapons inspections in Iraq failed to find evidence of the prohibited programs and began to report progress in their work. In his State of the Union Address in January 2003, Bush repeated the allegations about an Iraqi nuclear program, this time adding the dramatic assertion that "the British government has learned that Saddam Hussein recently sought significant quantities of uranium from Africa." He did not reveal at the time that the reason for attributing the intelligence to the British government was that U.S. intelligence services disputed the claim. For that reason, it had been removed from a speech he'd given in Cincinnati just three months before.

Similarly, Secretary of State Powell, in his UN presentation on February 5, asserted that "[there] can be no doubt that Saddam Hussein has biological weapons and the capability to rapidly produce more, many more . . . One conservative estimate is that Iraq today has a stockpile of between 100 and 500 tons of chemical weapons agents. . . . Saddam Hussein has chemical weapons . . . and we have sources who tell us that he recently has authorized his field commanders to use them." Powell then repeated the allegations about aluminum tubes and asserted that "Saddam Hussein is determined to get his hands on a nuclear bomb." In March 2003, even after the war had begun, Rumsfeld went so far as to claim that "we know where [the WMDs] are. They're in the area around Tikrit and Baghdad and east, west, south, and north somewhat."

These American officials no doubt did believe that Saddam Hussein had prohibited weapons programs. Most observers in the United States, the UN, and even France and Germany, agreed with that core assessment. Certainly it was unlikely that the Bush team would have pinned the case for war on finding WMDs they knew did not exist. Still, their willingness to exaggerate what they thought they knew about Iraqi weapons capabilities—making unqualified and unproven assertions that went well beyond what the UN weapons inspectors and other national intelligence agencies believed—created problems both at the time and later. It contributed to the original perception that Bush had long before decided to go to war for other reasons, and that the entire UN process, including the inspections, was just for show.

When it turned out that many of the confident American assertions were wrong—Saddam apparently did not have WMD stockpiles, the aluminum tubes were probably not nuclear related, the Africa uranium claim was largely based on forged documents, and the Iraqi nuclear program was far less developed than alleged—American credibility was damaged further. Europeans had been berated for failing to go to war to eliminate an Iraqi WMD capability that, it now appears, did not exist.

The Bush administration also made the crisis over Iraq worse than it needed to be by elevating the issue of military preemption to the level of "doctrine." While trying to persuade the world that force should be used to deal with Saddam, Bush identified Iraq as part of an "axis of evil," along with North Korea and Iran. He then formally declared America's readiness to act, alone if necessary, not only preemptively, against imminent threats, but even *preventively*, against potential threats. Treating the issue in this way turned a winnable debate about how to deal with Iraq into a call to set a precedent that the United States could take military action wherever and whenever Washington saw fit. This may not have posed a problem for Americans, but for others, even close allies within the Atlantic alliance, it amounted to the death notice of a rules-based international system and an end to their already limited ability to influence the American superpower. Bush seemed to be asking not for an exception to that system to deal with a particular problem—as NATO did in Kosovo in 1999—but for a blank check to take similar action whenever the President of the United States deemed it necessary. For many in Europe and beyond, this assertion of national, indeed personal, infallibility made it harder for them to sign on to the U.S. position on Iraq.

American rhetoric and policy toward some longstanding allies also unnecessarily exacerbated the crisis. Instead of acknowledging the reality that large majorities of the citizens in the European democracies (and the rest of the world) were against the war, and that the allies had legitimate concerns, Washington deemed any dissent to be disloyal that could only be explained by nefarious motives. Bush himself appeared genuinely incapable of grasping that even democratic allies did not accept it as a given that Americans always had pure motives and sound policies and that America was a "good nation," as the President kept insisting. It was easier to attribute the failure to win support for a war in Iraq to the greed and corruption of French politicians or the domestic political myopia of the German chancellor than to acknowledge that those who agreed with the United States were actually a small minority around the world.

Many of the French and German decisions about the war were unfortunate, even wrong. But instead of responding to them with humility born of strength—as Lyndon Johnson did when de Gaulle ejected U.S. troops from France—Washington responded with petulance. Instead of stepping up engagement, Bush hardly spoke to Chirac and Schröder throughout the entire run-up to the war, preferring to deal only with those allies who supported him. Rumsfeld denounced France and Germany as "old Europe" and compared Germany to Libya and Cuba—despite the fact that Germany ended up making a greater material contribution to the war effort than many of the official members of the administration's coalition. Berlin gave the United States basing and overflight rights, maintained chemical and biological warfare detection vehicles in Kuwait, and deployed antimissile defense systems to Turkey, but Rumsfeld preferred to ostracize his German counterparts rather than acknowledge their contributions.

Toward France, the American response was even harsher. It included changing the name of French toast to "Freedom toast" on Air Force One and French fries to "Freedom fries" in the House of

Representatives cafeteria. Such measures may have given some sense of satisfaction to their angry sponsors, but they hardly enhanced America's stature in most of the world, where they were seen to be silly and inappropriate. More substantively, the French were punished for their lack of loyalty by the Pentagon, which banned high-level U.S. military participation in the annual Paris Air Show and lobbied defense industry executives not to attend the show. In addition, the Pentagon prevented France from participation in long-planned military exercises, and Rumsfeld excluded the chief of the French air staff from a U.S.-hosted conference of air force commanders.

French visitors to Washington were berated by their counterparts, especially in the Pentagon, where officials like Paul Wolfowitz and Undersecretary of Defense for Policy Douglas Feith accused them of defending Saddam Hussein. To a French defense ministry visitor who had come to the Pentagon in December 2002 to discuss possible French participation in a war, Feith said, "We don't want you involved! You think you can be Saddam's lawyer for two months without consequences!" Instead of discussing the possible French support, Feith made the derisory proposal that if France wanted to help, it could provide medical units to the Sinai and fighter planes for Iceland to free up the four planes that the United States had deployed there.

American officials did not shy away from treating the UN weapons inspectors the same way, Cheney reportedly telling Hans Blix that if the administration found fault with his judgments, "we will not hesitate to discredit you." Separately, Wolfowitz ridiculed the inspectors' reluctance to claim knowledge that Iraq retained WMDs, telling them, "You do know they have weapons of mass destruction, don't you?"

The administration's aggressive campaign to bully its allies and denounce its critics was not only ugly, it was counterproductive. Far from cowing those critics, it reinforced the administration's reputation for arrogance and self-righteousness and only led the critics to dig in. The policy of berating opponents of the war, moreover, seemed to be based on an absolute conviction that all would go so well in Iraq—military victory, liberation, stabilization, and democratization—that the critics would soon be lining up to beg for forgiveness and a share of the spoils. When it turned out that the occupation of Iraq would instead be costly and deadly—as many of the skeptics both in the United States and in Europe had warned—the administration was hardly in a position to win the support of the Europeans whose arguments it had ridiculed. As Senator Joseph Biden put it in the summer of 2003, by snubbing our allies, we "missed an opportunity, in the aftermath of our spectacular military victory, to ask those who were not with us in the war to be partners in the peace. Instead we served 'freedom toast' on Air Force One. Wasn't that cute?"

Finally, U.S. diplomacy in the Iraq crisis was not only lacking in quality, it was insufficient in quantity. Bush's failure to engage directly with his French and German counterparts did not, as some predicted, lead them to back the American position out of a fear of isolation, but instead foreclosed any opportunity to persuade them either of the wisdom of the American course or at least the merits of not attempting to block it. In the German case, Bush's isolation of Schröder may have actually pushed him into the arms of Chirac at a time when his preference might have been to mend fences with the United States, had he been allowed to do so.

Diplomacy was also lacking at the next level down. In the run-up to the first Gulf War, then–Secretary of State James Baker visited forty-one countries on five continents. In comparison, as Ivo Daalder and James Lindsay have pointed out, Colin Powell hardly traveled anywhere in the months prior to the Iraq war, and he did not take a single trip "for the sole purpose of securing foreign support for a military undertaking that was far more challenging and controversial." Powell made just one trip to Europe in the run-up to the war—for 24 hours to Davos, Switzerland, in January 2003 to give a speech—but chose not to stop in Paris or Berlin, despite their key roles as Security Council members opposed to the war. Nor did he go to Ankara, whose support for an eventual war was as critical as it was uncertain.

Powell would later claim that modern technology like e-mail and telephones rendered personal diplomacy less important than it used to be, and that he saw his European counterparts frequently at UN meetings in New York during this period. But that view understates both the symbolic and practical importance of personal engagement on the ground in the foreign countries themselves. By limiting contacts with key allies in Europe, the Bush administration only reinforced the impression that they had little interest in or respect for the views of others, and that matters of war and peace were for Washington to decide.

The European Side

The United States did not make it easy for its European allies to support a war in Iraq. But it takes two to make a crisis, and if the Bush administration failed to live up to the standards of alliance behavior set during and after the Cold War, so, too, did some of its European counterparts. The Europeans who opposed the war did so at least in part to prevent an administration they strongly disagreed with from concluding that it had a blank check from Europe to pursue foreign policy as it saw fit. The problem with this stance was that it put an issue of principle and theory ahead of what was for the Bush administration and many Americans an urgent, practical issue of national security. As a result, their opposition only reinforced many Americans' prejudice that trying to work with Europeans was time consuming and ultimately futile.

That many Europeans were aware of this dynamic is evidenced by the superficially surprising willingness of most European leaders to support the United States over Iraq. Despite strong public opposition to the war and the huge unpopularity of the Bush administration in every country in Europe, a majority of European countries—led by Britain, Spain, Italy, Portugal, and the Central Europeans—ended up backing the United States. They did so in various ways—whether in the Letter of Eight or the Vilnius 10 letter, their votes on the Security Council (Britain, Spain, and Bulgaria), or by providing actual military support once the war came and in its aftermath. Of all of the members of either NATO or the European Union (a total of 23 countries), only the governments of France, Germany, and Belgium made active efforts to stand in Washington's way.

Some leaders, notably Tony Blair, seemed genuinely convinced of the need for military action. Blair consistently made clear that he was not just supporting the war because the Americans were "telling him to," but because he "believed in it." Most of these European leaders, however, also—or even primarily—backed Washington out of a sense of loyalty to the alliance and because of their belief in the enduring value of American leadership. Whatever the sins of American diplomacy in the run-up to the war—and Europeans across the board thought there were many—the leaders of these countries ultimately concluded that those sins were not so grave as to merit opposing an American-led war and risking the future of transatlantic cooperation. The leaders in France and Germany disagreed, and the result was the completion of the vicious circle.

Germany was the first to depart from alliance norms, which was surprising, given its strong tradition of trying to join consensus both within Europe and across the Atlantic. In a desperate effort to win votes in the summer of 2002, Gerhard Schröder wrote himself out of the diplomacy over Iraq. His declared refusal to support the use of force against Iraq even if authorized by the UN Security Council was, simply put, irresponsible. It went against everything German foreign policy had stood for since the founding of the Federal Republic. Germany's decision to stand with France in blocking NATO's preparation for the possible defense of Turkey in the context of an Iraq war was also difficult to defend. Whatever the American motives in calling for a NATO role in planning for the defense of Turkey, Germany's decision to refuse that role was deeply damaging to the notion of NATO as a defense alliance on which its members could rely. For over 50 years no country had benefited more from that understanding of NATO than Germany itself.

Some of the German rhetoric during the run-up to war, and especially during Schröder's political campaign, was also distinctly unhelpful—it paralleled and contributed to the anti-European rhetoric heard in the United States. Schröder appeared to discover during the campaign not only that his antiwar stance was winning him support, but that he did even better when attacking Bush personally. Thus Schröder not only did nothing to counter the widespread view in the German public and press that Bush was a trigger-happy cowboy who only wanted Iraq's oil, he actively encouraged and took advantage of that view.

The climate created was one in which the justice minister's comparison of Bush to Hitler was only a particularly egregious—and worse for her, public—example of the general tone of the German debate. Schröder's response to that insult to the President—a letter to Bush that essentially said, "I'm sorry you chose to be offended by something my minister did not say"—might not have merited the highly personalized American response it got, but it was deeply inept. More important, the letter hardly seemed to be the response of a leader who cared about his relationship with the President of the United States or the enduring health of the Atlantic alliance.

In short, German policy—the denunciation of American "adventures," the refusal to back even a UN-sponsored military action, and the objection even to NATO's planning for the defense of an ally—was a gift to the hard-liners and unilateralists in the American administration. If Europeans, the thinking went, especially those on the Security Council, were unprepared to enforce UN Security Council resolutions, implement NATO defense guarantees, or take seriously the issue of WMD proliferation, why should the United States agree to take seriously their argument to act through international institutions?

French policy was even more damaging to the concept of alliance. French arguments against the war derived at least in part from legitimate and reasoned principles. They were not merely the result of commercial interests, a reflexive desire to resist American power, or an unwillingness to face up to genuine threats. Like most Europeans, much of the world, and many Americans, the French feared that a war on Iraq could undermine the war on terrorism, destabilize the region, provoke the use of weapons of mass destruction, and lead to a difficult, costly, and possibly futile occupation of Iraq. Some of those concerns have proven unfounded, but others appear to have been validated by events. Certainly, the bloody, expensive, and uncertain experience of occupying Iraq has shown that French fears of the consequences of an invasion were not simply the product of anti-American fantasies.

But opposing the war was a different matter from opposing the United States—particularly after it had become clear that Washington was going to act. However arrogant and even misguided American policies might have been, they did not merit France's all out attempt to deny legitimacy to the operation once it had been decided. The French position that they would only support military action in Iraq if it was authorized by the UN Security Council was disingenuous given that, in the event, France itself held the key to that authorization. The French argument that containment and weapons inspections might have been a better policy course to pursue than a full-scale invasion and occupation of Iraq was not unreasonable. Nonetheless, Paris agreed in the fall of 2002 to a UN Security Council resolution obliging France to support "serious consequences" if Iraq failed to fully comply with that resolution, which even Paris acknowledged Iraq had not done. It was perfectly acceptable for France to conclude, as did many other countries, that even at that point force should not have been used. But without having deployed a single soldier to the Gulf region to reinforce the threat of action, for Paris to use its position on the Security Council to prevent the Americans from acting in those circumstances was not the act of an ally.

The French had a point, of course, that for the Security Council to be meaningful, it could not simply be a rubber stamp for American action. That is, regrettably, what many in the Bush administration apparently wanted it to be. But in the circumstances of 2003, French agreement to back the enforcement of Resolution 1441 and over a dozen previous resolutions would not have been an abdication of the Security Council's responsibility. Even if France felt that containment remained a better option than war, it could not argue that the Americans had no justification for their reading of Resolution 1441 and that Washington would be violating international law by acting. Paris could at that point have preserved what it felt was the moral high ground by refusing to associate itself with the war and withholding a positive vote in favor, but by accepting that the veto of a second resolution authorizing war was inappropriate.

Indeed, to the extent that French policy at the UN was designed to preserve the authority and role of the Security Council, the veto threat was almost certainly counterproductive. Had France forced the United States to go through the difficult UN process and then ultimately given authorization to action, it would have strengthened those in the United States who remained convinced that using international institutions was worth all the effort. Instead, the French only convinced many Americans that the hard-liners were right, that the UN was a deeply flawed organization, and that there is no point going back to it the next time around.

Once Paris had decided to oppose the war, a decision that only came gradually with the progress of weapons inspections and the growth of public opposition, there was little French diplomacy could do to avoid a serious clash with London and Washington.

Unfortunately, however, French diplomacy not only did little to prevent transatlantic relations from deteriorating, it almost seemed designed to undermine what little trust and confidence did exist. Jacques Chirac's enduring refusal not only to authorize military action but even to accept a firm deadline for compliance backed by force, as many countries were proposing in early 2003, was an abuse of France's position on the Security Council. His coopting the isolated Schröder in January 2003—and his surprising outburst at the Central Europeans following the publication of the Vilnius 10 letter a few weeks later— also seemed to indicate that there was more to his antiwar stance than he was letting on. At a minimum, his diplomacy allowed critics to credibly argue that Chirac was out as much to restore Franco-German hegemony over European affairs as he was to prevent a war he thought ill-advised.

Chirac often complained when the Americans refused to take his antiwar stand at face value and accused him of seeking to dominate Europe or to undermine the United States. His denials would have been more persuasive, however, had he and other French leaders not continually spoken of Europe in just such a way. For years Chirac had identified his geopolitical goal as the construction of a multipolar world in which Europe would be as important an actor as the United States. When asked on national French television in March 2003 why he opposed the war in Iraq, for instance, Chirac's very first answer was not fear of casualties, destabilization of the Middle East, or the threat of weapons of mass destruction, it was "because we want to live in a multipolar world." Whether deliberately or not, Chirac was essentially admitting that at least one of France's objectives was to constrain American power.

The diplomacy of French Foreign Minister de Villepin only exacerbated the problem. Whatever de Villepin's priorities during the diplomacy over the Iraq issue, maintaining decent relations with the United States and the viability of the Atlantic alliance did not seem to be among them. By undercutting Secretary of State Colin Powell at the UN in January 2003, for example, de Villepin undermined his best potential ally within the Bush administration and the most important American voice in favor of working closely with international institutions and European allies, which presumably were French goals. De Villepin's habit of casting his actions in terms of lofty philosophical principles and moral absolutes also infuriated his American and British interlocutors. They did not believe the French were behaving as "the guardians of an ideal . . . the guardians of a conscience," as de Villepin claimed, but rather, that France was failing to abide by the basic principle of enforcing a UN Security Council agreement reached by consensus only a few months before.

The French foreign minister was also capable of demonstrating a level of arrogance that matched that of some of the Americans, and it served him and his country no less badly. When asked after a speech in London in late March 2003 who he wanted to win the still-ongoing war, de Villepin refused to answer. He refused not because there was any doubt that he wanted the Americans to prevail—as he had said publicly many times—but because he resented the question. Thus he only deigned to tell the reporter, "I will not answer you. You have not listened to what I have said." The result, however, was extensive and deeply damaging press commentary about how the French were ambiguous about which side they were on.

Similarly, after the war was over and the occupation began to prove more difficult than many of the Americans had expected, de Villepin did much more than quietly note that these difficulties were among the reasons why France opposed the war, which might have won some begrudging credibility from the Americans. Instead he bragged about how, by opposing the war, "France and the Pope" had saved the world from a "clash of civilizations," and told interlocutors that the Americans did not understand the region and needed France in order to succeed. As one former American statesman commented, noting the irony of de Villepin's professional origins in the French Foreign Service, "the problem with the French foreign minister is that he's not a diplomat."

The French often said that their opposition to the war was in fact the action of a friend, since friends should always tell each other when they think they're making a mistake. That the French should have been honest with the Americans about their concerns about the consequences of war is correct, and the Americans should have been less sensitive about hearing French opposition. But once the French had tried and failed to stop the Americans from acting, the duties of alliance and a proper understanding of world order should have led Paris to support their friend and at least wish it well, not put further obstacles in its way. It was the refusal to do so, much more than the failure to actively support the United States, that distinguished France from even Germany and Russia, and caused such a deep rupture in transatlantic trust.

In defining the problem of U.S.-French relations of a different era, Henry Kissinger wrote:

> ... [the] conflict between France and the United States became all the more bitter because the two sides, profoundly misunderstanding each other, never seemed to be talking about the same subject. Although they were generally unpretentious personalities, American leaders tended to be cocksure about their practical prescriptions. De Gaulle, whose people had turned skeptical after too many enthusiasms shattered and too many dreams proved fragile, found it necessary to compensate for his society's deep-seated insecurities by a haughty, even overbearing, demeanor. The interaction of the American leadership's personal humility and historical arrogance, and de Gaulle's personal arrogance and historical humility, defined the psychological gulf between America and France.

By 2003 that gulf had, if anything, become greater, and the tempering ingredients of personal humility on one side and historical humility on the other seemed to have disappeared. What remained was personal and historical arrogance on both sides. The result was not only a failure to agree about Iraq, but such damage to the world's most successful alliance that it was a legitimate question whether it would endure.

PART III
WHAT NEXT?

Chapter

7

Restoring
the
Alliance ·

Even before the crisis over Iraq, commentators on both sides of the Atlantic proclaimed that the United States and Europe were growing apart strategically, culturally, and even morally. With America's emergence as the sole superpower, the two sides of the Atlantic no longer shared the same interests, the same values, or even the same understanding of world order and international law. The transatlantic alliance was dead or soon would be.

In this view, no tears had to be shed over the alliance's death, however, for it no longer mattered much for either side. An exceptionally powerful America could easily manage the world alone or with ad hoc coalitions assembled on the basis of short-term mutual interest and decisive U.S. leadership. A self-absorbed Europe was happy to free ride on the American order, sniping in moralistic tones from the gallery while standing aside and focusing its energies on internal European challenges. The Iraq crisis appeared to confirm this view. In the absence of a Soviet enemy to focus the mind, neither side was willing to subordinate its views on Iraq to the greater good of the Atlantic alliance.

No observer of recent events could fail to notice that the United States and Europe have different attitudes toward power, military force, and sovereignty, or even that the divide is growing. The question, however, is whether these differences are now so fundamental that the United States and the nations of Europe can or should dismiss the transatlantic alliance as irrelevant, concluding that they either do not need each other or that they might find better allies elsewhere. The answer is no.

The Atlantic alliance can be saved because the Americans and Europeans are not as far apart as is often portrayed. The Iraq crisis that nearly tore the alliance apart in 2003 was not inevitable. It could have been avoided, and resulted to a great extent from leaders' mistakes and miscalculations. It cannot be an experience that either side wants to repeat. There are real differences across the Atlantic, but the caricature of unilateral and militaristic American and a pacifist Europe masks the real differences within each side and obscures what the two sides have in common compared to much of the rest of the world.

The alliance should be saved, moreover, because it continues to serve a vital—indeed irreplaceable—role in maintaining international security and prosperity. American and European leaders have real choices to make that cannot be dismissed by blithe assertions of structure, laws of history, or unbridgeable cultural divides. The right choices could lead to an Atlantic alliance that is unified and capable enough to address pressing global issues, and to defend liberal democratic values around the world. The wrong choices could undermine a world order that has enriched and brought peace to the Atlantic community for more than 50 years.

Ties That Still Bind

The end of the alliance is not inevitable because the interests that the United States and Europe share do not stem merely from a fortuitous confluence of geopolitical circumstances. Rather, they reflect a unique commonality of culture and values that distinguish the United States and the nations of Europe from much of the rest of the world. By focusing on the Iraq crisis, we have naturally emphasized what divides them, both strategically and culturally. Indeed, there are very real differences between the two sides on basic issues such as their attitudes toward force and power, and on their respective understanding of world order and international law. Social issues like gun control, the death penalty, and the role of religion in public life also divide the two sides of the Atlantic. Iraq showed how such divides can matter and how the crisis itself made things worse.

But these differences do not define the relationship. Taking a broader view, the European democracies are certainly closer to the United States, both strategically and culturally, than any other region is or is likely to be anytime soon. Americans and Europeans still broadly share the same democratic, liberal aspirations for their societies and for the rest of the world.

Certainly, a president from Texas and a deeply conservative cabinet, including Vice President Dick Cheney, Defense Secretary Donald Rumsfeld, and Attorney General John Ashcroft, have little in common with most of their European counterparts. To use Robert Kagan's terms, the Bush team represents a particularly "American" perspective: On issues like religion, abortion, gun control, missile defense, use of force, multilateralism, and the environment, they are about as far from "European" positions as Americans get. It is thus not surprising that their election was read as a step toward an increasingly "American" America, and that their subsequent policies—given a further boost by the challenge of global terrorism—have crystallized the apparent differences across the Atlantic.

It is less clear, however, that Bush's election represented a fundamental shift in American values, or that these values have gotten more "American" over time, as Europe's values have gotten more "European." It should not be forgotten that Bush's opponent in the last election, Al Gore, won some 540,000 more votes than Bush on a platform that was much closer on most issues to the European norm. The 2000 and 2002 Congressional elections were also divided right down the middle between Democrats and Republicans, suggesting very little change in America's political and ideological balance, despite the fact that the approaches of the national leaders changed so dramatically. Polls ahead of the 2004 election suggest that the country remains evenly divided.

The point here is not to suggest that the Bush approach to domestic and world affairs is not widely supported in the United States or that most Democrats are not more "American" in their outlook than most Europeans. Rather, it is to underline that the alleged U.S.-European divide might look very different today had Al Gore polled a few more votes in Florida in 2000 or had the Supreme Court taken a different view of the Florida recount. There would still be real differences over the Middle East, the environment, and Iraq, as there were during the Clinton years, but they would not be anywhere near as brutal as is currently the case.

In fact, the view of Europeans toward the United States reflects an awareness of the distinction between the Bush administration and America. The European public is not as "anti-American" as is often assumed, but it is quite anti-Bush. In June 2003, for example, the Pew Global Attitudes Project found that Europeans who had unfavorable views of the United States overwhelmingly identified the problem as "Bush," rather than as "America in general." This was true for no less than 74 percent of the French and Germans, 67 percent of the Italians, and even 59 percent of the British.

A careful look at American and European perspectives and values, at least at the public level, suggests far more congruence than divergence between the two. Even while American and European leaders were publicly feuding over Iraq, public opinion polling conducted throughout the crisis showed, according to one survey, that "Americans and Europeans have remarkably similar assessments of the threats they face." As late as the summer of 2002, favorable opinions of each other were held by strong majorities (63 percent of the French and 61 percent of Germans had a favorable view of the United States), which have been fairly consistent over time. The war in Iraq did cause a significant dip in those figures in the United States and across Europe, particularly in Germany and France, where they bottomed out at 25 and 31 percent respectively. But such dramatic declines reflect a spike typical of transatlantic crises rather than secular trends. By June 2003 they had already begun to reverse.

Taking a broader perspective, Americans and Europeans identify very similar issues as their primary foreign policy concerns—including international terrorism, weapons of mass destruction, and global warming—demonstrate comparable perceptions of friends and allies, and express a strong affinity for each other. Before the Iraq war, Americans expressed discomfort with unilateralism, with 65 percent saying in a June 2002 poll that the United States should only invade Iraq with United Nations approval and the support of its allies. Even on the use of force, Europeans are at least in principle as ready to use force as Americans to uphold international law (80 to 76 percent), help a population struck by famine (88 to 81 percent), liberate hostages (78 to 77 percent), or destroy a terrorist camp (75 to 92 percent).

On other issues, polls also suggest much more similar public attitudes in Europe and America than the bitter public disputes between European leaders and the Bush administration would suggest. Seventy-five percent of Americans, for example, consider global warming a "serious problem," and a clear majority believes that the United States should join the European Union in ratifying the Kyoto accord. Even on genetically modified organisms, supposedly an example of the vastly diverging transatlantic attitudes toward science and technology, a plurality of Americans, like Europeans, believe that genetically modified organisms will "make food more poisonous," and 86 percent think the government should require labeling, which happens to be the EU's policy. U.S.-European differences on these and other important issues exist, but the data on public attitudes hardly seem a sign of two societies "living in different worlds."

The Europeans' harshest American critics suggest that whatever their sentiments in theory, Europeans are not likely to be useful allies when it really matters—that is, when military force must be threatened or used. It is certainly true that attitudes toward force differ, that Europeans are generally far more inclined to try diplomatic approaches to conflict. But the record of the 1990s and early 2000s does not match the caricature of a Europe that is so hopelessly pacifistic and appeasing that warlike Americans simply have no other choice but to seek other alliances or act alone. In the 1990–1991 Gulf War, Europeans were hardly keen to go to war (not unlike 47 U.S. senators and some prominent American generals), but they ultimately backed Operations Desert Shield and Desert Storm at the United Nations, provided tens of thousands of troops, and contributed over $10 billion to the American-led effort to expel Iraqi forces from Kuwait.

In the Balkans, it took the United States years to overcome its own reluctance to act militarily, and in both Bosnia and Kosovo there were times when both France and Britain were more ready than Washington to threaten or use force or to risk deploying forces on the ground. In 1995 it was Chirac who, in some ways, took the lead in galvanizing the international community to use force—ironically, given what would happen some seven years later, against the strenuous objections that Colin Powell had raised when he was Chairman of the Joints Chiefs of Staff in 1989–1993. While the Americans limited themselves to bombing, the British, French, and Dutch deployed a Rapid Reaction Force on the ground.

Europe and the United States eventually joined together to effectively undertake NATO's first military missions in Bosnia and Kosovo, in which European military forces flew hundreds of sorties, provided critical bases and logistical support, and played key combat and then peacekeeping roles. In the peacekeeping phase, particularly, Europeans eventually provided over 80 percent of the troops in Bosnia and Kosovo.

More recently, when the United States took military action in Afghanistan to retaliate against al Qaeda terrorists and to overthrow their host, the Taliban regime, European support—and desire to participate—was solid. As the fighting was going on, according to an October 2002 poll, majorities in 11 out of 15 EU states "agreed with the U.S. military action," and in the largest states the majority was substantial (France 73 percent, Germany 65 percent, and the UK 68 percent). Majorities of European populations even agreed that their own countries should take part in the fighting, and some European leaders chafed not at the fact that the United States was using force, but that their offers to contribute forces were rebuffed by a Pentagon that preferred to undertake the operation alone. Despite Pentagon reticence, European forces were involved by early 2002 in bombing, reconnaissance, cave-clearing, and Special Forces operations. European countries—first Britain, then Turkey, Germany, and the Netherlands, and eventually NATO itself—took on the lead role in the International Security Assistance Force (ISAF) deployed to keep the peace.

At one point in 2002, France had over 4200 troops deployed for operations in Afghanistan. At American request, France continues to deploy about 150 highly trained Special Forces on the Afghan-Pakistani frontier to hunt down Taliban and al Qaeda remnants. In Germany, the leftist-dominated German parliament approved the sending of 3900 combat troops to Afghanistan where, according to President Bush, "not only is Germany's participation important, it's robust, more robust than we would have anticipated." At the start of 2004, Germany maintained some 1600 troops in Afghanistan (as part of the NATO-led 5700-strong ISAF) and was taking the lead in the deployment of Provincial Reconstruction Teams of several hundred troops outside of Kabul.

The lesson of all of these episodes was not that Europe is unwilling to use force or has nothing to contribute, but that when the United States shows leadership, it is able to bring allies along—even to the fight.

Iraq, of course, demonstrated the limits of U.S. and European—or at least French and German—willingness to join together on such operations, and worsened the picture of alliance cooperation considerably. But a dramatic decline brought about by one event does not necessarily represent an irreversible trend. In the flush of apparent American victory after the fall of Baghdad in April 2003, the U.S.-European gap on Iraq seemed greater than ever. Nearly 80 percent of Americans thought the war had made them "more secure," and over 70 percent saw it as a "major step forward" in the war on terrorism. In contrast, large majorities across Europe—82 percent in France, 72 percent in Germany, 63 percent in Spain, and 55 percent in the UK—felt that the war in Iraq had made the world a "more dangerous place."

But as difficulties emerged in the U.S. occupation of Iraq and the "rally around the flag" effect that usually increases support for presidents during military operations began to fade, these differences between Europe and the United States started to shrink. Whereas just after the Iraqi war 70 percent of Americans said "the war with Iraq was worth fighting," by November 2003 that number had fallen to 52 percent, rising only slightly after the December 2003 capture of Saddam Hussein. While 56 percent of Americans felt France was wrong to oppose the war, 39 percent said France was right, implying that even the French position enjoyed substantial minority support in the United States. The divide over this issue, moreover—reflecting the overall polarization of U.S. politics—is highly partisan. In the fall of 2003, 78 percent of Republicans still supported the war in Iraq, but 78 percent of Democrats did not support it. By an overwhelming margin of 79 to 18 percent, Republicans said France was wrong to oppose war, while Democrats said the opposite by a margin of 59 to 34 percent.

Americans and Europeans, then, do not live in different worlds. Clearly, Bush's election, September 11, and the crisis over Iraq all exacerbated the structural and cultural differences that have always been difficult to manage in the transatlantic relationship. What is important, however, is not to allow the possibility of a transatlantic divorce to turn into a self-fulfilling prophecy. Assuming that Europeans and Americans are determined to go their separate ways would be the surest way of ensuring that very outcome. Unfortunately, this is precisely what many in the Bush administration—and some of its European critics—seem to be doing.

The Value of Alliance

The Bush administration came to office determined to overcome what it perceived to be its predecessor's penchant for compromise in the name of getting along with others. The new President, his team made clear, was going to lead based on a precise definition of American interests; European allies could and would grumble about American unilateralism, but in the end they would appreciate the new decisiveness from Washington, and the result would be better for all. The assumption backing up this approach seemed to be that if the Europeans did not see the light, it did not matter. Allied support would be nice, but it was certainly not indispensable to a United States that deemed itself by far the most powerful nation in history.

There is, of course, much to be said for assertive American leadership. As developments over the past decade—from the Gulf to the Balkans to Afghanistan—have shown, Washington's willingness to lead often seems to be the only way to get the rest of the international community to act. In all of these cases, moreover, the United States not only showed it could rally international support by charting a decisive political course, but it demonstrated in dramatic fashion the power of its military forces. Rapid and impressive U.S. military victories focused European minds on the indisputable fact that the U.S. military, even acting alone, can accomplish unprecedented feats. Thus, for example, the Security Council votes (UNSC Resolutions 1483, 1500, and 1511) authorizing the American-led occupation of Iraq, as well as the military contributions of some of the European allies in Iraq, were seen by many in Washington as vindication of the "if you build it, they will come" style of American leadership. While the United States may not have been able to win UN or NATO support for the Iraq war in advance, its quick success in toppling the Iraqi regime seemed to leave others with little choice but to acquiesce to American designs.

But it is also clear that when taken too far, assertive leadership can quickly turn into arrogant unilateralism, to the point where resentful others become less likely to follow the lead of the United States. The countries that did not support the war in Iraq, particularly France, Germany, and Russia, may have understood that in the wake of an Anglo-American victory they had little choice but to grant multilateral legitimacy to an occupation in Iraq that already existed. But their resentment and lack of involvement in the reconstruction of Iraq meant they were unwilling to provide the military or financial support the United States desired. Ironically, few anticipated this type of reaction better than candidate Bush in October 2000 when he warned that potential allies around the world would "welcome" a humble United States but "resent" an arrogant one.

The Bush team's policies thus far, however, have been based on the opposite premise. Telling allies that if they did not support Washington's approach to the war on terrorism, they were "with the terrorists," slighting key NATO allies (and NATO itself) in Afghanistan, and refusing genuine consultations before important decisions—

all these were, and are, far more likely to foster resentment than to muster support. Whatever the merits of the administration's opposition to the long list of multilateral agreements it has fought since coming to office—and many of those agreements were genuinely flawed—it should have been clear that the United States could not abruptly pronounce the Kyoto Protocol "dead," seek to undermine the International Criminal Court, raise tariffs on steel and increase agricultural subsidies, and oppose a range of arms control agreements without such actions having a cumulative impact on the attitudes of European leaders and publics toward the United States. The German election of September 2002, where for the first time in the postwar period a leading candidate concluded that major electoral gains could be had by running against the United States, should be taken as a warning that American unilateralism could come at a price.

Some would argue that it does not matter whether the Germanys of this world—and their $28 billion defense budgets—support the United States. And it is true that with its vast military budget and vibrant economy, the United States seems well placed to go it alone. Yet this would be an extremely shortsighted approach. Even a country as powerful as the United States needs a certain level of legitimacy and consent, not to mention the financial and military support that come with it, to achieve lasting success in ventures as complex and fraught as the war on terrorism and the reconstruction of Iraq.

The "if you build it, they will come" theory of coalition management that has been applied with such vigor and purpose by the Bush administration has the virtue of allowing quick and decisive action. But it requires that the coalition move from success to success. When even one setback occurs—and setbacks inevitably occur, as they already have in Iraq—the theory fails, and fails badly, because there is no reservoir of legitimacy and consent to see the coalition through hard times. Not to do the minimum necessary to ensure that Europeans remain positively disposed to American aims—or worse, to actually provoke

Europe into playing a sort of "balancing" role—would be to squander the potential advantages of a position of strength.

In the past, the United States maintained a sort of "European empire" so successfully because it was an "empire by invitation" as historian Geir Lundestad puts it: The United States was predominant in European affairs because Europeans wanted it to be. Today, that feeling remains strong among many European governments, but European publics are less certain. U.S.-European cooperation is sustained by the conscious decision of most European governments to defy domestic public opinion in the interests of maintaining an alliance with the United States.

Such situations are not sustainable in democracies. Unless circumstances change, the electoral strategy of the German Social Democrats—running an election campaign against the United States—will become an increasingly attractive option for European politicians. The result might be an entire European Union that resembles the common U.S. perception of France: resentful of American power, reluctant to lend political support, and out to counter American interests at every turn. Pushed even further, most of Europe might coalesce into a bloc against the United States, with spillover into other areas. The EU and the UN Security Council would become forums for anti-Americanism, forcing the United States to assume global security responsibilities all by itself or to retreat into less than splendid isolation. America would have successfully invaded Iraq and freed itself from the constraints of the ABM and Kyoto treaties, but it would find itself bearing the burdens of maintaining international security not only alone, but in the face of concerted opposition from powerful states.

The approach of many Europeans to the Atlantic alliance has also contributed to transatlantic tensions. The more Europeans reject the notion that some international problems have to be dealt with by force, the more they reinforce the conclusion among some Americans that consultation is a waste of time and Washington must go it alone. When

Europeans appear to play down American concerns about issues such as terrorism and weapons of mass destruction, they also play directly into the hands of those in the United States who argue that there is no point even trying to get the Europeans on board. The European argument that Bush's approach to terrorism and his "axis of evil" speech are "simplistic" has the merit of being true, but it does not offer much of an alternative plan for confronting the common threats that Europeans and Americans face. Europe's repeated "insistence" that Saddam Hussein comply with UN Security Council resolutions and allow weapons inspectors to return to Iraq, without the backing of potential military force, was a hollow threat that had no chance of having any effect.

Europeans will also have to wake up to the fact that their security now depends more than ever on developments that will take place beyond their borders. One reason for the current transatlantic divergences is that while Washington is focused on global developments, Europeans are preoccupied with the enormous challenges of finishing the peaceful integration of their continent, through EU enlargement, the single currency, and a new EU constitution. These are hugely important projects, themselves major contributions to world peace and stability, but they are no longer enough. The new Europe will have to set its sights beyond its borders if it wants to preserve the close global partnership with the United States that both sides need.

At a more fundamental level, some European governments during the Iraq crisis failed to acknowledge the reality that the United States really is, in former Secretary of State Madeleine Albright's formulation, an "indispensable power"—that it has a special role in the world that derives from its unique responsibilities. Outside of the European zone of peace, power and force still matter in the world. The notion of dealing with the United States on the basis of sovereign equality has a nice ring of principle about it, but it does not correspond to the way the world works, or indeed to a world in which most Europeans would want to live. As the Iraq crisis demonstrated, opposing the United States on this basis risks creating a divided Europe and an angry America.

Avoiding that outcome lies in recognizing the new context for U.S.-European relations. The two sides now exist in a globalized world in which the notion of disentangling their mutual interests—whether economic, strategic, or cultural—has no practical meaning. U.S.-European trade and investment relationships dwarf any others in the world, indeed any other such relationships in history. The network of economic ties and dependencies across the Atlantic are so dense, so certain, and so common, that they have almost ceased to be noticed. Indeed, often lost in bold predictions about the "rise of Asia" and dire headlines about U.S.-EU trade disputes is the basic fact that transatlantic economic ties are not decreasing, but in fact increasing. Transatlantic investment links, which are perhaps the key measure of such ties, are not only growing steadily, but even increasing relative to investment links with other regions. The share of U.S. foreign investment going to Europe rose from 48 percent of all investment in 1994 to 52 percent in 2002, and the share of overall European investment going to the United States rose from 61 to 74 percent over the same period.

To say that America and Europe are vastly interdependent does not preclude differences between them; indeed, such interdependencies will create differences. Nor is it to say that interdependence makes outright hostility and conflict futile and therefore unlikely, as Norman Angell argued just before the outbreak of World War I. It is simply to say that such conflict would be a very bad idea for both sides.

The crux of the problem is that today's issues are global, not European or transatlantic. During the Cold War, when disputes involved out-of-area issues that fell outside of NATO's mandate, the requirements of consultation and obedience were often unclear, and the routes to compromise or at least acquiescence were many and varied. They often did not involve the formal institutions of the alliance at all. Indeed, NATO's growing involvement in issues outside of its historic area of competence—from democratization in Eastern Europe to peacekeeping in Afghanistan to a proposed role in Iraq—has increased the strain on the old consensus. The United States, in particular, is unwilling to see its freedom to maneuver outside Europe limited by the ritualized interactions and messy compromises of the institutions of the Atlantic alliance. Conversely, many Europeans see the NATO model that accords such a special place to the United States as an undesirable basis on which to build a twenty-first-century world order.

Clearly, the current institutions of alliance were designed for a threat and a world that no longer exists. They are not ideal for dealing with post–Cold War threats that are transnational and global rather than intergovernmental and European. But creating such institutions is far more difficult than adapting them. In this context, the institutions of the alliance—for all of their limitations—represent the only even semiformal method for achieving consensus and compromise between these two main centers on difficult global issues, particularly those issues that concern security.

A Common Agenda

Can America and Europe reestablish their alliance while leaders as incompatible as Bush, Chirac, and Schröder remain in power? Doing so will not be easy. The personal relations between these leaders are now so frayed, and the trust between their administrations so eroded, that the reflexes of cooperation that should be at the core of any alliance will be difficult to restore. But even if these leaders remain in power, there is much that can and should be done.

At the very minimum, the issue of diplomatic style needs to be addressed. In retrospect, the most striking feature of the crisis over Iraq in comparison to past crises was the absence of effective diplomacy. The most egregious offenders in this regard were certainly the United States and France. Other countries, like the United Kingdom, played more constructive—and frankly, more dignified—roles. Not only were transatlantic diplomatic contacts strikingly limited in comparison to past crises, but both American and French statesmen often appeared almost unaware, and certainly uninterested, in maintaining norms and a style of diplomacy that had long reigned within the Atlantic alliance. The story of the crisis reveals an extraordinary number of intemperate outbursts and inexcusable gaffes—from Rumsfeld's cranky denunciation of "old Europe" to Chirac's hot-headed scolding of EU candidate countries for daring to take a position opposed to that of France.

Traditional diplomatic niceties often lack the communicative advantages of bluntness, but they exist for a reason. Reasoned debate and deference to the other side's sensitivities help to ensure that disagreements do not become personalized and spiral out control, resulting in unnecessary disunity. From the American perspective, as Tony Judt has put it, "even the appearance of taking the world seriously would enhance American influence immeasurably—from European intellectuals to Islamic fundamentalists, anti-Americanism feeds voraciously off the claim that the United States is callously indifferent to the views and needs of others." A U.S. policy of "punishment," immediately after the American military victory in Iraq, similarly elevated pique over strategy and alienated precisely those countries America needed most to make a long-term success of the invasion of Iraq. French statesmen similarly serve their country poorly when their actions reinforce the stereotype of a nation whose ambition and arrogance far outstrip its actual power.

The simple expedient of rediscovering diplomacy—that is, subordinating personal feelings to the national interests, showing more respect for others, and sometimes accepting compromise—would go a long way toward avoiding the type of vicious circle that caused the Iraq crisis. But Americans and Europeans will need to do more than simply behave better. The two sides need to establish a common agenda no less ambitious than was the containment of the Soviet Union and defeat of communism during the Cold War. Some of the basic elements of that agenda would include the following points.

Bring Allies into Iraq

The most important near-term issue is the stabilization and reconstruction of Iraq. The problems within the alliance did not begin within the Iraq crisis, but Iraq now functions as a cause and even a symbol of transatlantic differences. The United States and Europe can of course still work together on other issues even if Iraq never evolves into a stable democracy, but it is an illusion to think that the core notions of an alliance can be preserved while American soldiers are dying in a war in Iraq that key Europeans governments continue to oppose in principle and do little to support in practice. For this reason, the administration's failure to better plan and prepare for inevitable problems in the aftermath of victory was not only a gift to its critics, but also a serious blow to the alliance. Even if evidence of weapons of mass destruction programs is someday found, the wisdom of the American invasion will ultimately be judged on whether the United States can foster a viable and stable democracy in Iraq.

Despite the sweeping military victory of spring 2003 and the capture of Saddam Hussein, Americans would be deeply mistaken to believe that Europe's Iraq debate—or Europe's America debate—is now over. While the desire to side with the powerful United States did lead most European governments to override public opinion and back the war, it has not led to the widespread faith in the quality and integrity of American leadership that the Bush administration believes it deserves. Doubts about the quality of U.S. leadership have fueled desires in some quarters for building Europe as a counterweight to the United States. While the United States has many advantages in this fight for Europe's soul, it needs to do more than rely on raw power if it wants to ensure a future Europe that is not hostile to its aims.

The next battle in this struggle will be over how the war in Iraq is perceived by history. At the moment, the outcome of the war remains understood very differently on the two sides of the Atlantic. Most Americans—despite the difficulties of occupation and especially since the December 2003 capture of Saddam Hussein—continue to see a war of liberation that eliminated a dangerous threat. Most Europeans still see a military adventure by a reckless cowboy that has created a dangerous chaotic mess in the center of the Middle East. As result, European support for the long-term project of Iraq reconstruction is very shallow.

To overcome this gap in perception, Washington needs to do more to give others—including war opponents in France and Germany— a stake in success. Until critics have such a stake in a positive outcome, they will—at least subconsciously—wish for failure to justify their prior opposition and to curb American arrogance. Because the administration initially saw postwar Iraq as a prize rather than a burden, it missed a chance early on to do more to give war opponents a way to meaningfully participate in postwar Iraq. The condescending and moralistic attitude of much of the administration, exemplified by the Pentagon's efforts to "punish" recalcitrant allies, only exacerbated the problem. The U.S. decision in December 2003 to ban firms from countries that opposed the war from bidding on primary contracts for Iraq showed that the Bush administration was still not prepared to put differences over the war behind it nine months after the war, or at least major conflict, had ended. Even many of the administration's supporters complained that the policy only "made credible European charges of vindictive pettiness and general disregard for the opinion of even fellow liberal democracies."

By the end of 2003 there were nonetheless signs that France and Germany were beginning to consider ways to help with the stabilization of Iraq. Concretely, in mid-December, just days after the capture of Saddam Hussein, French President Chirac and German Chancellor

Schröder welcomed President Bush's envoy James A. Baker III with pledges to support substantial debt relief for Iraq. The French and German governments also said they were prepared to consider other ways they might help, including providing training for Iraqi police and security forces, funding humanitarian and reconstruction projects in Iraq, and possibly even providing troops in the context of an eventual NATO role.

Whether France and Germany ultimately contribute to the stabilization of Iraq in these ways will mostly depend on their domestic political dynamics, but the response from the Bush administration will matter as well. A wise administration would vigorously explore the possibility of winning this wider support for the operation in Iraq, even if that means trading a degree of control over postwar Iraq for that support. Sharing such control—with NATO, the UN, or some smaller "contact group" of leading coalition members—would not be without a price: Washington's ability to dictate the course of the Iraqi political process would be diminished. But it would be worth it, not only because Europeans have a lot to contribute to the stabilization and reconstruction of Iraq, but also because the future of the alliance itself may depend on working together on this project.

For all Bush's talk of a broad coalition in Iraq, at the start of 2004 the United States was still providing more than 80 percent of the coalition troops, and U.S. troops had suffered more than 90 percent of the casualties. Including military and reconstruction costs, the American taxpayer was committed to spending some $70 billion in Iraq in fiscal year 2004. In contrast, international pledges of aid to Iraq amounted to less than $4 billion in grants and $9 billion in loans, most of which remained unfulfilled as of December 2003. In that context, the additional resources that France, Germany, and other countries that had opposed the war could provide—as well as the new resources that might come from elsewhere if the occupation was given new legitimacy through this wider support—should be seen as more than welcome.

Just as the West only truly overcame its deep divisions in the Balkans once NATO was deployed on the ground, in Iraq the Atlantic alliance will remain divided until there is a collective interest in stability and success. So long as divisions in responsibilities and stakes persist, so will serious questions about the future of the transatlantic alliance and about America's ability to win European support the next time it needs it. If the leaders who backed America on Iraq are either not prepared to do so next time—or worse, are booted from power by resentful electorates—America will be forced to act alone if it wants to act at all.

Consolidate the Antiterror Coalition

The coalition assembled by the Bush administration to fight the war on terror was perhaps the broadest group of nations ever jointly committed to a single, pragmatic purpose. Only such a coalition, which included the key European states, could hope to effectively counter the transnational threat of global terrorism. All of those governments came together because they genuinely saw international terrorism as a common threat. Europeans, in particular, needed little convincing that the perpetrators of the September 11, 2001, attacks made no distinction between the various subtleties of Western positions toward the Islamic world. As a result, cooperation between the United States and Europe concerning terrorism, including countries that would actively oppose the war in Iraq, reached new heights after September 11 and has been a critical tool in tracking down known terrorists, cutting off terrorist financing, and preventing further attacks.

This cooperation remains effective, but the very visible divides between the United States and other members of the antiterrorist coalition over Iraq present a long-term challenge to that coalition. In the first instance, this is because the United States never effectively made the case that the Iraq war was a necessary or even a helpful step in the war on terrorism, thus threatening the solidarity of the coalition. As a result, the countries that opposed the war in Iraq are now willing to consider the notion that Islamist terrorists may distinguish between the United States and Europe. Al Qaeda, for instance, previously insensitive to divides within the Western world, was quick to exploit the dispute by reserving their venom for those countries that aligned with the United States over Iraq. More broadly, the unsuccessful attempt to link the Iraq war with 9/11 encouraged the notion in Europe that the U.S.-defined "war on terrorism" was in fact an all-purpose excuse for promoting selfish American interests.

In the context of this effective but fragile cooperation against terrorism, reestablishing a firm basis for the antiterrorist coalition should become an urgent priority for the United States. As with any heterogeneous coalition, this will require difficult compromise and trade-offs. The policy of keeping terrorist suspects in indefinite detention on the U.S. Naval Base in Guantanamo, Cuba, for example, may not yield sufficient dividends relative to the costs it entails in alienation of important allies. Even the traditionally pro-American British publication *The Economist* has been severely critical of this policy:

> The claim that America is free to do whatever it wishes with the Guantanamo prisoners is unworthy of a nation which has cherished the rule of law from its very birth, and represents a more extreme approach than it has taken even during periods of all-out war. It has alienated many other governments at a time when the effort to defeat terrorism requires more international cooperation in law enforcement than ever before. America's casual brushing aside of the Geneva Conventions, which require at least a review of each prisoner's status by an independent tribunal, made America's invocation of these same conventions on behalf of its own soldiers during the recent Iraq conflict sound hypocritical.

Whatever one feels about the validity of the criticism, the fact that such judgments exist, even in the minds of America's closest friends, is a problem that must be addressed more constructively than it has been. If America's antiterror policy damages its reputation as a land of law and justice throughout the world—to the point of alienating the populations of its closest allies—the costs of that policy could prove greater than the benefits.

Before the war in Iraq, the U.S. government felt little need to respond to allied concerns over the conduct of the war on terrorism, or even to specifically define who the enemy was. President Bush declared war not against an enemy, but against a technique, asserting that "either you are with us or you are with the terrorists." In the wake of the feelings of solidarity and sympathy after the September 11 attacks, such an approach was at least plausible. However, as the memory of those attacks fades, and after the divisions demonstrated by the crisis over Iraq, achieving the level of cooperation necessary for success will require some high-profile efforts to show that allied concerns are now being taken into account and that the U.S. antiterror strategy goes well beyond the use of military force. It will also require defining the enemy more precisely, in order to convince allies that the war on terror is not simply a cover for pursuing other, less noble American strategic or commercial interests. Absent such efforts, the pernicious notion that the United States and Europe no longer face the same threat from Islamist terrorism may take root. And that notion would be devastating to the alliance and the safety of its citizens.

Promote a Two-State Solution in the Middle East

The Israel-Palestine problem represents a running sore that infects the Atlantic alliance almost as much as it poisons the Middle East. The continuing bloodshed fuels resentment against the West in the Arab and Muslim world and helps create the conditions, or at least the excuse, for anti-Western terrorism. There are no simple solutions to this problem, but given that the United States and Europe agree on the desired outcome—a viable Palestinian state that coexists alongside a secure Israel—they could cooperate much more effectively than they have done in recent years.

Europeans tend to sympathize with the weaker Palestinians and often appear to want to curry favor with the Arab world. In so doing, they often show little understanding of Israel's genuine security dilemma and appear soft on the horrors of suicide bombings, provoking anger and mistrust from both Israel and the United States. Americans, however, often support Israel so reflexively and unconditionally that they appear unconcerned about the no less genuine plight of the Palestinians, thereby provoking the anger not only of the Arab world, but of many Europeans as well. The Bush administration's track record of inconsistent and episodic engagement leaves the impression that the President finds it more expedient to stand passively aside and denounce terrorism than to take real risks and expend real political capital for peace.

The lack of a common U.S.-European position encourages both parties to the conflict to resist change, prolongs the stalemate, and undermines the whole project of creating a peaceful Middle East. Unconditional U.S. support for Israel has encouraged those within Israel who would prefer not to make the painful concessions necessary for peace. European equivocation on terrorism has encouraged moderate Palestinians to believe they can avoid confronting the extremists within their midst. The hard truth is that as long as either side can dare to hope that their maximalist goals are attainable, they will not settle for compromise.

The United States and the Europeans did work extensively and cooperatively together on the Middle East during the 2002–2003 preparation of the "Road Map," a jointly sponsored U.S.-EU-UN-Russian plan designed to chart a course toward a two-state solution.

They also worked together to persuade the Palestinian Authority to create the position of prime minister and to appoint to that job someone committed to peace, which they did with the March 2003 appointment of Mahmoud Abbas. But when implementation difficulties emerged, the Bush administration quickly disengaged and failed to sustain any high-level effort to keep the Road Map alive.

After having publicly pledged to British Prime Minister Tony Blair during the Iraq war that he would "expend the same amount of energy in the Middle East" as Blair had while working for peace in Northern Ireland, Bush instead failed even to appoint a high-level envoy to the region, let alone get personally involved. And then, in fall 2003, Bush did little to try to prevent the Israeli government from building a security fence across Palestinian territory, despite having told Abbas that summer that "a wall snaking through the West Bank" would be "a problem." Other than sending Commerce Secretary Donald Evans on a mission to explore trade with Palestinians, Bush also did little to support Abbas, who was easily sidelined by Arafat and resigned in September 2003. This unwillingness to do more than go through the motions of pursuing Middle East peace while making a top-level priority of war in Iraq not only did nothing to bring Israelis and Palestinians together, but it eroded European trust in the U.S. commitment to the Road Map, and on the Israel-Palestine issue in general.

For there to be any hope of progress in the Middle East, Europeans and Americans together need to make clear that no Palestinian state can be born of violence and that they are committed to the future of Israel as a secure, democratic, Jewish state. The United States and Europe together need to hold Israel to its responsibilities on settlements, and to persuade it that military superiority and possession of territory alone will never bring a real peace. They will also have to work together to extinguish the hope of extremists on both sides and to realize the common vision of safe and secure Israeli and Palestinian homelands. Doing that would be an enormous step forward not only for Israelis and Palestinians, but for the war on terrorism and the restoration of transatlantic trust.

Coordinated Carrots and Sticks Toward Iran

Another Middle East issue that could potentially form the basis of either a common U.S.-European approach or, if mishandled, another major transatlantic crisis is Iran. As already noted, in the mid- to late 1990s Iran was actually a greater source of transatlantic division than Iraq, as the United States sought to isolate the Tehran regime while Europeans hoped they could woo it with conditional engagement. By the early 2000s both sides had to admit that their respective approaches were failing. Not only had the reformers led by President Mohammed Khatami (whose election in 1997 led to such hope in the West) failed to gain the upper hand over the conservative clerics who ruled the country, but in 2003 evidence began to emerge that Iran was violating its commitments under the Nuclear Nonproliferation Treaty and pursuing a nuclear weapons program more actively than even many of its critics had alleged.

The Iranian nuclear program has the potential to drive America and Europe apart much as Iraq did, with the Americans potentially pursuing regime change or military strikes while the Europeans appeal for engagement or containment. But it could and should also form the basis for a common policy toward Iran. Indeed, given the well-demonstrated difficulty of influencing Iranian behavior, only a concerted U.S.-European effort to combine their considerable carrots and sticks has any hope of halting the Iranian nuclear program, let alone winning Iranian cooperation in other areas of common transatlantic interest, like terrorism or interference in Iraq or the Middle East.

An important first step toward a common approach was taken in October 2003, when Foreign Ministers Joschka Fischer of Germany,

Jack Straw of Britain, and Dominique de Villepin of France traveled to Tehran to press the Iranians for progress on the nuclear issue. After years of relying on engagement and resisting any form of coercion, the Europeans this time presented Tehran with a tough message: The EU would only move forward with its long-planned trade and cooperation agreement with Iraq—attractive to Iranian leaders, whose economy is failing and whose growing population needed the economic support of the EU—if Iran fully met all of the International Atomic Energy Agency's nuclear demands.

After long and difficult negotiations, and even a European threat to walk away from the table when the Iranians were dragging their feet, a deal was struck. Iran agreed to account fully for its past nuclear activities, to sign an enhanced protocol on nuclear inspections, and to suspend its uranium enrichment and reprocessing activities. It was unclear whether the main factor in persuading the Iranians to make such an unprecedented agreement was the new approach from the EU, Iranian concerns about possible American military strikes, or simply changed domestic circumstances in Iran. But some combination of those factors seemed to have persuaded Tehran to accept what it had never accepted before.

Moving forward, the United States and Europe need to join together to propose a package of incentives and disincentives to change Iranian behavior. If Iran would not only suspend but permanently and verifiably end its nuclear enrichment and reprocessing programs, the EU would proceed with the trade and cooperation agreements that Iran so desperately needs. The United States would also have to put engagement on the table. In exchange for verifiable Iranian commitments on the nuclear issue as well as progress on other issues of importance, the United States should be prepared to reestablish diplomatic relations with Iran and begin discussions with Iran on regional security issues. To the extent that Iran ceases support for terrorist groups in the Middle East and works constructively with the United States in Iraq and Afghanistan—where Iran's potential for creating trouble could be significant—Washington should also offer trade and investment incentives, including potentially supporting Iranian membership in the World Trade Organization.

The concomitance of such Western carrots would be real transatlantic agreement that in the absence of Iranian compliance—or if there is cheating on the nuclear agreement—the United States *and* the EU would respond with sticks. The main problem with the European countries' nuclear agreement with Iran is that the German, British, and French leaders still refuse to state clearly what the consequences would be in the event that Tehran proceeded with an overt nuclear weapons program. Those consequences should include not only the halting of enhanced trade and diplomatic agreements, but suspension of all European trade and investment with Iran. Such a threat would make the Iranians think twice since the EU is by far Iran's leading trading partner, accounting for more than 37 percent of Iran's total imports and absorbing some 28 percent of its exports. As a last resort, Americans and Europeans should also leave open the option of military strikes, if that turned out to be the only possibility of preventing a fundamentalist Islamic regime in Iran from developing nuclear weapons.

Even with concerted U.S.-European agreement on a package of carrots and sticks for Iran, it may prove impossible to persuade the regime to abandon its nuclear plans, or to keep it from taking other actions that are counter to Western interests. Indeed, support for a nuclear Iran is so widespread in Iranian society that even a new, reformist regime might not back away from the nuclear plans. Given the history of foreign interventions in Iran and the existence of other nuclear powers like Israel, India, and Pakistan in the region, any Iranian government will be reluctant to get completely out of the nuclear business. And a nuclear Iran would be a major threat to Western interests—not only because it might give Iran the confidence to seek hegemony over its neighbors, but because it could lead other regional powers to follow it.

It is therefore a compelling national interest for both the United States and Europe to join together to increase the costs for Iran of going nuclear and to increase the benefits to Iran if it foregoes that option. If Iranians can be persuaded that the price of nuclear weapons is economic and diplomatic isolation from the Western world, they might conclude that it isn't worth it.

Promote Reform in the Greater Middle East

It is not a coincidence that the first four issues on this agenda involve problems emanating from one region of the world: the Middle East. No region is more central to the set of important international security issues faced by the Western world, and none generates more friction between Americans and Europeans. The Middle East is far from the poorest region on the planet, but it suffers from some distinct and deep-seated social, demographic, and political problems. In particular, lack of political and economic freedom, anemic and unbalanced economic growth, and a large, poorly educated, and chronically unemployed youth population plague almost every country in the region. These factors make the Middle East a particularly fertile ground for unrest and violent conflicts. Because of the region's strategic location and critical energy resources, those conflicts frequently draw in outside parties and have effects well beyond the region, and into the United States and Europe.

This regional malaise is understood by Western observers, as well as by intellectuals and officials in the region itself. A 2002 report written by Arab social scientists, published by the UN Development Program, concluded that "the wave of democracy that transformed governance in most of Latin America and East Asia in the late 1980s and early 1990s has barely reached the Arab States." The report calls for a similar transformation of governance in the Arab states in order to overcome "deeply rooted shortcomings in Arab institutional structures."

Western policies have too often contributed to these dynamics. For decades, the United States basically had a deal with repressive governments throughout the Middle East: They could run their countries as they chose, as long they were willing to sell oil at reasonable prices on world markets and to act as strategic allies of the United States. This policy has long been self-evidently at odds with professed American values of freedom and democracy.

But since September 11 it has also been understood by American officials to be a serious threat to U.S. and Western security. As President Bush acknowledged in November 2003: "[Sixty] years of Western nations excusing and accommodating the lack of freedom in the Middle East did nothing to make us safe.... As long as the Middle East remains a place where freedom does not flourish, it will remain a place of stagnation, resentment, and violence ready for export. And with the spread of weapons that can bring catastrophic harm to our country and our friends, it would be reckless to accept the status quo." Americans, Europeans, and many in the region thus agree that lasting success in the greater Middle Eastern region is only possible if policies toward specific issues or crises are complemented by longer-term initiatives to promote political, economic, and social reform throughout the region.

That is easier said than done, of course. Widespread agreement on the problem has not led to widespread agreement on the solution. The Bush administration has articulated a neo-Wilsonian vision of political and economic liberalization in the Middle East that builds on the American experience in establishing liberal democracy in Germany and Japan and in encouraging democratic transformation in the former Soviet bloc. The speeches putting forth that vision contain universally admired sentiments, but there is widespread skepticism that American actions reflect that rhetoric now, or indeed that they ever will.

In part, this results from a realistic assessment of American interests. Bush's statements reflect the fact that the United States has a moral stake and a long-term security interest in democratic transformation of the Middle East. In the short term, however, it is much less obvious that a democratic transformation of the Middle East is in U.S. interests. Democratization is a difficult, destabilizing process that often increases violence in the short term. Moreover, many of the regimes on which the United States depends for maintaining the stability of the oil market and even for cooperation against terrorist threats—most notably the ruling al-Saud family in Saudi Arabia—would themselves be directly threatened by greater political openness and by economic liberalization.

At the moment, the main alternative to such regimes, and most likely the main beneficiaries of democratization, are Islamist parties that once in power would likely prove hostile to the United States and perhaps even to democracy. If a U.S. policy of democratization created instability in the oil market, decreased the critical cooperation against terrorism now provided by countries like Egypt, Saudi Arabia, and Pakistan, or threatened to bring a virulently anti-Western political party to power, it is not clear that the recognition of the long-term moral and security value of democracy articulated by President Bush could sustain the policy.

This assessment is not lost on non-Americans, many of whom begin with a less benign interpretation of American motives than that of the Bush administration. Many Europeans look at these stark facts, as well at the long American record in accommodating repressive governments in, for example, Saudi Arabia and Egypt, and doubt that any American government will sacrifice short-term American economic or strategic interests to promote democracy and freedom in allied states.

Arab intellectuals, for their part, resent the very notion that such fundamental reform can originate from abroad, particularly when put forward by the same country that in their view has a history of lending unconditional support to Israel and of resorting to force of arms to solve regional issues. According to the 2003 Arab Human Development report, "reform from within, based on rigorous self-criticism, is a far more proper and sustainable alternative." The unspoken message is that any project of reform that originates from abroad will only add to the perception that the West views the Middle East as culturally inferior and backward. In that case, it will not only fail, but may make matters worse by encouraging a backlash against regional actors that cooperate or share the vision of Western democracy.

In this context, American power and legitimacy will clearly not suffice to carry forward such an ambitious project. European support will be critical, but even that will not be sufficient. The region's ills require a broad-based approach that involves all of the regional players in an overarching structure that explicitly links security, economic development, and human rights issues. Modeled on the Organization for Cooperation and Security in Europe (OSCE), such an organization would at first merely provide a forum for reaching arms control agreements and free trade agreements within the regional states and with the United States and Europe in exchange for establishing human rights norms and democratization goals that all countries can pledge to accept. Eventually, as with the OSCE, the forum might evolve into an organization that names and shames violators of their agreements, encourages transparency, and sets the standards for regional economic development and human rights.

This is clearly a generational project, and one that contains no guarantee of success. It will have to proceed in tandem with the other projects mentioned above, but it can and must begin now. There is no reason to accept that the Israel-Palestine problem or the reconstruction of Iraq must be solved before an overarching project of reform can begin. On a regionwide basis, the first step is for the United States and Europe to get on the right side of the issue of reform in the Middle East and to stay there, in order to establish that Western oil interests will not always trump human rights and concerns about democracy. If done with sufficient humility, this will make it possible to engage the regional actors in the type of forum envisaged. Concurrently, the United States and its partners must follow through on their promises to stabilize, reconstruct, and liberate both Iraq and Afghanistan as demonstrations of their goodwill, strength of purpose, and capacity.

From a transatlantic perspective, the project of promoting political reform in the Middle East represents an opportunity to reinvigorate the alliance by creating a joint project that rests on common U.S. and European values and that addresses their common security interests.

Develop New Norms on Legitimacy and the Use of Force

The crisis over Iraq did not just reflect differences over how to deal with Saddam Hussein's regime, but in fact revealed wider divides between the United States and Europe over issues of world order and the appropriate use of force. Simultaneously, the crisis served to demonstrate how differences on seemingly arcane issues of international law can matter in practical circumstances.

One important lesson all parties should take from this experience is that it makes sense to begin now to address basic disagreements that have emerged over world order before the next crisis begins. Since September 11, the Bush administration has forcefully made the point that the old laws and institutions established for the post-World War II and Cold War realities are not effective in today's world. The combination of terrorism, weapons of mass destruction, and rogue states mean that the world can no longer define aggression in simple cross-border terms, nor does it have the luxury of waiting for threats to definitively manifest themselves before it reacts with purpose and resolve.

Before the Iraq crisis, Europeans paid some lip service to these notions, but they generally refused to take concrete action to reform the institutions of international order to account for their implications. In this context, the Bush administration's preemption doctrine, so actively scorned in Europe, does not just represent the unilateralist tendencies of a hard-line administration. It also reflects a general American frustration that the institutions of world order are too slow and too ineffective to confront the immediate problems of twenty-first-century security—to include the physical security of the American homeland.

The idea of anticipating threats and preventing them through the use of force, while always controversial, is hardly new. In fact, even recent French military doctrine contains provisions for using force under such circumstances. Similarly, the EU's first effort at a European Security Strategy—a document drafted by High Representative for EU Common Foreign and Security Policy Javier Solana—also acknowledged that threats such as terrorism and weapons of mass destruction may require action even before crises arise.

Americans and Europeans are unlikely to ever agree completely on what new principles should govern the use of force. But the solution is not to dismiss the importance of maintaining any international rules and norms, as some Americans would have it, and simply ask the world to trust that a benign and wise United States will make the right decisions. Unfortunately, whatever the objective truth of this American self-image, it is not a view that is sufficiently shared throughout the world, or even in Europe, to constitute an effective basis for legitimating the use of force against sovereign entities.

Nor, however, is the "European" solution of unwavering attachment to principles adopted by the United Nations over 50 years ago—long before the specter of terrorists with weapons of mass destruction appeared—viable in today's world. As Europeans implicitly accepted in the Kosovo conflict, an agreement among the 19 Western democracies of NATO can be as legitimate as agreement among 15 members of the Security Council.

A mature official and unofficial dialogue among Americans and Europeans could help yield a new understanding of the principles that should apply to the use of force in the twenty-first-century. The answer must be somewhere between "only when the UN agrees" and "whenever the United States sees fit."

Revive NATO and Encourage European Defense

NATO has always been at the heart of the Atlantic alliance. If that alliance is to survive and prosper, the United States and its European partners must reorganize and reinstitutionalize NATO so it can be a useful tool for the problems we are likely to face.

During the 1990s, that project seemed well begun. The expansion of NATO membership and NATO's first combat and peacekeeping missions in the Balkans gave the institution a sense of purpose and dynamism and demonstrated the organization's continued relevance. After September 11, the United States displayed less interest in reinvigorating NATO, but the alliance still played a role in substituting for some of the U.S. assets that were sent to fight the war in Afghanistan and in managing the International Security Assistance Force after the conflict. However, the severe crisis within NATO on the issue of Iraq—indeed, the institutional breakdown—demonstrated that NATO cannot rely on its recent successes to ensure its continued relevance, any more than it can rely on its victory in facing down the communist threat. For NATO to survive and flourish, it needs to continue to adapt to new threats and challenges.

A part of that effort will involve reforming NATO's structure and tools, which is to say, further streamlining its command structure and creating a rapid deployment force that can respond to emergencies around the world. Plans for a NATO Response Force, approved at the Prague Summit in November 2002, are a good step forward. But the member states of NATO have for some time known what they needed to do to reform NATO internally. The larger issues are deciding to commit the resources to that known task and accommodating NATO to the existence of common European Union security and defense policy.

Without a substantial and balanced commitment of resources to defense by the countries of NATO, the most efficient command structure in the world will be of little use. European military capabilities will clearly have to be enhanced if Europeans want to be taken seriously— both in Washington and throughout the world. In the current climate of fiscal stringency, European defense budgets are unlikely to rise dramatically, but they will need to increase at least to some degree. Even short of that, better spending—through more joint acquisitions, rationalization of the defense industrial base, and cutting bloated, immobile forces—could go a long way.

More conceptually, Europeans need to think of their forces as part of a global alliance with global responsibilities to fulfill. This means they need fewer mass armies and more deployable forces and niche capabilities, such as special operations forces or airlift capability that can complement U.S. forces. The existence of usable forces in large enough numbers would give the prospect of gaining European agreement for the use of force a more pragmatic rationale than just abstract notions of legitimacy. At the moment, the United States has little reason to pay attention to Europe during the heat of military crises—an incentive structure that does little to enhance long-term U.S. policy.

The trends are not good. U.S. forces are continually updating, even transforming themselves. Without more and better European defense spending to create capabilities the United States needs and wants, European forces will find themselves increasingly unable to operate alongside a transformed U.S. military. That situation would only exacerbate a division of labor—U.S. troops for combat, European for peacekeeping—that has already helped undermine the sense of shared risk that an alliance requires. A more balanced alliance would enhance European influence, as well as American wisdom, ultimately working in the interests of both sides.

The devotion of these resources is even less likely, however, if the United States and the member states of the European Union fail to agree on how to develop a common European defense policy that complements, rather than duplicates, the functions of NATO. The exact balance of responsibilities between the EU and NATO is less important than reaching agreement and for Europe to offer a coherent policy and an effective force to its American partners. Absent those developments, it is likely that even a new U.S. administration will continue to engage with Europe as individual European countries, rather than as a whole—or will not engage at all.

From the American perspective, there is little to fear from an EU capable of such actions, and much to gain, as EU missions to the Balkans and Africa have already demonstrated. The greater problem is Europe's current weakness, not its potential strength. A European counterweight to the United States only exists in the dreams of nostalgic Frenchmen and in the nightmares of paranoid Americans. Indeed, the only way to convince Europe that such a counterweight would make sense would be through an arrogant American refusal to countenance any independent European defense capability. The United States has little to fear from European unification, but much to fear from other enemies and challenges already apparent on the horizon. America will need a European great power as a partner in the years to come.

An Alliance of Choice

These major projects—stabilizing Iraq, combating terrorism, transforming the Middle East, and adapting our institutions—of course represent only some of the new challenges with which the United States and Europe are faced. But even so, the agenda is daunting. In fact some argue that it is so daunting and American and European perspectives on these issues are often so dissimilar that pursuing the agenda in common is not even worth the effort. The powerful United States, in this view, should simply do what it knows is right, and if

Europeans choose not to follow along, that is their problem and theirs alone.

We strongly disagree. The strategic, political, and cultural differences between Europe and the United States are real. And so is the immense U.S. power that has led many Americans to believe that this country can meet the threats it faces in the world today largely alone. But if the Iraq experience tells us anything, it is that power and determination—even for the world's strongest nation—are not enough to ensure security in an increasingly interdependent world. To help deal with the vast challenges it faces, the United States still needs the legitimacy and resources only an alliance with a democratic Europe can bring. Acting as if the United States needs no one, on the other hand, will lead to resentment, isolation, and even a degree of outright opposition to American leadership that no amount of U.S. military power could overcome.

Without the glaring simplicity of the Cold War threat to convince Americans and Europeans of their common interests, perhaps they will fail to unite against the threats that they face today. But there is no law of history or international relations that says that they must, and it is the duty of the current leaders on both sides of the Atlantic to ensure that they do not. We shall all be much poorer and less secure if they fail in that central task.

NOTES

INTRODUCTION

Page 2: *In March 2003 a significant majority of Americans . . ."* March 2003 Gallup International Iraq 2003 poll, www.gallup-international.com.

Page 3: *"Though clear majorities of Europeans still had favorable opinions as late as summer 2002 . . ."* In Spain, favorable opinions toward the United States fell from 50 percent in 1999–2000 (no figure available for summer 2002) to 14 percent in March 2003. Pew Global Attitudes Project, *Views of a Changing World*, Pew Research Center for the People & the Press, June 2003, p. 19.

Page 3: *"Between February 2002 and spring 2003, the number of Americans with favorable views . . ."* Pew Global Attitudes Project, *Views of a Changing World*, June 2003, p. 20.

Page 3: *" . . . Bush administration officials warned that there would be 'consequences' . . ."* See, for example, "Interview with Charlie Rose of PBS," U.S. Department of State, April 22, 2003.

Page 3: *"By summer of 2003, even mainstream columnists . . ."* Thomas L. Friedman, "Our War with France," *New York Times*, September 18, 2003.

Page 4: *" . . . 'deep differences' within the Euro-Atlantic community . . ."* Francis Fukuyama, "The West May Be Cracking," *International Herald Tribune*, August 9, 2002; and Francis Fukuyama, John Bonython Lecture, "Has History Restarted Since September 11?" August 8, 2002.

Page 4: *" . . . 'we are witnessing the dissolution of an international system . . .'"* Tony Judt, "The Way We Live Now," *New York Review of Books*, March 27, 2003.

Page 4: *". . . 'if the existing trend in transatlantic relations continues . . .'"* Henry A. Kissinger, "Repairing the Atlantic Alliance," *Washington Post*, April 14, 2003.

Page 4: "*. . . the United States and Europe may be headed 'down the same road as Rome and Constantinople' . . .*" Charles Kupchan, *The End of the American Era: U.S. Foreign Policy and the Geopolitics of the Twenty-First Century* (New York: Knopf, 2002), 153; and Kupchan, "The alliance lies in the rubble," *Financial Times,* April 10, 2003.

Page 4: " *. . . NATO—once the centerpiece of the transatlantic alliance—is 'dead.'*" Charles Krauthammer, "Reimagining NATO," *Washington Post,* May 24, 2002.

Page 4: "*Not everyone agrees. . .*" Antony J. Blinken, "The False Crisis Over the Atlantic," *Foreign Affairs* (May/June 2001), 35–48; Ronald D. Asmus and Kenneth M. Pollack, "The New Transatlantic Project," *Policy Review* (October & November 2002), 3–18; James B. Steinberg, "An Elective Partnership: Salvaging Transatlantic Relations," *Survival* (Summer 2003), 113–146; Joseph R. Biden Jr. and Chuck Hagel, "Winning the Peace," *Washington Post,* April 6, 2003; Richard G. Lugar, "Redefining NATO's Mission: Preventing WMD Terrorism," *Washington Quarterly* (Summer 2002), 7–13.

Page 4: "*. . . 'transatlantic relations are in 'very serious trouble.'*" Ivo H. Daalder, "The End of Atlanticism," *Survival* (Summer 2002), 147–166.

Pages 4–5: "*Probably the most powerful case that America and Europe are growing apart . . .*" Robert Kagan, "Power and Weakness," *Policy Review* (June & July 2002), 3. Kagan later expanded his article into a book, *Of Paradise and Power: America and Europe in the New World Order* (New York: Alfred A. Knopf, 2003).

Page 5: "*. . . 'setting national priorities, determining threats, defining challenges . . .'*" Kagan, "Power and Weakness," *Policy Review,* 4.

Page 6: "*But the notion that these other relationships could adequately substitute for a permanent alliance . . .*" For two such suggestions, see Jeffrey Gedmin, "This Alliance is Doomed," *Washington Post,* May 20, 2002; and Charles Krauthammer, "A Costly Charade at the UN," *Washington Post,* February 28, 2003.

CHAPTER 1

Page 19: "*A list of book titles published since the 1950s . . .*" Geir Lundestad, *The United States and Western Europe Since 1945* (New York: Oxford University Press, 2003), 4.

Page 20: "*Roosevelt's outlook . . . combined an old American confidence . . .*" John L. Harper, "American Visions of Europe after 1989," Center for Strategic and International Studies (CSIS: Washington, D.C.), March 2003.

Page 22: " . . . 'to settle all of our difficulties with Russia and then go to the movies . . .'" Quoted in Walter Isaacson and Evan Thomas, *The Wise Men: Six Friends and the World They Made—Acheson, Bohlen, Harriman, Kennan, Lovett, McCloy* (New York: Simon & Schuster, 1986), 348.

Page 22: *"By the end of 1946 . . ."* James Dobbins et al., *America's Role in Nation Building: from Germany to Iraq* (Washington, D.C.: RAND, 2003): 9–10.

Page 23:" . . . *their very 'way of life' was at stake."* Harry S Truman, "Special Message to the Congress on Greece and Turkey," The Truman Doctrine, March 12, 1947, *Truman Public Papers 1947*, 178–179; and Harry S Truman, "Special Message to Congress on the Marshall Plan," December 19, 1947, *Truman Public Papers 1947*, 515–529.

Page 23: ". . . 'clearer than the truth . . .'" Dean Acheson, *Present at the Creation: My Years in the State Department* (New York: Norton, 1969), 374–375.

Page 23: " . . . 'familiarity with federalism discouraged the view . . .'" John Lewis Gaddis, *We Now Know: Rethinking Cold War History* (Oxford, UK: Clarendon Press, 1997), 201; and Lawrence S. Kaplan, *The United States and NATO: The Formative Years* (Lexington: University Press of Kentucky, 1984), 11, 100–101, 181.

Page 25: *"The logic linking all of these decisions was that of politics . . .'"* Gaddis, *We Now Know*, 201. Original was in italics for emphasis.

Page 25: " . . . 'any areas encroaching in some form or manner . . .'" See statement by Secretary of State Dulles at a press conference on October 2, 1956, quoted in Anthony Eden, *Memoirs: Full Circle* (Cambridge, Mass.: Riverside Press, 1960), 556.

Page 26: " . . . *voting against the United States in the Security Council for the first time."* Frank Costigliola, *France and the United States: The Cold Alliance Since World War II,* (New York: Twayne Publishers, 1992), 112–115.

Page 26: *"When an agreement to withdraw was not forthcoming . . ."* On the chronology of events and the debate within the UN see Anthony Eden, *Memoirs: Full Circle* (Cambridge, Mass.: Riverside Press, 1960), 545–626.

Page 26: *"But the American action showed that such backing had a limit . . ."* Eden, *Memoirs: Full Circle,* 512.

Page 27: " . . . 'the Americans would not hesitate to leave them in the lurch.'" Pierre Melandri, "The Troubled Friendship: France and the United States, 1945–1989," in Geir Lundestad, *No End to Alliance: the United States and Western Europe: Past, Present, Future* (New York: St. Martin's Press, 1998), 124.

Page 27: *"Thus the French resolved to pursue an autonomous foreign policy . . ."* On the link between Suez and later French military policies, see Philip H. Gordon, "Charles de Gaulle and the Nuclear Revolution," in John Lewis Gaddis, Philip H. Gordon, Ernest May and Jonathan Rosenberg, eds., *Cold War Statesmen Confront the Bomb: Nuclear Diplomacy Since 1945* (New York: Oxford University Press, 1999), 216–235.

Page 27: *"By demonstrating the dangers of intra-alliance disputes the Suez crisis set the standard . . ."* Douglas Stuart and William Tow, *The Limits of Alliance: NATO Out-of-Area Problems Since 1949* (Baltimore, Maryland: Johns Hopkins University Press, 1990), 8.

Page 27: *" . . . withdrawal of France from NATO's military structure . . ."* Costigliola, *France and the United States,* 144–145.

Page 27: *"This was the fate American neoconservative writer Robert Kagan suggested . . ."* For de Gaulle's version of the argument, see Philip H. Gordon, *A Certain Idea of France. French Security Policy and the Gaullist Legacy* (New Jersey: Princeton University Press, 1993), especially 21. For Kagan's version, see Robert Kagan, "Power and Weakness," *Policy Review* (June/July 2002), 3.

Page 28: *"'I trust you,' de Gaulle told Acheson."* Maurice Vaïsse et al., *L'Europe et la crise de Cuba* (Paris, Armand Colin, 1993), 95, fn. 37.

Page 28: *" . . . if that included the dead ones in the cemeteries."* Secretary of State Dean Rusk cited in Thomas J. Schoenbaum, *Waging Peace and War: Dean Rusk in the Truman, Kennedy, and Johnson Years* (New York: Simon & Schuster, 1988), 421.

Page 28: *"'When a man asks you to leave . . .'"* Lyndon Johnson cited in Richard Barnet, *The Alliance: America, Europe, Japan, Makers of the Postwar World* (New York: Simon & Schuster, 1983), 248. Also see Thomas Alan Schwartz, *Lyndon Johnson and Europe: In the Shadow of Vietnam* (Cambridge, Mass.: Harvard University Press, 2003).

Page 28: *"In contrast to the Soviet Union when Hungary tried to distance itself . . ."* For an instructive comparison between the American reaction to the French withdrawal from NATO and the Soviet reaction to Hungary's efforts to chart a more independent course in 1956, see Gaddis, *We Now Know,* 219.

Page 29: *"'[Europe's] legalistic argument was to the effect that . . .'"* Henry A. Kissinger, *Years of Upheaval* (Boston: Little Brown & Company, 1982), 711.

Page 30: *"In response, Kissinger called the Europeans 'craven' and 'contemptible' . . ."* Quoted in Costigliola, *France and the United States,* 164.

Page 30: "... *the French government went so far as to hold aerial defense exercises* ..." Pierre Melandri, "The Troubled Friendship: France and the United States, 1945–1989," in Geir Lundestad, *No End to Alliance,* 125.

Page 30: "*Polls showed that a majority of West Germans opposed* ..." Dana H. Allin, *Cold War Illusions: America, Europe and Soviet Power 1969–1989* (New York: St. Martin's Press, 1994), 91.

Page 31: "*Henry Kissinger has rightly observed* ..." Kissinger, *Diplomacy,* 819.

Page 32: "*It is necessary to point out that our economic interests are paramount* ..." Peter Tarnoff quoted in John M. Goshko, "Reduced U.S. Role Outlined But Soon Altered," *Washington Post,* May 26, 1993.

Page 33: "*Then U.S. policy moved away from the notion of air strikes* ..." Ivo H. Daalder, *Getting to Dayton: the Making of America's Bosnia Policy* (Washington, D.C.: Brookings Institution Press, 2000), 15–19; and David Halberstam, *War in a Time of Peace: Bush, Clinton and the Generals* (New York: Scribner, 2001), 224–231.

Page 33: "*The Christopher mission would later come to be seen, especially among Republican critics* ..." For such critiques, see, for example, Bob Dole, "Shaping America's Global Future," *Foreign Policy,* March 22, 1995, 22; and Robert Kagan, "Coalition of the Unwilling," *Washington Post,* October 17, 2001, A35.

Page 33: "... '*the hour of Europe, not the hour of the Americans.*'" Jacques Poos quoted in Joel Haveman, "EC Urges End to Yugoslav Violence, Threatens Aid Cut," *Los Angeles Times,* June 29, 1991, A11.

Page 34: "... *they would be obliged to rescue European peacekeepers* ..." Richard Holbrooke, *To End a War* (New York: Random House, 1998), 68.

Page 34: "*After much early hesitation, in 1995 it charted a clear course for NATO enlargement* ..." James M. Goldgeier, *Not Whether But When: The U.S. Decision to Enlarge NATO* (Washington, D.C.: Brookings Institution Press, 1999); and Ronald D. Asmus, *Opening NATO's Door: How the Alliance Remade Itself for a New Era* (New York: Columbia University Press, 2002).

Page 35: "*The administration believed in the concept* ..." Senator Richard Lugar, "NATO: Out of Area or Out of Business," remarks delivered to the Open Forum of the U.S. State Department, August 2, 1993, Washington, D.C.

Page 35: "*The European allies, led by France, insisted on acknowledging the importance of the UN* ..." North Atlantic Council, "The Alliance's Strategic Concept," NAC-S(99)65, April 24, 1999; and see the discussion in Asmus, *Opening NATO's Door,* 275–282.

Page 36: *"'Let me state categorically, without strong continued cohesion . . .'"* William S. Cohen, Testimony to Senate Armed Services Committee, October 14, 1999.

Page 36: *"'NATO wasn't an obstacle to victory in Kosovo . . .'"* Wesley Clark, "An Army of One?" *Washington Monthly*, November 21, 2002. Clark makes this case more broadly in Wesley K. Clark, *Waging Modern War*, 426.

Pages 37–38: *"America would use 'decisive and, if necessary, unilateral' force . . ."* William J. Clinton, "A National Security of Engagement and Enlargement," February 1995, 12.

Page 38: *" . . . the threat from what the Americans called 'rogue' or 'backlash' states . . ."* For an early use of the term and exposition of the American approach, see the article by Clinton's first National Security Adviser, Anthony Lake, "Confronting Backlash States," *Foreign Affairs* (March/April 1994), 45–55.

Page 43: *"'Saddam Hussein's intentions will never be peaceful.'"* Madeleine Albright, "Remarks by Secretary of State Madeleine Albright at Georgetown University," Washington, D.C., published as Madeleine Albright, "Preserving Principle and Safeguarding Stability: United States Policy Toward Iraq," U.S. Department of State, March 26, 1997.

Page 43: *" . . . 'it should the policy of the United States to support efforts to remove the regime . . .'"* See "Iraq Liberation Act of 1998," Public Law 105-338, October 31, 1998.

Page 43: *" . . . '[so] long as Saddam Hussein remains in power . . .'"* William J. Clinton, "Remarks of the President on Iraq," December 19, 1998, www.fas. org/news/iraq/1998/12/19/98121913_tlt.html.

Page 44: *" . . . Europeans were 'relatively rich and ungrateful introverts.'"* Geoffrey Williams, *Global Defense: Motivation and Policy in a Nuclear Age* (New Delhi: Vikas, 1983), 55.

Pages 44–45: *" . . . the failure of their European allies to support U.S. policy . . ."* See, for example, Irving Kristol in 1980 cited in Stuart and Tow, *The Limits of Alliance*, 91 and Senator Ted Stevens in 1982 cited in George C. Wilson, "Western Europe warned of GI withdrawal over Soviet pipeline," *Washington Post*, March 3, 1982, A3.

CHAPTER 2

Page 48: *"He cautioned against too much foreign intervention . . ."* Governor George W. Bush, "A Distinctly American Internationalism," Ronald Reagan

Presidential Library, Simi Valley, California, November 19, 1999, www. globalsecurity.org/wmd/library/news/usa/1999/991119_bush_foreign policy.htm.

Page 48: *"Even more prominently . . ."* On Colin Powell as the scourge of the neoconservatives, see Lawrence F. Kaplan, "Yesterday's Man: Colin Powell's Out-of-date Foreign Policy," *New Republic*, January 1, 2001; Robert Kagan, "The Problem with Powell," *Washington Post*, July 23, 2000, B7.

Page 48: *"Bush himself summed up this balance . . ."* George W. Bush, News Conference with Donald Rumsfeld, Transition Headquarters, Washington, D.C., December 28, 2000, available at www.presidency.ucsb.edu/docs/tran sition2001/bush_rumsfeld_1228.php.

Page 50: *"The Bush administration's well-noted desire to distance itself . . ."* On the Bush administration's tendency to reject the policies of its predecessor, see Ivo H. Daalder and James L. Lindsay, *America Unbound: The Bush Revolution in Foreign Policy* (Washington, D.C.: Brookings Institution Press, November 2003), 35–49, especially 37.

Page 50: *"Scholar Robert Kagan articulated the theory . . ."* Robert Kagan, "The Benevolent Empire," *Foreign Policy* (Summer 1998), 33.

Page 50: *"Former CIA Director James Woolsey . . ."* Quoted in an interview that aired on "War on Terror," Fox News, November 26, 2001.

Page 51: *"As William Kristol put it . . ."* Cited in Maureen Dowd, "Hypocrisy and Apple Pie," *New York Times*, April 30, 2003, A27.

Page 51: *"Writer Max Boot agrees . . ."* Max Boot, "Power: Resentment Comes with the Territory," *Washington Post*, March 3, 2003.

Page 51: *"While there have certainly been differences . . ."* Examples can be found in Lawrence F. Kaplan, "Containment: Cheney versus Powell, round two," *New Republic*, February 5, 2001, 17; John Maggs, "Reading Tea Leaves," *National Journal*, May 19, 2001, vol. 33, no. 20, 1486; and Evan Thomas and Roy Gutman, "See George Learn Foreign Policy," *Newsweek*, June 18, 2001, 20.

Page 51: *"[Where] we have a principled position . . ."* Colin Powell, "Press Briefing on the President's Trip to Europe," Rome, Italy, May 28, 2002, www.state.gov/ secretary/rm/2002/10516.htm.

Page 52: *"The United Nations in particular . . ."* Quoted in an interview that aired on *Meet the Press*, NBC News, March 16, 2003.

Page 52: *"Indeed, Cheney argued . . ."* Richard B. Cheney, "Remarks by the Vice President to the Heritage Foundation," October 10, 2003.

Page 53: *"Only hours before the first trip of his presidency . . ."* See "President Bush Discusses Global Climate Change," June 11, 2001, www.whitehouse.gov/news/releases/2001/06/20010611-2.html.

Page 54: *"In retrospect, the manner in which the U.S. government . . ."* Peter M. Leitner, "A Bad Treaty Returns: The Case of the Law of the Sea Treaty," *World Affairs* 160 (Winter 1998), 134. On the process through which the Reagan administration consulted the allies, see John Norton Moore, "Follow Reagan's Lead," Letter to the Editor, *Wall Street Journal*, June 22, 2001; and Jeffrey Gedmin and Gary Schmitt, "Allies in America's National Interest," *New York Times*, August 5, 2001, A13.

Page 55: *" . . . multilateralism à la carte . . ."* The quote is from then Policy Planning Staff Director Richard Haass, quoted in Thom Shanker, "White House Says the U.S. Is Not a Loner, Just Choosy," *New York Times*, July 31, 2001.

Page 57: *"U.S. policymakers slowly concluded that the use of force is a more viable option . . ."* No official public record is kept of such operations. These numbers were compiled from a list of "named" operations available at www.globalsecurity.org/military/ops/index.html. Many of these operations were minor and thus only indicative of the rate of increase from the 1980s to the 1990s, rather than an indication of the overall level of U.S. military operations.

Page 57: *" . . . though Europe has some 1.5 million men and women in its ground forces . . ."* Michael E. O'Hanlon, *Expanding Global Military Capacity for Humanitarian Intervention* (Washington, D.C.: Brookings Institution Press, 2003), 56. Figures are for the European members of NATO and refer to the ability to deploy the force in one to three months and to sustain it for a year.

Page 58: *"As British diplomat and author Robert Cooper has written . . ."* Robert Cooper, *The Breaking of Nations: Order and Chaos in the Twenty-First Century* (London: Atlantic Books, 2003), 159.

Page 59: *"Americans have often complained that this lack of support represents parochialism . . ."* See, for example, Stuart Taylor Jr., "How free-riding French and Germans risk nuclear anarchy," *National Journal* 35 (March 1, 2003), 633–635.

Pages 59–60: *"According to former President George H.W. Bush . . ."* Patrick Tyler and Jane Perlez, "World Leaders List Conditions on Cooperation," *New York Times*, September 19, 2001, A1.

Page 60: *" . . . 'an act of war against our country.'"* George W. Bush, "Address to a Joint Session of Congress and the American People," September 20, 2001, available at www.whitehouse.gov/news/releases/2001/09/20010920-8.html.

Page 61: *"European commentators denounced the Bush administration's use of the word 'war' . . ."* Michael Howard, "What's in a Name? How to Fight Terrorism," *Foreign Affairs 81* (January-February 2002), 8–13, especially 8. For a similar American view, see Zbigniew Brzezinski, "Where do we go from here?" *Transatlantik Internationale Politik,* March 2003, 3. For an official perspective, see Jacques Chirac, "Joint Press Conference with President George W. Bush," Washington, D.C., September 18, 2001, available at www.diplomatie. gouv.fr/actual/dossiers/attentatsusa/chirac180901.html.

Page 61: *"In Secretary of Defense Donald Rumsfeld's formulation . . ."* Vernon Loeb, "Rumsfeld Says War Will Need Backing of 'Revolving Coalitions,'" *Washington Post,* September 26, 2001, A7.

Page 62: *"Former NATO Secretary General Javier Solana . . ."* James Kitfield, "Pox Americana?" *National Journal,* April 6, 2002, 986.

Page 62: *"In a speech on September 20, 2001 . . ."* George W. Bush, "Address to a Joint Session of Congress and the American People," September 20, 2001, available at www.whitehouse.gov/news/releases/2001/09/20010920-8.html.

Page 63: *"Already on September 12, NATO, for the first time . . ."* Marc Champion et al., "Allies at Odds: Behind U.S. Rift with Europeans: Slights and Politics," *Wall Street Journal,* March 27, 2003, A7.

Page 63: *"Similarly, the UN Security Council . . ."* For French President Jacques Chirac's discussion of the initiative, see excerpts of an interview with the *New York Times* in "French Leader offers America both Friendship and Criticism," *New York Times,* September 9, 2002, A9. The interview is available, in French, at www.elysee.fr/actus/arch0209/020909/english.htm.

Page 63: *"He also made clear . . ."* The quotation from Deputy Secretary of Defense Wolfowitz on coalitions is from Judy Dempsey, et al., "White House Avoids Seeking NATO-Wide Aid," *Financial Times,* September 27, 2001. The quotation from Secretary of Defense Rumsfeld is from U.S. Department of Defense, "Secretary Rumsfeld Media Availability En Route to Poland," News Transcript, September 22, 2002.

Page 64: *"Whereas many in Europe saw the Kosovo air campaign . . ."* See, for example, Dana Priest, "The Commanders' War: Bombing by Committee; France Balked at NATO Targets," *Washington Post,* September 20, 1999; and General Michael C. Short, interview with *Frontline,* available at www.pbs.org/wgbh/pages/frontline/shows/kosovo/interviews/short.html, February 1998.

Page 65: *"European governments—with what the U.S. administration saw as typical pessimism . . ."* For examples of immediate European government reactions to events in Afghanistan, see Laurent Zecchini, "À Luxembourg, les ministres des affaires étrangères redoutent un affaiblissement rapide de la coalition," *Le Monde*, October 31, 2001; R. W. Apple Jr., "Under the Tent; the Coalition Is Broad. But Can it Hold?" *New York Times*, November 4, 2001, Section 4, page 1.

Page 66: *"Even among supporters of national missile defense . . ."* Joseph R. Biden, "Missile Defense Delusion," *Washington Post*, December 19, 2001, A.39; Leon Fuerth, "Arms Race Reconsidered: Return of the Nuclear Debate," *Washington Quarterly* 24:4 (Autumn 2001), 97.

Page 66: *"The real turning point . . ."* George W. Bush, "State of the Union Address," Washington, D.C., January 29, 2002, available at www.whitehouse. gov/news/releases/2002/01/20020129-11.html.

Page 67: *"European reaction was swift and scathing . . ."* Judy Dempsey, "Washington turns deaf ear to Europe's divided voices: President Bush's 'Axis of Evil' speech has exposed the EU's gaping rifts over foreign policy," *Financial Times*, February 13, 2002; and Steven Erlanger, "Germany Joins Europe's Cry that the U.S. Won't Consult," *New York Times*, February 13, 2002.

Page 68: *"Lest anyone not get the message . . ."* George W. Bush, "Remarks by the President at 2002 Graduation Exercise of the United States Military Academy," West Point, New York, June 1, 2002, available at www.whitehouse.gov/news/ releases/2002/06/20020601-3.html.

Page 68: *"By September 2002, the doctrine implied . . ."* U.S. National Security Council, *The National Security Strategy of the United States of America*, September 17, 2002.

Page 70: *"According to Secretary of Defense Rumsfeld . . ."* Donald Rumsfeld, "Speech at Camp Pendleton Town Hall Meeting," August 27, 2002, available at www.dod.mil/transcripts/2002/t08282002_t0827thm.html

CHAPTER 3

Page 75: *"Throughout 2001–2002, public opinion polls showed . . ."* See "Top Ten Findings About Public Opinion and Iraq," *Poll Analyses*, October 8, 2002, www.gallup.com/poll/releases/pr021008.asp?Version=p); and *Worldview 2002: American Public Opinion and Foreign Policy* (Chicago Council on Foreign Relations, Washington: 2002), 27.

Page 77: *"As former CIA Director James Woolsey explained . . ."* *Lehrer News Hour*, February 10, 2003.

Page 77: *"Fox News anchor Tony Snow was even more categorical . . ."* See Tony Snow, "Parting Thoughts," Fox News, February 10, 2003, www.foxnews.com/ story/0,2933,78096,00.html.

Page 77: *"Even Secretary of State Colin Powell . . ."* U.S. Department of State, "Interview on Fox News Sunday with Tony Snow," March 16, 2003.

Page 77: *"From 1997 through 2002, French exports to Iraq averaged . . ."* For the French statistics, see French Economics, Finance and Industry Ministry, Echanges Commerciaux France/Irak, DREE, douanes françaises, www. commerce-exterieur.gouv.fr/CdTabEchangesPays.htm.

Page 78: *"For Germany, the Iraqi trade share was even smaller . . ."* Federal Statistical Office of Germany, www.destatis.de/download/e/aussh/rang2.pdf.

Page 78: *"The United States in the early 2000s was importing . . ."* For U.S. imports of Iraqi oil, see International Trade Administration, Trade and Economy: Data and Analysis, http://ese.export.gov/SCRIPTS/hsrun.exe/ Distributed/ITA2003_NATIONAL/MapXtreme.htx;start=HS_newMap.

Page 78: *"Neither the French government nor French oil companies . . ."* Valerie Marcel, "The Future of Oil in Iraq: Scenarios and Implications," *Royal Institute for International Affairs Briefing Paper* (London: December 2002).

Page 79: *"Attributing European opposition to . . ."* Patrice de Beer, "Mieux comprendre les Européens," *Le Monde*, February 2, 2003. For the figure for Turkey, see John Ward Anderson, "Party Discipline Won Out in Turkey's Vote on U.S. Request," *Washington Post*, February 13, 2003.

Page 80: *"According to a December 2002 poll . . ."* Pew Global Attitudes Project, "What the World Thinks in 2002," Pew Research Center for the People and the Press, Washington, D.C., December 4, 2002.

Page 80: *"The German newsweekly* Der Spiegel *also argued . . ."* "Blüt für Öl: Worum es in Irak wirklich geht," *Der Spiegel*, January 13, 2003, 94–109.

Page 81: *"Generously assuming that Iraq's oil production . . ."* See John Tatom, "Iraqi oil is not America's objective," *Financial Times*, February 13, 2003; Martin Wolf, "Stable oil supplies are worth defending from Iraqi aggression," *Financial Times*, February 26, 2003; and Pierre Noël, "La vérité sur le pétrole irakien," *Le Figaro*, February 5, 2003, and "Le contrôle de l'or noir irakien en question," *Le Figaro*, February 6, 2003.

Page 81: *"And given the immense potential costs . . ."* Projected costs for the war, security, and reconstruction could only be estimated, and these figures were widely used by experts in the run-up to the war. Testifying to the Senate Foreign Relations Committee in July 2002, experts put costs for post-conflict security, humanitarian assistance, and reconstruction at $20 to $25 billion per year over 10 years. Cited in Joseph R. Biden Jr. and Chuck Hagel, "Winning the Peace," *Washington Post*, April 6, 2003. For similar estimates, see Gordon Adams, "Not Enough Oil in Iraq," *The Globalist*, March 28, 2003; and Neela

Banerjee, "Can Oil Pay for Iraq's Rebuilding? The U.S. Hopes So," *New York Times*, March 2, 2003.

Page 82: *"'We can go to the country on this issue'* . . ." Cited in Thomas B. Edsal, "GOP Touts War as Campaign Issue; Bush Adviser Infuriates Democrats With Strategy Outlined at RNC Meeting," *Washington Post*, January 19, 2002.

Page 83: *"According to a Gallup poll* . . ." Thirty-four percent thought Saddam was not involved and 13 percent had no opinion. See "Conflict with Iraq: Iraq's Possible Links to Terrorists," Americans and the World Public Opinion on International Affairs, Program on International Policy Attitudes http://www.americans-world.org/digest/regional_issues/Conflict_Iraq/ linkstoTerr.cfmwww.americans-world.org. On Bush's own initial belief that Saddam must have been involved, see Bob Woodward, *Bush at War* (New York: Simon & Schuster, 2002), 99.

Pages 83–84: *"According to a January 2003 poll* . . ." See Knight Ridder poll conducted by Princeton Survey Research Associates, Jan. 3–6, 2003, cited in Martin Merzer, "Poll: Majority of Americans oppose unilateral action against Iraq," Knight Ridder Washington Bureau, January 12, 2003.

Page 86: *"'A man armed with only a knife* . . .'" Kagan, *Of Paradise and Power*, 31.

Page 87: *"Prominent neoconservatives* . . ." See Robert Kagan and William Kristol, "What to do about Iraq," *Weekly Standard*, January 21, 2002.

Page 88: *"Democratic foreign policy experts* . . ." Ronald D. Asmus and Kenneth M. Pollack, "The New Transatlantic Project," *Policy Review* (October/ November 2002).

Page 88: *"As a senior Bush administration official told the British journalist* . . ." The examples given by the official included Bosnia, NATO enlargement, missile defense, the European security and defense identity, free trade, and Ronald Reagan's reference to the 'Evil Empire.'" Martin Walker, "U.S. Diplomat's View of Europe: Contempt Now Glitters in the American Eye," *Washington Times*, November 14, 2002.

Page 88: *"French Ambassador Jean-David Levitte explained* . . ." Jean-David Levitte, "A Warning on Iraq, from a Friend," *New York Times*, February 14, 2003.

Page 88: *"Indeed, historians liked to point out* . . ." For a good discussion of how British colonizers expected to be welcomed in the Middle East after World War I, see David Fromkin, *A Peace to End all Peace: The Fall of the Ottoman Empire and the Creation of the Modern Middle East* (New York: Avon Books, 1989), especially chapters 9, 10, 24, 31, 35, and 36; and Margaret Macmillan,

Paris 1919: Six Months That Changed the World (New York: Random House, 2001), especially 386–400.

Page 89: *"The statement British General Francis Maude made . . ."* See the Maude statement juxtaposed with George W. Bush's statements in Niall Ferguson, "Hegemony or Empire," *Foreign Affairs* (September/October 2003).

Page 90: *"'People in France and more broadly in Europe . . .'"* Jean-David Levitte, "A Warning on Iraq, From a Friend," *New York Times*, February 14, 2003.

Page 90: *"Osama bin Laden's February 11, 2003, audio tape . . ."* The tape is available at news.bbc.co.uk/2/hi/middle_east/2751019.stm. For Powell's reaction, see his testimony before the Senate Budget Committee on the President's International Affairs Budget for 2004, U.S. Department of State, Washington, D.C., February 11, 2003.

Page 90: *"As French President Chirac put it . . ."* Cited in "France is Not a Pacifist Country," *Time*, February 24, 2003.

Page 91: *"As former Secretary of State Henry Kissinger put it . . ."* Henry A. Kissinger, "Iraq is Becoming Bush's Most Difficult Challenge," *Chicago Tribune*, August 11, 2002.

Page 91: *" . . . success in Iraq could . . ."* See Bush's speech to the American Enterprise Institute, "President Discusses the Future of Iraq," Washington Hilton Hotel, February 26, 2003.

CHAPTER 4

Pages 93–94: *"In January 2000, for example, Bush's chief foreign policy adviser . . ."* Condoleezza Rice, "Promoting the National Interest," *Foreign Affairs* 79:1 (January / February 2000), 45–62.

Page 94: *"Similarly, in his January 2001 confirmation hearings . . ."* U.S. Senate Foreign Relations Committee, "Confirmation Hearing of General Colin Powell to be Secretary of State," Washington, D.C, January 17, 2001.

Page 95: *"On September 13, for example, Deputy Secretary of Defense . . ."* See "DOD News Briefing, Deputy Secretary Paul Wolfowitz," Department of Defense, September 13, 2001, and the discussion in Woodward, *Bush at War*, 60–61.

Page 95: *"'I believe Iraq was involved' . . ."* Woodward, *Bush at War*, 81–85; quotation on 99.

Page 95: *"Three days later Bush told . . ."* Quoted by Christopher Meyer, Britain's ambassador to the United States, in "Blair's War," PBS's *Frontline*,

March 18, 2003, www.pbs.org/wgbh/pages/frontline/shows/blair/interviews/ meyer.html.

Pages 95–96: *"The warning that . . ."* Office of the Press Secretary, "President's State of the Union Address," U.S. Capitol, Washington, D.C., January 29, 2002. For examples of how the speech was interpreted as a warning about Iraq, see William Kristol, "Taking the War Beyond Terrorism," *Washington Post*, January 31, 2002; and Jean-Jacques Mével, "Etats-Unis Après l'Afghanistan, le président américain étand la bataille antiterroriste au reste du monde; Bush déclare la guerre à 'l'axe du mal,'" *Le Figaro*, January 31, 2002.

Page 96: *"Bush's arguments that containment was 'not possible' . . ."* Office of the Press Secretary, the White House, "President Bush Delivers Graduation Speech at West Point," Remarks by the President at 2002 Graduation Exercise of the United States Military Academy," West Point, New York, June 1, 2002.

Page 96: *"And it did not take much of a logical leap . . ."* Director of the State Department's Policy Planning Staff Richard Haass, quoted in Nicholas Lemann, "How it Came to War," *The New Yorker*, March 31, 2003.

Pages 96–97: *"Baker did not argue against. . ."* James A. Baker III, "The Right Way to Change a Regime," *New York Times*, August 25, 2002.

Page 97: *"Former Secretary of State Henry Kissinger . . ."* See the interview with Lawrence Eagleburger on Fox Special Report with Brit Hume, August 16, 2002.

Page 97: *"Zinni argued that regime change . . ."* See Zinni's comments to the Florida Economic Club, August 23, 2002, www.npr.org/programs/morning/ zinni.html.

Page 97: *"All these debates seemed to be having an affect . . ."* See *Washington Post*–ABC News Poll, February 2, 2003, www.washingtonpost.com/wp-srv/ politics/polls/vault/stories/data020203.htm.

Page 97: *"He used the opportunity . . ."* Karen De Young, "For Powell, A Long Path To a Victory; Pragmatism, Persistence Led to 15–0 U.N. Vote," *Washington Post*, November 10, 2002.

Page 98: *"The administration's original idea . . ."* DeYoung, ibid. Interviews with senior U.S. officials.

Page 98: *"Powell again made the case . . ."* Tyler Marshall, Maggie Farley, and Doyle McManus, "A War of Words Led to Unanimous Iraq Vote; The long-sought U.N. resolution shows the extent of U.S. power—and its limits," *Los Angeles Times*, November 10, 2002.

Page 99: *"Two groups within the administration . . ."* DeYoung, ibid.

Page 99: *"And in France, officials said . . ."* The positions of all three countries, the poll numbers. and the Schröder quote are all found in Glenn Frankel, "Britons Grow Uneasy About War in Iraq," *Washington Post*, August 7, 2002.

Page 99: *"In his view, this approach had been tried . . ."* Office of the Press Secretary, Vice President Cheney Speaks at Veterans of Foreign Wars 103rd National Convention, August 26, 2002.

Pagae 99: *"Given Cheney's perceived importance . . ."* See Stephen Fidler and Carola Hoyos, "White House makes the case for attack: Cheney's speech suggests signs of consensus in U.S. administration behind use of force," *Financial Times*, August 28, 2002; and "Cheney's path to war," editorial, *Financial Times*, August 29, 2002.

Page 100: *"Earlier in the year he had told a German journalist. . ."* Journalist Michael Inacker, cited in Steven Szabo, *Parting Ways: 9-11, Iraq, and the German-American Relationship*, (Baltimore, MD: Johns Hopkins University Press, forthcoming).

Page 100: *"A few days later . . ."* Interview with Schröder, "No One Has a Clear Idea About What the Effects Would Be," *New York Times*, September 5, 2002.

Page 101: *"Instead, he asserted, the arguments . . ."* Ibid.

Page 101: "On September 12, while Bush was at the U.N. . . ." Cited in Julia Preston, "Bush's Step Toward UN Is Met by Warm Welcome; Council Seems Ready to Act," New York Times, September 13, 2002.

Page 101: *"Two days before the election . . ."* Steven Erlanger, "Bush-Hitler Remark Shows U.S. as Issue in German Election," *New York Times*, September 20, 2002.

Page 101: *"The comparison of Bush to Hitler . . ."* See Haig Simonian, Gerrit Wiesmann, et al., "U.S. condemns 'poisoned' relations with Berlin," *Financial Times*, September 21, 2002. Also see "Empörung im Weissen Haus CDU: Däubler-Gmelin der Lüge überführt," *Frankfurther Allgemeine Zeitung*, September 21, 2002; and "Rice nennt Beziehung zu Deutschland vergiftet," *Frankfurther Allgemeine Zeitung*, September 22, 2002.

Pages 101–102: *"'I would hereby like to let you know . . .'"* For the complete text of the letter, see "Brief von Bundeskanzler Schröder an U.S.-Präsident Bush," September 20, 2003, www.bundeskanzler.de/Findulin-Spiel-.8442.440681/ Brief-von-Bundeskanzler-Schroeder-an-US-Praeside...htm.

Page 102: *"White House officials called his letter to the President insulting . . ."* Authors' interviews with senior administration officials, October 2003.

Page 102: *"According to senior administration officials . . ."* Ibid.

Page 103: *"When Schröder ended up doing so . . ."* For the complaint that Schröder broke his promise, interviews with senior U.S. officials, May 2003 and October 2003. The quote about Bush is from "War in Iraq: how the die was cast before transatlantic diplomacy failed," *Financial Times*, May 27, 2003.

Page 103: *"A few days after the election . . ."* For Rumsfeld's comment, see U.S. Department of Defense News Briefing, "Press Conference with Polish National Security Adviser Minister Marek Siwiec at the Presidential Palace, Warsaw," September 23, 2002. For the alleged snub, see Steven Erlanger, "NATO Chief Urges Allies Not to Let Iraq Divide Them," *New York Times*, September 26, 2002.

Page 103: *"Rumsfeld denied any snub . . ."* Erlanger, ibid.

Page 103: *"Months later, in May 2003 . . ."* See Rice quoted in "USA-Reise: Mission Impossible," *Focus Magazin* (May 26, 2003), 34–36. Also see "Bush-Schröder relations fatally affected by Iraq: Bush adviser," Agence France Presse, May 24, 2003.

Page 103: *"Schröder denied having misled Bush . . ."* A senior aide to Schröder who spoken to him about the episode said that Schröder denies having agreed to support Bush on the issue of Iraq. Interview with senior German official, fall 2003.

Page 103: *"With Schröder at his side . . ."* See Bush's comments in "President Bush Meets with German Chancellor Schröder," White House Office of the Press Secretary, May 23, 2002.

Page 104: *"To prevent this scenario . . ."* Authors' interviews with French officials, Paris, August 2003.

Page 104: *"De Villepin stressed the importance . . ."* See de Villepin's opening speech to the 10th Conférence des Ambassadeurs, Paris, August 27, 2002.

Page 104: *"Chirac repeated his opposition to 'unilateral actions' . . ."* See "Perspectives/Jacques Chirac: French Leader Offers America Both Friendship and Criticism," *New York Times*, September 9, 2002; and see excerpts of the interview in "Jacques Chirac: French Leader Offers America Both Friendship and Criticism," *New York Times*, September 9, 2002.

Page 105: *"Former UN Ambassador Richard Holbrooke . . ."* Richard Holbrooke, "Take It to the Security Council," *Washington Post*, August 27, 2002.

Page 106: *"Singling out Milosevic and Saddam Hussein . . ."* See Blair's speech "Doctrine of the International Community" at the Economic Club of Chicago, April 24, 1999.

Page 106: *"According to people close to him . . ."* Authors' discussion with Downing Street officials, summer 2003. See also John Kampfner, *Blair's Wars* (London: Simon & Schuster, 2003); and Steven Philip Kramer, "Blair's Britain After Iraq," *Foreign Affairs* (July/August 2003), 90–104.

Page 106: *"According to British journalist . . ."* Hugo Young, "Blair has one final chance to break free of his tainted fealty: US idealism of the Kennedy era has given way to rampant imperialism," *The Guardian*, April 1, 2003; and authors' communication with Young, August 25, 2003. Senior Downing Street advisers agree with Young's interpretation. Authors' interviews, October and November 2003.

Page 106: *"The British government thus had no problem . . ."* Jack Straw, "Saddam must allow weapons inspectors into Iraq or suffer the consequences," *Times*, March 5, 2002.

Page 107: *"What Blair didn't realize . . ."* Authors' interviews with U.S. and British officials, Washington and London, June and July 2003.

Page 107: *"But in a statement that some . . ."* Bob Woodward, *Bush at War*, 348.

Page 108: *"As one administration official had put it . . ."* Cited in Michael R. Gordon, Julia Preston, Craig S. Smith, and Sabrina Tavernise, "U.S. Plan Requires Inspection Access to All Iraq Sites," *New York Times*, September 28, 2002.

Page 108: *"The latter point was critical for France . . ."* Cited in Tyler Marshall, Maggie Farley, and Doyle McManus, "A War of Words Led to Unanimous Iraq Vote; The long-sought U.N. resolution shows the extent of U.S. power— and its limits," *Los Angeles Times*, November 1, 2002.

Page 109: *"As one U.S. official commented . . ."* Ibid.

Page 109: *"First floated on September 26 . . ."* Draft of September 26, 2002.

Page 109: *"Told by his advisers . . ."* Karen DeYoung, "For Powell, A Long Path To a Victory; Pragmatism, Persistence Led to 15–0 U.N. Vote," *Washington Post*, November 10, 2002.

Page 110: *" . . . the French told the Americans . . ."* Authors' discussions with American and French diplomats involved in the negotiations.

Page 112: *"In the final text of 1441 . . ."* Authors' discussion with senior French official involved in 1441 negotiations, August 2003.

Page 113: *"While some of the most enthusiastic American proponents . . ."* See Holbrooke's comments on the *Lehrer News Hour*, February 10, 2003, www.pbs.org/newshour/bb/middle_east/jan-june03/divisions_2-10.html.

CHAPTER 5

Pages 115–116: *"After taking some time to translate . . ."* Secretary Colin L. Powell, "Press Conference on Iraq Declaration," December 19, 2002, Washington, D.C., U.S. Department of State.

Page 116: *"U.S. Ambassador to the United Nations . . ."* See Remarks by Ambassador John D. Negroponte, United States Permanent Representative to the United Nations. Following the Consultations on Iraq, Security Council Stakeout, December 19, 2003, USUN Press Release 218.

Page 116: *"It 'added little that was new' . . ."* "Déclaration à la presse du Représentant permanent de la France à l'issue des consultations du Conseil de Sécurité des Nations Unies," December 19, 2002.

Page 116: *"Consistent with their interpretation of 1441 . . ."* Julia Preston, "Diplomatic Strain on Iraq: Allies See U.S. as Hasty," *New York Times*, December 22, 2002.

Page 116: *"The French also insisted . . ."* Resolution 1441, emphasis added.

Pages 116–117: *"British Ambassador to Washington . . ."* Interview with Christopher Meyer, in "Blair's War," *Frontline*, March 18, 2003, www.pbs. org/wgbh/pages/frontline/shows/blair/interviews/meyer.html.

Page 117: *"According to U.S. officials . . ."* Authors' interviews with senior U.S. and UK officials, April 2003 and November 2003.

Page 117: *"UK Defense Secretary Geoff Hoon . . ."* Hoon cited in Claire Tréan, "Pour la France, on ne peut conclure à ce stade à une 'violation patente,'" *Le Monde*, December 21, 2002.

Page 117: *"Blair was personally convinced . . ."* Authors' interview, Downing Street official, July 2003.

Page 117: *"'War is looking less likely' . . ."* Authors' interview with senior French official, Paris, April 2003.

Page 117: *"That same week . . ."* Authors' interviews with senior German official, fall 2003.

Page 118: *"In Britain, on January 5 . . ."* "War is Not Inevitable, Straw Says," *The Guardian*, January 6, 2003.

Page 118: *"British strategist Lawrence Freedman agreed . . ."* Lawrence Freedman, "A war against Iraq can still be averted," *Financial Times*, January 8, 2003.

Page 118: *"Already on January 3, Bush spoke . . ."* Mike Allen, "Bush Tells Troops: Prepare for War; 'We Are Ready,' President Says," *Washington Post*, January 5, 2003.

Page 118: *"Newspapers began reporting . . ."* Vernon Loeb, "Buildup Accelerates For Invasion of Iraq; Top Divisions to Participate in War Scenarios," *Washington Post*, January 6, 2003; and Allen, "Bush Tells Troops," *Washington Post*, January 5, 2003.

Page 119: *"On January 7, speaking to the French diplomatic corps . . ."* Discours de Monsieur Jacques Chirac Président de la République lors de la présentation des voeux du corps diplomatique," January 7, 2003, www.elysee.fr/cgi-bin/auracom/aurweb/search/file?aur_file=discours/2003/0301VXDI.htm.

Page 119: *"Just one day later, Foreign Minister de Villepin . . ."* Victor Mallet, "France keeps up demand for proof on Iraqi arsenal," *Financial Times*, January 14, 2003.

Page 119: *"De Villepin then traveled to Moscow . . ."* Agence France Presse, "France Calls on U.S. to deliver proof of Iraq weapons possession," January 8, 2003.

Pages 119–120: *"Rice bluntly dismissed the Frenchman's arguments . . ."* A summary and partial transcript of the meeting was leaked to the press and was reported in Claude Angeli and Jérôme Canard, "Le Pentagone traite Chirac d' 'irresponsable' et l'accuse d"encourager" Saddam. . ." *Canard Enchainé*, January 22, 2003.

Page 120: *"Upon returning to Paris . . . "* Gourdault-Montagne quoted in Marc Champion, Charles Fleming, Ian Johnson, and Carla Anne Robbins, "Allies at Odds: Behind U.S. Rift With Europeans," *Wall Street Journal*, March 27, 2003; and Authors' interviews. Also see "War in Iraq," *Financial Times*, May 27, 2003.

Page 120: *"In one senior French official's words . . ."* Cited in James Kitfield, "Damage Control," *National Journal*, July 19, 2003.

Page 121: *"When Gourdault-Montagne was asked . . ."* Authors' Interview with U.S. participant in meeting with Gourdault-Montagne, December 2003.

Page 121: *"As one senior French official . . ."* Authors' interview with Senior French offical, Paris, April 2003.

Page 122: *"Rice, Rumsfeld, and Powell all argued . . ."* See "Dr. Condoleezza Rice discusses Iraq, North Korea and affirmative action," *Meet the Press*, January 19, 2003; Secretary Colin L. Powell, "Interview on CBS's *Face the Nation* With Bob Schieffer," January 19, 2003; and "Interview with Donald Rumsfeld," Fox News Sunday, January 19, 2003.

Page 122: *"Echoing Cheney's arguments . . ."* Powell, ibid.

Page 122: *"Citing Hans Blix's view . . ."* Authors' interview with French Foreign Ministry official, Paris, May 2003.

Page 122: *"Powell, however, responded with a warning . . ."* Cited in Marc Champion et al., "Allies at Odds," *Wall Street Journal*, March 27, 2003.

Page 122: *"At the UN meeting the next day . . ."* Réunion du Conseil de Sécurité des Nations Unis au Niveau Ministeriel sur la Lutte Contre le Terrorisme, Discours du Ministre des Affaires Etrangères, M. Dominique de Villepin, New York, January 20, 2003.

Page 122: *"German Foreign Minister Joschka Fischer did talk about Iraq . . ."* Speech by Fischer to the UN Security Council, New York, January 20, 2003, available at www.auswaertiges-amt.de.

Pages 122–123: *"Ivanov warned against 'unilateral steps . . .'"* See "Statement by His Excellency Mr. Igor S. Ivanov, Minister for Foreign Affairs of the Russian Federation, at the UN Security Council meeting January 20, 2003" ; and Glenn Kessler and Colum Lynch, "France Vows to Block Resolution on Iraq War; U. S. Schedule Put at Risk By UN Debate," *Washington Post*, January 21, 2003.

Page 123: *"Caught off guard by the debate . . ."* Kessler and Lynch, ibid.

Page 123: *"He said little about Iraq in his opening statement . . ."* Press Conference: "H.E. Mr. Dominique de Villepin, Minister for Foreign Affairs of France," January 20, 2003, available at www.un.org/webcast/PC2003a.html.

Page 123: *"Asked about Iraq by a reporter . . ."* See Corine Lesnes, "Irak: la France menace d'utiliser son veto contre un guerre américaine," *Le Monde*, January 22, 2003.

Page 123: *"The U.S. reaction to de Villepin's comments . . ."* Kessler and Lynch, ibid.

Page 123: *"According to his close aides, Powell . . ."* James Kitfield, "Damage Control," *National Journal*, July 19, 2003.

Page 124: *"During the negotiations over Resolution 1441 . . ."* Cited in Steven R. Weisman, "A Long, Winding Road to a Diplomatic Dead End," *New York Times*, March 17, 2003.

Page 124: *"As Powell's friend General Anthony Zinni observed . . ."* Cited in Glenn Kessler, "Moderate Powell Turns Hawkish On War With Iraq," *Washington Post*, January 24, 2003.

Page 124: *"Within days, Powell . . ."* Ibid.

Page 126: *"Schröder, still ostracized by the White House . . ."* Marc Champion, Charles Fleming, Ian Johnson. and Carla Anne Robbins, "Allies at Odds: Behind U.S. Rift with Europeans," *Wall Street Journal*, March 27, 2003.

Page 126: *"At the press conference . . ."* "Conférence de Presse Conjointe de Monsieur Jacques Chirac, Président de la République et de Monsieur Gerhard Schröder, Chancelier de la République Fédérale d'Allemagne à l'issue du Conseil des Ministres Franco-Allemand," Paris, Palais de l'Elysée, Wednesday, January 2003.

Page 126: " *. . . called the Franco-German agreement a 'stunning power play' . . ."* William Safire, "Breaking up the Alliance," *New York Times*, January 24, 2003.

Page 128: *"When asked about 'European' opposition . . ."* "Secretary Rumsfeld Briefs at the Foreign Press Center," Department of Defense, January 22, 2003, available at www.defenselink.mil/transcripts/2003/t01232003_t0122sdfpc .html.

Page 128: *"'Frankly,' Powell told Jim Lehrer . . ."* Cited in Steven R. Weisman, "U.S. Set to Demand that Allies Agree Iraq is Defying UN," *New York Times*, January 23, 2003.

Page 128: *"A few days later Rumsfeld . . ."* Hearing of the House Armed Services Committee, February 5, 2003, www.house.gov/hasc.

Page 129: *"It underlined the signatories' . . ."* José Maria Aznar, José-Manuel Durao Barroso, Silvio Berlusconi, Tony Blair, Vaclav Havel, Peter Medgyessy, Leszek Miller, and Anders Fogh Rasmussen, "United We Stand," *Wall Street Journal*, January 30, 2003.

Page 130: *"The leaders from France, Germany, Belgium, and Luxembourg . . ."* A good account of the origins of the Letter of Eight, confirmed by interviews with several of the officials involved and with the *Wall Street Journal*'s Michael Gonzalez, can be found in William Safire, "And Now: Op-Ed Diplomacy," *New York Times*, February 3, 2003.

Page 130: *"'For 40 years, Chirac and Schröder had asserted . . ."* "Fortieth Anniversary of the Elysée Treaty—Speech by M. Jacques Chirac, President of the Republic, to Members of the German and French Parliaments," January 22, 2003, available at www.info-france-usa.org/news/statmnts/2003/chirac 012203.asp; and "Discours de Monsieur Jacques Chirac, Président de la République, devant les députés allemands et français," January 22, 2003, www.elysee.fr/cgi-bin/auracom/aurweb/search/file?aur_file=discours/ 2003/D030122.html.

Page 130: *"Spain, with a growing economy . . ."* The quote is from former Aznar cabinet member Pio Cabanillas, cited in John Vinocur, "In backing U.S. on Iraq, Spain charts its own global role," *International Herald Tribune*, February 28, 2003.

Page 131: "*Solana, who had spent . . .*" See "The Divided West: Part II. The rift turns nasty: the plot that split old and new Europe asunder," *Financial Times*, May 28, 2003.

Page 131:"*Tony Blair told associates repeatedly . . .*" Authors' interview with Downing Street official, July 2003.

Page 131: "*French Foreign Minister de Villepin . . .*" Ibid.

Page 132: "*At NATO's Prague summit . . .*" See Statement by the Heads of State and Government of Albania, Bulgaria, Croatia, Estonia, Latvia, Lithuania, Macedonia, Romania, Slovakia and Slovenia on the occasion of NATO Summit in Prague, November 21, 2002, available at http://domino.kappa.ro/mae/home.nsf.

Page 133: "*According to his senior aides . . .*" Authors' discussion with French official close to Chirac in February 2003.

Page 134: "*The EU candidates who signed the Vilnius 10 letter . . .*" See Conférence de Presse de Monsieur Jacques Chirac, Président de la République, à l'issue de la Réunion Informelle Extraordinaire du Conseil Européen, Lundi 17 février, 2003 (February 17, 2003).

Page 134: "'*Beyond the somewhat amusing or childish aspects . . .*'" Ibid.

Page 135: "'*I don't regret it*' . . ." See Chirac interview, "French Leader Offers America Both Friendship and Criticism," *New York Times,* September 22, 2003.

Page 135: "*Rumsfeld called on them . . .*" Thomas E. Ricks, "NATO Allies Trade Barbs Over Iraq; Rumsfeld: Critics Are Undermining Alliance's Strength," *Washington Post*, February 9, 2003.

Page 135: "*The Germans and French, however, were not persuaded.*" Ibid.

Page 136: "*Portuguese Defense Minister Paulo Portas . . .*" See Peter Spiegel, "Old Europe unpersuaded by U.S. therapy," *Financial Times*, February 10, 2003.

Page 136: "*At the same meeting . . .*" See "The Divided West: Part II," *Financial Times*, May 28, 2003.

Page 136: "*U.S. Senator Joseph Lieberman . . .* "Remarks by Senator Joseph Lieberman 39th Munich Conference on Security Policy, "NATO's Future Role," February 8, 2003.

Page 137: "*To officials at the U.S. mission to NATO . . .*" Authors' interviews at NATO headquarters, Brussels, May 2003.

Page 138: "*According to one participant . . .*" Authors' interview with meeting participant at NATO, May 2003.

Page 138: *"As Belgian Foreign Minister Louis Michel put it . . ."* Cited in Paul Ames, "France, Germany, Belgium block NATO plans to protect Turkey; Ankara calls for emergency consultations," Associated Press, February 10, 2003.

Page 138: *"U.S. Ambassador to NATO Nicholas Burns called . . ."* Cited in Ames, ibid.

Page 138: *"Other Americans, including the most senior officials . . ."* For Powell, see interview with Tony Snow, Fox News Sunday, "Interview with Colin Powell," February 9, 2003. For Rumsfeld, see Ames, ibid. Holbrooke is cited in *Lehrer News Hour*, February 10, 2003.

Page 138: *"Representative Tom Lantos, a Democrat . . ."* Thomas Fuller, "U.S. backs deal to salvage NATO aid for Turkey," *International Herald Tribune*, February 13, 2003.

Page 138: *"Powell feared that the alliance . . ."* Powell cited in Julia Preston and Steven R. Weisman, "France Offering Plan to Expand Iraq Arms Hunt," *New York Times*, February 12, 2003.

Page 139: *"Washington, NATO Secretary General Robertson. . ."* Authors' interviews with U.S. and NATO officials at NATO headquarters, May 2003.

Page 139: *"'We cannot, via a decision of NATO . . .'"* Thomas Fuller, "U.S. backs deal to salvage NATO aid for Turkey," *International Herald Tribune*, February 13, 2003.

Page 140: *"As a German official put it . . ."* See Kitfield, "Damage Control."

Page 141: *"The French Defense Minister also insisted . . ."* Cited in Ames, ibid.

Page 142: *"Many Americans would later come to conclude . . ."* See Thomas L. Friedman, "Moment of Truth," *New York Times*, December 18, 2003.

Page 142: *"As late as January 7, Chirac . . ."* Discours de Monsieur Jacques Chirac, President de la République, en Réponse aux Voeux des Armées, Palais de l'Elysée, January 7, 2003.

Page 142: *"Chirac had authorized . . ."* Authors' interviews with Elysée, foreign ministry, and defense ministry officials, spring 2002 and August 2003.

Page 143: *"As de Villepin put it in his January 20 press conference . . ."* Kessler and Lynch, ibid.

Page 143: *"In October 2002 a senior French official . . ."* French official to NATO-sponsored U.S. delegation, Paris, October 2002.

Page 143: *"Blix's first report to the Security Council . . ."* Hans Blix, "An Update on Inspection," Report of the Executive Chairman of UNMOVIC to the

United Nations Security Council, January 27, 2003, available at www.un.org/ Depts/unmovic/recent%20items..html.

Page 143: *"Now, three weeks later . . ."* See Executive Chairman of UNMOVIC, Dr. Hans Blix, "Briefing of the Security Council," February 14, 2003, UN News Service.

Page 143: *"Those inspections, he added . . ."* Executive Chairman of UNMOVIC, ibid.

Page 144: *"In addition, Blix challenged a number of the allegations . . ."* Ibid.

Page 144: *"ElBaradei also painted an improved picture. . ."* See IAEA Director General Dr. Mohamed ElBaradei, "The Status of Nuclear Inspections in Iraq," New York, February 14, 2003.

Page 144: *"In France itself, for example . . ."* "Le jugement des Français sur les preuves américaines et sur une intervention en Irak," Institut Français de l'Opinion Publique, February 10, 2003.

Page 144: *"In Britain, the percentage of those who approved . . ."* See "Blair Losing Public Support On Iraq," MORI poll, January 21, 2003.

Page 144: *"And in Russia, opposition to military action . . ."* Pew Global Attitudes Project, Pew Research Center for the People and the Press, March 18, 2003.

Page 145: *"As former U.S. Assistant Secretary of State Martin Indyk later wrote . . ."* Martin Indyk, "We Forgot the Russians," *Washington Post*, March 23, 2003.

Page 146: *"As Robert Kagan put it . . ."* Robert Kagan, "Napoleonic Fervor," *Washington Post*, February 24, 2003.

Page 146: *"In the face of hostility toward the war . . ."* The quotation is from Blair's response during Prime Minister's Questions of January 15, 2003, www.publications.parliament.uk/pa/cm200203/cmhansrd/vo030115/debtext/ 30115-03.htm#30115-03_dpthd0.

Page 147: " . . . *'should the United Nations decide to pass a second resolution . . .'"* Quoted in "Remarks by the President and British Prime Minister Tony Blair," London, January 31, 2003, available at www.whitehouse.gov/news/ releases/2003/01/20030131-23.html.

Page 148: *"The French and the Germans . . ."* Authors' discussions with French and German diplomats in Washington, D.C., January and February 2003.

Page 148: *"On February 21, the French ambassador . . ."* Authors' interview with Levitte, September 2003. Also see Gerard Baker, et al., "Blair's mission impossible: the doomed effort to win a second UN resolution," *Financial Times*, May

29, 2003; and Levitte's public discussion of the matter at the Council on Foreign Relations, http://www.cfr.org/publication.php?id=5774.

Page 149: *"U.S. diplomats at the UN . . ."* Authors' interviews at U.S. and UK Missions to the United Nations, March 3, 2003.

Page 150: *"'We will not allow a proposed resolution . . .'"* See "Déclaration Russie-Allemagne-France," Paris, March 5, 2003.

Page 150: *"French Foreign Minister de Villepin was equally clear . . ."* De Villepin press conference, March 5, 2003, available at www.diplomatie.gouv.fr.

Page 150: *"'[The resolution says Saddam Hussein] is in defiance . . .'"* See "President George Bush Discusses Iraq in National Press Conference," East Room, March 6, 2003.

Page 150: *"In Yaounde, the Cameroon capital . . ."* See "Africans understand French stance against Iraq war: de Villepin," Agence France Press, March 11, 2003.

Page 151: *"In fact, Colin Powell later acknowledged . . ."* See Powell's interview on *Charlie Rose,* April 22, 2003, Federal Information and News Dispatch, Inc., State Department, www.state.gov/secretary/rm/2003/19816.htm.

Page 151: *"Coming across a French official . . ."* Authors' interview with French diplomat in Paris, April 2003. The story is also recounted in "Blair's Mission Impossible: the doomed effort to win a second UN resolution," *Financial Times,* May 29, 2003.

Page 151: *"Over the weekend of March 8–9 . . ."* Authors' interview with senior British officials, London, August 2003; and Karen DeYoung and Colum Lynch, "Bush Lobbies for Deal on Iraq; Plan Would Set Deadlines, Goals," *Washington Post,* March 12, 2003.

Page 152: *"He submitted his list to Blix's team . . ."* Authors' interviews with officials at U.S. and UK Missions to United Nations, New York, March 2003; and with British officials in London, July 2003.

Page 152: *"Many of the undecided six . . ."* Patrick Wintour and Martin Kettle, "Special investigation: Blair's road to war," *Guardian,* April 26, 2003.

Page 152: *"The interview began with Chirac explaining . . ."* Authors' interview Télévisée de Monsieur Jacques Chirac, Président de la République par Patrick Poivre d'Arvor (TF1) et David Pujadas (France 2), Palais de l'Elysée, March 10, 2003.

Page 153: *"When Blair called Chirac later that week . . ."* Authors' interviews with Blair advisers, August and November 2003.

Page 153: *"On March 11, Canada proposed . . ."* See "Statement by Ambassador Paul Heinbecker, Permanent Representative of Canada to the United Nations Security Council Open Meeting on the Situation Between Iraq and Kuwait," New York, March 11, 2003. For the White House reaction, see Press Briefing, Ari Fleischer, March 11, 2003.

Page 153: *"White House press spokesman Ari Fleischer . . ."* Press Briefing, Ari Fleischer, March 14, 2003.

Page 154: *"Some British officials believe that Blair . . ."* For the speculation and assessment of the British position, see "Blair's mission impossible: the doomed effort to win a second UN resolution," *Financial Times*, May 29, 2003.

Page 154: *"Others speculated about what would have happened . . ."* See James P. Rubin, "Stumbling Into War," *Foreign Affairs* (September/October 2003), 56.

CHAPTER 6

Page 158: *"Faced with strong domestic opposition to the war . . ."* Authors' discussions with Labor members of Parliament, April 2003.

Page 158: *"Ultimately, however, pursuing the new UN authorization . . ."* On how Britain ended up pursuing this mistaken course, see Charles Grant, *Transatlantic Rift: How to Bring the Two Sides Together,* (London: Centre for European Reform, 2003), Appendix II, "Britain's Diplomatic Defeat," 115–119.

Page 160: *"The Atlanticism Schröder seemed interested in promoting . . ."* Senior U.S. and German diplomats agree that Schröder and Bush had a good early relationship, and several very positive meetings together in the fall of 2001.

Page 160: " *. . . asked whether Vice President Cheney had considered the potential impact . . ."* Cited in Stephen Szabo, *Parting Ways: 9–11, Iraq, and the German-American Relationship* (Baltimore, MD: Johns Hopkins University Press, forthcoming).

Page 161: *"Chirac's foreign minister, Dominique de Villepin, was a part-time poet . . ."* See Dominique de Villepin, *Les Cent-Jours ou l'esprit de sacrifice* (Paris: Librarie Académique Perrin), February 2001.

Page 161: *"De Villepin wrote that 'not a day goes by . . .'"* See Elaine Sciolino, "France's Perpetual-Motion Foreign Minister Can't Slow Down," *New York Times*, March 8, 2003; and Robert Kagan, "Napoleonic Fervor," *Washington Post*, February 24, 2003.

Page 161:. *"According to former French Foreign Minister Hubert Védrine . . ."* Authors' discussion with Védrine, June 2003.

Page 162: *"The powerful Turkish military . . ."* The story of the successive mistakes and mishaps that led to Turkish rejection of the resolution on U.S. troops is best told by *Hurriyet* columnist Sedat Ergin, who presented his research on the subject at a Brookings Institution conference, "Turkey and the United States after the War in Iraq," June 26, 2003. His detailed assessment, as published in *Hurriyet*, is available (in Turkish) at www.hurriyetim. com.tr.

Page 163: *"Indeed, Bush prepared the ground politically . . ."* See "President Bush Outlines Iraqi Threat," Speech to Cincinnati Museum Center, Cincinnati, Ohio, October 7, 2002.

Page 164: *"The President's firm conviction . . ."* White House Office of the Press Secretary, "President Delivers 'State of the Union,'" January 28, 2003.

Page 164: *"'When it comes to our security,' Bush asserted . . ."* White House Office of the Press Secretary, "President George Bush Discusses Iraq in National Press Conference," March 6, 2003.

Page 164: *"'At some point we may be the only ones left,' . . ."* Cited in Bob Woodward, *Bush at War*, 81.

Page 164: *"The degree to which allied and other views . . ."* Cited in Karen DeYoung, "U.S. Officials Say UN Future at Stake in Vote; Bush Message Is that a War Is Inevitable, Diplomats Say," *Washington Post*, February 25, 2003.

Page 166: *"Even Paul Wolfowitz . . ."* Deputy Secretary Wolfowitz Interview with Sam Tannenhaus, *Vanity Fair*, U.S. Department of Defense News Transcript, May 9, 2003.

Page 167: *"For a time he even suggested . . ."* See DOD News Briefing, Secretary Rumsfeld and General Pace, Tuesday, August 20, 2002.

Page 167: *"Powell even suggested . . ."* See Powell's assertion in his testimony before the Senate Budget Committee, President's International Affairs Budget for 2004, February 11, 2003, U.S. Department of State, Washington, D.C. The text of the purported bin Laden tape was made available at the BBC News site, news.bbc.co.uk/2/hi/middle_east/2751019.stm.

Page 167: *"The administration's inability to agree internally . . ."* Wolfowitz interview with Sam Tannenhaus, *Vanity Fair*, U.S. Department of Defense News Transcript, Friday, May 9, 2003.

Page 168: *"As James Rubin put it . . ."* James P. Rubin, "Stumbling into War," *Foreign Affairs*, September/October 2003, 48.

Page 168: "*In August 2002, for example . . .*" Dick Cheney, "Remarks to the Veterans of Foreign Wars 103rd National Convention," Nashville, Tennessee, August 26, 2002.

Page 168: "*Two weeks later Bush told the United Nations . . .*" George W. Bush, "Remarks to the United Nations General Assembly," New York, September 12, 2002, www.whitehouse.gov/news/releases/2002/09/20020912-1.html.

Page 168: "*In October, Bush made the unqualified assertion . . .*" George W. Bush, "Remarks on Iraq," Cincinnati, October 7, 2002.

Page 169: "*In his State of the Union Address . . .*" George W. Bush, "President Delivers State of the Union," Washington, D.C., January 28, 2003.

Page 169: "*Similarly, Secretary of State Powell, in his UN presentation . . .*" Colin Powell, "Remarks to the United Nations Security Council," New York, February 5, 2003.

Page 169: "*In March 2003, even after the war had begun . . .*" Donald Rumsfeld, "Remarks on ABC *This Week with George Stephanopoulos,*" March 20, 2003.

Page 171: "*Bush himself appeared genuinely incapable . . .*" In October 2001, for example, Bush commented that he was "amazed that there is such misunderstanding of what our country is about. Like most Americans, I just can't believe it. Because I know how good we are." George W. Bush, "President Holds Primetime News Conference," Washington, D.C., October 22, 2001, www.whitehouse.gov.

Page 171: "*Berlin gave the United States . . .*" Daalder and Lindsay, *America Unbound*, 190.

Page 172: "*French visitors to Washington were berated . . .*" Authors' interview with a participant in the meeting with Feith, summer 2003.

Page 172: "*American officials did not shy away . . .*" Cheney and Wolfowitz both cited in Rubin, "Stumbling into War," 55.

Page 173: "*As Senator Joseph Biden put it . . .*" See "Dealing with Iraq: Is U.S. Policy Working?" Speech at Brookings Institution, Washington, D.C., July 31, 2003.

Page 173: " *. . . Colin Powell hardly traveled anywhere . . .*" Daalder and Lindsay, *America Unbound*, 192.

Page 174; "*Powell would later claim . . .*" Colin Powell, "Press Availability with NATO Secretary General Lord Robertson," Washington, D.C., February 20, 2003.

Page 175: "*Blair consistently made clear . . .*" See Blair's comments to a meeting of the Parliamentary Labor Party in February 2003, cited in Peter Riddell, *Hug*

Them Close: Blair, Clinton, Bush and the "Special Relationship" (London: Politico's, 2003), 24.

Page 179: *"When asked on national French television . . ."* Interview Télévisée de Monsieur Jacques Chirac, Président de la République par Patrick Poivre d'Arvor (TF1) et David Pujadas (France 2), Palais de l'Elysée, March 10, 2003.

Page 180: *"They did not believe the French were behaving . . ."* See "Intervention du Ministre des Affaires Etrangères, M. Dominique de Villepin, au Conseil de Sécurité des Nations Unies," February 14, 2003.

Page 180: *"Instead he bragged about how . . ."* De Villepin made such remarks on numerous occasions, including, according to participants, at a high-level gathering of American and European officials, experts, and journalists at the Bilderberg conference on May 17, 2003. The comments about France and the Pope are cited in Charles Grant, *Transatlantic Rift: How to Bring the Two Sides Together* (London: Centre for European Reform, July 2003), 43.

Page 180: *"As one former American statesman commented . . ."* A former senior U.S. official speaking to one of de Villepin's colleagues. Authors' interview in Paris, May 2003.

Page 181: *" . . . conflict between France and the United States . . ."* Henry Kissinger, *Diplomacy* (New York: Simon & Schuster, 1994), 603.

CHAPTER 7

Page 188: *"In June 2003, for example, the Pew Global Attitudes Project . . ."* Pew Global Attitudes Project, *Views of a Changing World,* June 2003, 22.

Page 189: *"Americans and Europeans have remarkably similar assessments . . ."* German Marshall Fund, *Transatlantic Trends 2003,* September 2003, 12–13. For similar results, see Pew Global Attitudes Project, *Views of a Changing World,* June 2003; Worldviews 2002, *American Public Opinion and Foreign Policy,* June 2002; Worldviews 2002, *European Public Opinion and Foreign Policy,* September 2002; PIPA/Knowledge Networks, *Americans on Terrorism: Two Years after September 11,* September 9, 2003.

Page 189: *"By June 2003 they had begun to reverse."* Pew Global Attitudes Project, *Views of a Changing World,* June 2003, 19.

Page 189: *"Americans expressed discomfort with unilateralism . . ."* Worldviews 2002, *American Public Opinion and Foreign Policy,* June 2002, available at www.worldviews.org/detailreports/usreport/index.htm.

Page 189: *"Even on the use of force . . ."* Worldviews 2002, *Europeans see the World as Americans Do, but Critical of U.S. Foreign Policy,* September 4,

2002, 5; available at www.worldviews.org/docs/TransatlanticKeyFindings. pdf.

Page 189; " . . . *polls also suggest much more similar attitudes in Europe and America . . .*" For polls on global warning, see Jeffrey Kluger, "A Climate Of Despair," *Time Magazine*, April 9, 2001, 30; and Dalia Sussman, "Global Warming Trend: Six in 10 Say U.S. Should Join Kyoto Treaty," ABC News, April 17, 2001, available at abcnews.go.com/sections/us/DailyNews/poll 010417.html. On genetically modified foods, see HarrisInteractive, "Genetically Modified Foods: An Issue Waiting to Explode?" *Harris Poll* 33, June 28, 2000, www.harrisinteractive.com/harris_poll/index.asp?PID=96.

Page 191: *In the peacekeeping phase . . .*" James Dobbins, John G. McGinn, Keith Crane, et al., *America's Role in Nation-Building: From Germany to Iraq* (Washington, D.C.: RAND, 2003), 116; and Elaine Sciolino, "Don't Forget the Balkans," *New York Times*, October 8, 2003, 1.

Page 191: *"At one point in 2002, France had over 4200 troops . . ."* U.S. Department of Defense, *Report on Allied Contributions to the Common Defense*, July 2003, II-8. On special forces see Jacques Isnard, "A l'OTAN, des responsables américains louent le savoir faire de l'armée française," *Le Monde*, October 9, 2003.

Page 191: "'. . . *not only is Germany's participation important . . .*'" George W. Bush, "Remarks by the President and Secretary of Defense Donald Rumsfeld in Press Availability," Prairie Chapel Ranch, Crawford, Texas, August 8, 2003.

Pages 191–192: *"At the start of 2004, Germany maintained . . ."* See "Afghanistan will need security force for a decade," *Agence France Presse*, December 4, 2003. On Provincial Reconstruction Teams, German Federal Press Office, "ISAF mission in Afghanistan extended and expanded," October 16, 2003, available at http://www.german-embassy.org.uk/isaf-mission_in_afghani stan_ex.html.

Page 192: *"Nearly 80 percent of Americans . . ."* Jeffrey M. Jones, "Speech Watchers Believe Iraq Victory Aids U.S. in War on Terrorism," Gallup Poll News Service, May 2, 2003.

Page 192: *"In contrast, large majorities across Europe . . ."* Gallup International, "Post War Iraq 2003 Poll," May 16, 2003.

Page 192: *"Whereas just after the Iraqi war . . ."* *Washington Post*/ABC News Poll, April 30, 2003, November 16, 2003 and December 14, 2003.

Pages 192–193: *"In the fall of 2003, 78 percent of Republicans . . ."* See Lydia Saad, "Americans still reluctant to call France an 'Ally,'" Gallup Poll, September 26, 2003; David S. Broder and Dan Balz, "Nation Again Split on Bush,"

Washington Post, November 2, 2003; and Richard Benedetto, "Poll: Independents' support on Iraq eroding," *USA Today*, October 28, 2003.

Page 194: *"Ironically, few anticipated this type of reaction . . ."* See "The Second Presidential Debate," *Online Newshour*, Winston-Salem, North Carolina, October 11, 2000, available at www.pbs.org/newshour/bb/election/2000 debates/2ndebate1.html. Candidate Bush's exact words were: "If we are an arrogant nation, they will resent us; but if we're a humble nation, but strong, they'll welcome us."

Page 195: *" . . . American unilateralism could come at a price."* For a good discussion of how foreign domestic politics undermine support for American policy, see Fareed Zakaria, "The Arrogant Empire," *Newsweek*, March 24, 2003.

Page 196: *"In the past, the United States successfully maintained a sort of 'European empire' . . ."* Geir Lundestad, "Empire by Invitation in the American Century," *Diplomatic History*, 23:2 (1999), 189–217.

Page 198: *" . . . transatlantic economic ties are not decreasing . . ."* Joseph P. Quinlan, *Drifting Apart or Growing Together? The Primacy of the Transatlantic Economy* (Washington, D.C.: Center for Transatlantic Relations, 2003), 25–26.

Page 198: *"The share of U.S. foreign investment going to Europe . . ."* Calculated on an historical cost basis from U.S. Bureau of Economic Analysis, *International Economic Accounts*, available at www.bea.doc.gov/bea/di1.htm.

Page 198: *"Nor is it to say that interdependence make outright hostility and conflict futile . . ."* Norman Angell, *The Great Illusion: A Study of the Relationship of Military Power to National Advantage* (London: W. Heineman, 1910).

Page 200: *" . . . 'even the appearance of taking the world seriously . . .'"* Tony Judt, "Its Own Worst Enemy," *New York Review of Books*, August 15, 2002.

Page 202: *"Even many of the administration's supporters . . ."* See William Kristol and Robert Kagan, "Contracts for Iraq: Reverse the Pentagon's Decision," Memorandum to Opinion Leaders, Project for the New American Century, December 11, 2003.

Page 203: *"In contrast, international pledges to Iraq amounted to . . ."* See Steven R. Weisman, "Funds for Iraq Are Far Short Of Pledges, Figures Show," *New York Times*, December 7, 2003.

Page 205: *"Al Qaeda, for instance, previously insensitive to divides within the Western world . . ."* An October 2003 al Qaeda videotape declared, for example: "We reserve the right to respond at the appropriate time and place against all the countries participating in this unjust war, particularly Britain, Spain, Australia, Poland, Japan, and Italy." Quoted in "Excerpts from latest tape attributed to Bin Laden," Associated Press, October 18, 2003.

Page 205: *"The claim that America is free to do whatever it wishes . . ."* See "A Place in the Sun, Beyond the Law," *The Economist*, May 8, 2003.

Page 206: " . . . *'either you are with us or you are with the terrorists.'"* George W. Bush, "Address to a Joint Session of Congress and the American People", September 20, 2001, available at www.whitehouse.gov/news/releases/2001/09/20010920-8.html.

Page 206: *"It will also require defining the enemy more precisely . . ."* This point is made with particular eloquence by Zbigniew Brzezinski, "Where do we go from here," *Transatlantik Internationale Politik,* March 2003, 3–10.

Page 208: *"After having publicly pledged to British Prime Minister Tony Blair . . ."* For the pledge to Blair, see "President Bush Meets with Prime Minister Blair in Northern Ireland," Hillsborough Castle, Belfast, Northern Ireland, Office of the Press Secretary, April 8, 2003.

Page 208: " . . . *'a wall snaking through the West Bank' . . ."* George W. Bush, "President Bush Welcomes Prime Minister Abbas to White House," Washington, D.C., July 25, 2003, available at www.whitehouse.gov/news/releases/2003/07/20030725-6.html.

Page 210: *"After long and difficult negotiations . . ."* Interviews with members of the European negotiating team, October 2003 and December 2003.

Page 211: " . . . *including potentially supporting Iranian membership in the World Trade Organization . . ."* As Steven Everts has pointed out, WTO membership would not only increase trade and investment with Iran, but WTO transparency rules on subsidies would undermine the role of the *bonyads*— the religious foundations that distort the Iranian economy and supply funding for extremist religious groups. Steven Everts, "Iran: The Next Big Crisis," *Prospect* (December 2003), 46–49.

Page 211: " . . . *the EU is by far Iran's leading trading partner . . ."* See European Union, "Bilateral Trade Relations: Iran,", February 2003 available at europa. eu.int/comm/trade/bilateral/iran/index_en.htm.

Page 211: *"A 2002 Report written by Arab social scientists . . ."* UN Development Program, *Arab Human Development Report 2002* (New York: United Nations), 1–2.

Page 213: " . . . *'[Sixty] years of Western nations excusing . . .'"* George W. Bush, "Freedom in Iraq and the Middle East," Remarks at the 20th Anniversary of the National Endowment for Democracy, U.S. Chamber of Commerce, Washington, D.C., November 6, 2003.

Pages 214–215: *"According to the 2003 Arab Human Development report . . ."* UN Development Program, *Arab Human Development Report 2003*, 2.

Page 216: "*From a transatlantic perspective . . .*" On the potential for Middle Eastern transformation to serve as a basis for transatlantic cooperation, see Ronald D. Asmus and Kenneth M. Pollack, "The New Transatlantic Project," *Policy Review* (October/November 2002), 3–19.

Page 217: "*In fact, even recent French military doctrine . . .*" See "Loi no. 2003-73 relative à la programmation militaire pour les années 2003 à 2008," Annex, Section 2.3.1, *Journal Officiel,* January 29, 2003, http://www.legifrance.gouv.fr/WAspad/UnTexteDeJorf?numjo=DEFX0200133L.

Page 217: "*Similarly, the EU's first effort at a European Security Strategy . . .*" Javier Solana, *A Secure Europe in a Better World,* Paper for the European Council in Thessaloniki, Greece, June 20, 2003, available at ue.eu.int/press data/EN/reports/76255.pdf. The final, official version of the paper deleted all references to the word "preemption," underscoring how controversial these issues remained within the EU. See *A Secure Europe in a Better World: European Security Strategy,* Brussels, December 12, 2003 available at ue.eu.int/pressdata/EN/reports/78367.pdf.

INDEX